AUG 0 8 2019

DATE DUE

Library Store #47-0108 Peel Off Pressure Sensitive

Under The Same Roof

by

Anthony Ellis McGee

Bloomington, IN	Milton Keynes, UK
authorHOUSE

AuthorHouse™
1663 Liberty Drive, Suite 200
Bloomington, IN 47403
www.authorhouse.com
Phone: 1-800-839-8640

AuthorHouse™ *UK Ltd.*
500 Avebury Boulevard
Central Milton Keynes, MK9 2BE
www.authorhouse.co.uk
Phone: 08001974150

This book is a work of fiction. People, places, events, and situations are the product of the author's imagination. Any resemblance to actual persons, living or dead, or historical events, is purely coincidental.

© 2006 Anthony Ellis McGee. All rights reserved.

No part of this book may be reproduced, stored in a retrieval system, or transmitted by any means without the written permission of the author.

First published by AuthorHouse 6/6/2006

ISBN: 1-4259-2104-3 (sc)

Library of Congress Control Number: 2006901624

Printed in the United States of America
Bloomington, Indiana

This book is printed on acid-free paper.

DEDICATION

To my loving grandmother Sarah Broida,
your nurturing spirit will remain in my heart forever.

To the memory of my father, Charles W. McGee,
the ways in which you impacted my life are revealed to me daily.

To the memory of Charles H. McGee,
Chucky, I hope you're proud of your little brother.

I love you and miss you!

ACKNOWLEDGMENTS

First I want to thank God for blessing me with a vision and giving me the courage and faith to follow the steps He ordered in my life. Thank You Lord for allowing me to keep my eyes on You instead of being blinded by fear and self-doubt.

Next I need to thank my mother, Jessye H. McGee, for providing me with an unconditional love. Your words of wisdom will follow me all the days of my life. Thanks for being supportive and believing in my dreams. I love you Mama.

I also need to thank all the people at Trinity United Church of Christ who have prayed with me and for me and encouraged me as I took a leap of faith. Thank you Pastor Wright for preaching sermons that allowed me to dream and believe that with the grace of God, ordinary people can do extraordinary things. To my BMIC (Black Men in Christ) brothers, James Hart, Joseph Sanders, Deacon Lawrence Myles, Ronald Linton and Tony Hawthorne for lifting me up in prayer on a regular basis. Our Thursday morning phone calls of prayer have been a huge blessing in my life.

I have to give a word of thanks to my Godparents, Albert and Ida Feggins for your words of encouragement, and to my aunt and uncle, Rose and S.R. Hubbard for being a second set of parents to me. I have much love for Charlease Bufford and Carron Woods; they're the older sisters I never had. I also can't forget to thank all of my relatives who are too numerous to name.

I want to give a special thanks to Kimberly Vann, Yvette Stringer, Chyrel Graham, Pat Thomas, Rita Lewis and Tony Bracey for reading sample chapters over and over again, and giving me positive feedback when I wondered if I were on the right track.

I also have to give a shout out to some of the folks who have been with me over the years. Having people in our life for the long haul during good and bad times are a blessing so I need to give props to the TUCC Men's Chorus, Michael and Phyllis Adams, Charles White, Gregory Glenn, Raymond Riley, Michael Newson, and the many other people God has allowed to enrich my life. I love you all.

And to all the people I missed, I'll be sure to mention you next time.

1

JULIAN

"Hear we go again," I thought, as I drove like a madman on a mission, chasing the screaming siren and flashing lights of an ambulance along rain slick streets. Hope Collins, my sixty-five-year-old mother, had just suffered another asthma attack and was en route to Roseland Community Hospital located on Chicago's south side. Over the last three years, I've watched Mama battle an array of ailments resulting in numerous calls to 9-1-1 and frequent trips to the hospital. Once again, I was praying to keep Hope alive.

Raised from roots planted deep in the soils of Mississippi, Mama is a courageous and resilient woman. She has an elastic spirit, which allows her to keep bouncing back from physical setbacks. Some of the nurses at the hospital have even joked in the past that Mama has nine lives. I know she's tired of being sick, but somehow she manages to maintain her sense of humor and dignity, unwilling to give up on life.

For me, dealing with Mama's sickness is like living on an emotional rollercoaster. As soon as I begin riding high on the thought of her condition possibly improving, another setback happens, sending her back to the hospital, and me on a downward spiral. I'm up one moment and down the next. It's mentally and physically draining.

A male and female crisis team wheeled the stretcher carrying Mama into the emergency area. Beads of sweat dance on Mama's fever stricken forehead. She's weary. They work to stabilize her. A male nurse, who appeared to be Filipino, came in and covered Mama's mouth with an oxygen mask. Soon after, another male nurse set up a machine used to drain the excess fluid from Mama's body.

When Mama first got sick, I was overwhelmed by the sight of seeing all the medical equipment connected to her body, but now I've become accustomed to seeing and hearing the health related gadgets used in the emergency room and ICU. Lately, I've been in the emergency room with Mama so much, that I feel like I should get a certificate from one of those accelerated nursing schools because I know why all the different machines are used and which questions to ask the doctors while they're treating Mama.

Beeping monitors with flashing numbers occupy significant space in the small room. A BiPAP machine is helping Mama breathe by pushing air into her weakened lungs and keeps them open to allow more oxygen to filter through. Sometimes Mama is irritated by wearing the mask associated with the BiPAP machine, but at least it's more comfortable than having a breathing tube inserted down her throat. Other digital instruments track her blood pressure and heart rate. She's struggling, but the Lord is helping her to hold on. I pray to God to heal my mother.

As the oldest of three children born to Hope Collins and a father I hardly knew, I'm the responsible one. My number is usually the first one Mama dials. I feel good about holding that place in her heart, but sometimes I think I'm in it all alone. Mama phones me for just about everything, and that includes calls for everything from repairs needed to be done to the house to why the remote control wasn't working on the television. Sometimes I think Mama calls me because she's lonely and tired of living alone.

The physical resemblance between us is striking and undeniable. Our round faces are dipped in a hue of rich, dark chocolate; both complexions shaded to perfection; smooth and blemish free. Both of us possess small lips that smile even when our eyes want to cry. Mental fatigue is making my spirit eager to shed a few tears now.

Sometimes I want to ask God why I have to deal with so much responsibility, but it wouldn't be fair to ask God why now because I never questioned Him about the blessings I received. I try to take the good with the bad. Besides, Mama always said "God never puts on us more than we can bear." However, I believe God has a sense of humor and makes a point of pushing us very close to our breaking point, or at least out of our comfort zone.

At age thirty-five, I feel like I'm on the cusp of making an impact in my life, almost as if I'm about to do some great things. I consider myself a lifetime member of the overachiever, workaholic club. I graduated with honors from the University of Michigan and later obtained a law degree from the University of Chicago. My credentials are solid. I had job offers from major law firms, but never had an interest in pursuing employment with any of them. Taking a position with a major firm would've meant turning my life over to them. They would've been able to dictate my existence while I labored long hours in an attempt to make partner. I'd rather hustle for myself than worry about meeting billable hour quotas and making the partners rich.

A lot of people questioned my decision, but I had to step out on faith. It took me a little time to decide what area of law I wanted to practice, but real estate always appealed to me. I knew a law degree and a real estate license would provide me with a lot of opportunities.

I have a lovely home in Beverly, an affluent area on Chicago's south side. The neighborhood is comprised of mostly upwardly mobile whites and a speckle of blacks, dwelling in big, beautiful, brick houses, where massive trees shade long driveways and meticulously manicured lawns. Beverly is covertly segregated. I live amongst whites, but by no means am I isolated from my people.

In Chicago, neighborhoods can change fast. Beverly, on the other hand, has remained stable and relatively safe because of expensive housing costs, steep property taxes and redlining. All it takes is a viaduct here or an intersection there, to shed an entirely different light on a community. New developments and condo conversions are taking place all over the city, and I'm trying to get some of it for myself. The way I see it: In ten years, if a man doesn't have a place to lay his head in the city, he won't be able to because living in the city will be too expensive. Folks are being priced out to the suburbs.

Professionally, things are going well, but my love life definitely needs some extra spice. I yearn to be in a committed relationship with a special lady in my life. I need someone to hang out and have fun with. I'm ready to settle down and start a family.

I've grown tired of living like a serial dater, spending lots of money on the weekend, trying to impress women who want more than I can ever give. Besides, it's time consuming and very expensive! I've gotten bored with it. No longer am I interested in pursuing women just for sex. Getting a piece of tail is always nice, but I want more right now. Sometimes, after listening to a few females whine about lousy credit, bad kids and stalker ex-husbands and boyfriends, I lose the motivation I have to hang around long enough even to get the sex. Sometimes the drama just isn't worth it.

My last serious relationship was with a woman by the name of Terri. We dated for almost a year and a half, and I thought we were headed down the aisle towards wedding bells. It seemed almost as though the romance faded overnight. I don't know what happened. One moment we were in love, the next moment we weren't. The time and energy put into the relationship seemed like nothing more than a bad emotional investment; no return on romance and zero profits in passion. I'm still trying to recover from the loss of that relationship. Accepting the fact that the relationship has ended and realizing it's time to start all over again is always the most difficult part.

I sat down in a chair by the bed and tried to get comfortable. Mama's condition had finally stabilized. The oxygen mask was gone and Mama was able to speak freely.

"How do you feel, Ma?"

"Better . . . than I did," she whispered between labored breaths. "Ah … I was feelin' fine last night when I went to bed, but … I got sick in the middle of the night . . . couldn't catch my breath. I had a rough night Julian. Ooh, I had a rough one baby," she said, shaking her head in a way that suggested she was very tired of being sick and going through this routine.

This is the third time in the last two and a half months Mama has been rushed to the hospital because of breathing problems. It's gotten to the point now that many of the people on staff in the emergency area know Mama by name. One of the female nurses in the intensive care unit even teases Mama saying she loves them so much that she just can't stay away.

As usual, the emergency area is crowded with new patients entering constantly. The small hospital, located in one of the city's roughest areas, is often, the place of recovery for the many victims of the vices occurring nearby. I'm guessing it will be a while before they move Mama into a regular hospital room. Most likely they'll put her in an intensive care unit so they can monitor her closely overnight. I try to adjust my body by getting in a position that will allow me to relax better, but the chair is just too uncomfortable.

Mama tapped her hand on the bed. "Have you spoken with Kendall and La-La?"

"Not yet, Ma,"

"You need to call 'em and let 'em know . . ."

"I will."

I don't even want to call my younger brother, Kendall. Only two years separates us in age, but a lifetime separates our souls. He's everything I'm not. Kendall possesses a cockiness that mocks my humbleness, a swagger that scorns my subtlety, and a defiantness that dilutes my discipline. And it's always been like that! Mama says I have a heart of gold and the dignity of a king, but Kendall is an ace in the hole always looking to stack the deck in his favor.

Lauren, the self centered diva, and baby of the family, is too loyal to her position with a downtown insurance company to realize she will only have one Mama. The perennial sista on the go doesn't always have time to incorporate family matters into her schedule. You know: she's busy. I'm blessed to have my siblings, but a lot of times I feel like I'm in this all alone.

Mama tries to encourage me to go home, but I'm determined to stay with her until they move her to a regular room. I look at my watch. It's almost midnight. I've been sitting in the same uncomfortable chair since four o'clock this afternoon. My back is sore and my stomach is aching with hunger. A new shift is just beginning. A stout, middle-aged black woman enters the room. She speaks softly to greet me and then goes over to the bed to check on Mama. During the course of the evening, Mama has been sleeping off and on.

The nurse's movement around the bed causes Mama's eyes to open. Now I understand what Mama means when she says she's never able to rest in the hospital because every time she closes her eyes someone wakes her up to check on this and monitor that. At least this time, the nurse is bringing good news. She informs us that Mama is going to be moved from the emergency room area to the intensive care unit on another floor.

I gathered Mama's belongings and put them in a large, plastic shopping bag to take home with me. I don't want anything getting misplaced. On a previous hospital stay, Mama lost a coat being transported from one room to another.

A young guy came into the room and asked Mama if she was ready to take a trip. She smiled and nodded her head. I kissed Mama on the forehead and said goodbye. It's time for me to go home and get it my own bed. This wasn't how I had planned on spending my Saturday night.

2

KENDALL

There's nothing better than being in Las Vegas on the Saturday night of a big fight. Bernard "The Executioner" Hopkins is ready to go to war with boxing's Golden Boy, Oscar De La Hoya for the middleweight championship of the world. The electricity is overflowing in the desert.

Folks in all shapes, forms and fashions are in town to engage in their festivities of choice; to see and be seen. As Hollywood movie stars stepped out of limos in outfits primed for a night at the Oscars, intoxicated rock idols and blunt smoking rappers rolled up in stretch Hummers with eager entourages staggering along for the ride. Meanwhile Big Willie Dynamite style pimps paraded along the strip in flamingo pink suits with matching gators on their feet. They strutted around town with peacock feathered hats on their heads and shiny pimp cups in their hands. While the mack daddies took the term coordinated to a new level, their prostitutes strolled seductively in tight leather dresses and six inch stiletto heels, advertising their goodies to turn a quick trick.

Black and Latino gang factions are in town to represent their crews and bash a few heads along the way. Everyone's out to enhance their reputations. As the action heats up the strip, drug dealers transact future business and perform quietly under the marquee lights. Las Vegas has the reputation as being sin city, but for people like me its heaven.

Bernard Hopkins executed a perfect body punch that sent the Golden Boy sprawling on the MGM Grand canvas. Oscar was knocked down and couldn't get up. The ninth round knockout instigated the raucous crowd into contenders of mini showdowns between rival Latino and black gangs. Hopkins' punch took De La Hoya's breath away, and sucked a life of cash out of many Latino pockets. It was a wild scene. I wasn't feeling the extra curricular nonsense, so I returned to my suite in the Luxor to prepare for the rest of the evening. The fight was over, but the night was still young. It was only ten-thirty and the parties were just getting started.

I took a quick shower and laid a tan suit out on the side of the bed. The reflection in the mirror allowed me to admire myself. My bronze skin glistened and exuded the power of an Egyptian god. At six-foot two inches tall, my body was strong and lean; anchored with broad shoulders and long, muscular arms. Thick eyebrows and lengthy lashes shielded a piercing stare which attracted and repelled at the same time. I was always able to engage people with my personality and magnetically drew folks close to me; especially women. I had all the traits that made me lovable and dangerous at the same time. Mama always said, "Boy you just like Kenny." People either loved me or hated me. I guess naming me Kendall Lamar Collins Jr. was appropriate.

Mama had done the best she could in raising three kids without a man in the house. We were young when Daddy left us. I'm the middle child, sandwiched by an older brother and younger sister, each of two years. We'd grown up under the same roof, but were so different it seems as though we were raised by a different mother on opposite sides of town. Our personalities are extremely different!

I'm considered the outcast, the black sheep of the family. They don't approve of my lifestyle. That's cool with me. Even so, I feel Julian and I should be on better terms since we're brothers, but we're as different as night and day and just don't see things eye to eye. My older brother thinks he's smarter than everyone else because he's a college graduate and has a law degree. He always had his head buried in a book. I ain't hatin' on him. That's his thing.

I remember when we were kids and used to play outside; he would always want to go in the house and do homework. Since he's older, I was always expected to follow his lead. It was a problem because Julian's pace was too slow for me. As kids, he was always the one to play it safe, trying to avoid danger and risk. I was more adventurous.

My sister, Lauren is living single in her own world; tucked away in Hyde Park with the rest of her bourgeois and proper speaking friends. She's so busy yearning for the perfect planet in an imperfect universe that she'll probably never be happy; just too set in her ways and hard to get along with. Her expectations of people are too great. Lauren wants every man to kiss her ass and tell her she's right all the time. She's very high maintenance and wants to have her way all the time. Somewhere along the line she started believing her shit didn't stink.

I'm probably the smartest of the three of us, but I never applied myself in the classroom the way Julian and Lauren did. School bored me and getting good grades failed to motivate me. Math was a subject that came easy for me because I liked numbers and keeping figures, but usually, I did just enough to pass. I was too busy fighting, messing with girls, and being rebellious. Besides, what I lacked in formal education, I more than made up for it in mother wit and street smarts. I know how to survive. Neither one of my siblings could make it in my world, but I would excel in theirs.

I love Julian and Lauren, but I . . .

I admire my appearance again in the mirror. Fresh and clean, just like the money in my pocket. Dirty money makes the world go round and Las Vegas is one of the largest Laundromats in the land. Unfortunately, federal laws are making it more difficult to keep money clean. Dope addicts usually buy drugs with small bills, so I needed to do laundry and pack before coming to Vegas. I had gone to several currency exchanges back in Chicago and purchased $98,000 worth of money orders. I made sure all the money orders were less than $3,000 to keep the currency exchanges involved from having to report it to the government.

Once I got to Vegas, I had to convert the money orders into gambling chips. The money orders were made out to several casinos on the strip and downtown in amounts smaller than $10,000 to avoid currency reports being submitted by the cashiers. By the time I had the chips in my hand, the money had already been laundered twice: first in Chicago and then again in Vegas. It was time consuming going to so many different casinos, but it was the safest way to do it. Now I was ready to meet with Hector.

    I don't know a whole lot about Hector and I don't want to know a lot either. I called him Hect Connect because he supplied me with drugs for me to circulate on the south side of Chicago. This will be our third meeting. The higher-ups back home have sanctioned my activities with Hector as long as I paid a monetary tribute to them and shared a piece of my earnings. Chasing the cheese in the drug game is always very dangerous because traps are set everywhere, but a plate full of cheddar makes eating so much better and the risk much more rewarding. Money is addictive and so is power and respect. And that's what keeps me in the game.

    It was midnight when Hector knocked on my door. He was always on time. Hector entered the room and greeted me with a firm handshake and the aroma of a freshly lit cigar.

    "Que Paso?" I said, with a sheepish grin, knowing damn well I couldn't engage in a lengthy conversation with Hector in Spanish.

    "Muy bien, amigo," he replied, as he took a puff, leaving my once fresh clothes fuming with smoke. He reached into his pocket and pulled out a silver cigar container and gave it to me. He suggested we get down to business and let the smoke rise. I obliged.

    The always dapper Hector was dressed in a black, single breasted suit with a burgundy silk shirt, opened at the middle of his chest, displaying a large gold medallion. Hector was not physically imposing, but he possessed an aura of power and confidence in a very controlled yet sneaky way. He unbuttoned his jacket and took a seat; crossing his legs in a relaxed mode; his black leather shoes shone brighter than the lights on the strip. The pose made me think of a magazine I saw recently with the singer, Marc Anthony on the cover. Hect "Connect" was incognito cool.

    Hector and I discussed a few details and set up a date for a transaction. Out of the $98,000 in chips in my possession, I gave Hector $85,000 for a future cocaine delivery and kept the remaining

$13,000 for myself to cash in later. Both of us could say we won playing craps or blackjack. I ushered Hector to the door and said goodbye.

My business with Hector was done, so I decided to go back downstairs to unwind and try my luck at roulette. I found a table that wasn't too crowded and grabbed a chair next to a young Asian woman working the game. I decided to pass on the roll and watched to see how things would play out. In the meantime, I studied the board to check which numbers had won recently. I watched the little white ball zip around the carousel about a dozen times before it stopped on number 15. I don't usually play that number so I would've lost. I waited for the Asian lady to reward the winners with fresh chips and then decided to get in the game.

I pulled out a hundred dollar bill and put it on the table for the cute Asian chick to grab it from the game table. She pushed the crisp bill into a tiny slot, and gave me blue chips to play with. To my left, a sexy, caramel toned woman in a FUBU jogging suit stared at me seductively as I stacked chips in neat piles of ten. We made eye contact and I gave her a wink. That's all it took for her to come my way. Because that's what I do: I stack up chips and lay down chicks.

"My lucky number is 8," she said, gently rubbing her body against mine.

"Then *you* should play 8," I responded with a sly smile. I put a stack of ten chips on number 12 and 3 and gave the sexy Ms. FUBU the once over. I played with the rest of my chips and wondered if there was any room for me inside her jogging pants.

"What about the number 8?" she asked. "That's my son's age."

"Well *you* should play it then," I said with a penetrating stare.

The white ball raced around the carousel. The Asian cutie waved her slender hand across the board signaling the end of all bets for this particular roll. The ball flipped over a few numbers and landed on 3. I had just hit at 35-1 odds and had $350 in chips coming my way. I gave the Asian lady a ten dollar tip in chips. Ms. FUBU folded her arms and looked at me as if she was supposed to get a tip also. The board was covered with chips, with some people playing even and odd number bets, colored bets, or sections. Usually, I selected numbers that represented the birthdays of my mother, siblings or me.

I glanced at Ms. FUBU. "What happened to number 8?" I asked arrogantly.

"It's comin' this time," she declared. "Just wait and see."

"Yeah right," I said, and placed ten dollars in chips on 2, 14, 9 and 24. I was winning big but always betted small. I'll never let the casino get all of my money. This time the ball stopped on 14, the day of the month I was born. Another $350 in chips came my way.

Money was coming easy. I was on a roll and was ready to stay in the game for a few more spins. Unfortunately my cell phone kept vibrating non-stop inside my right pants pocket. I pulled out my cell phone and checked the caller ID. It's Lauren. I advised the Asian babe to cash me out. I left the game with about $650; not bad for a few minutes work.

I headed to the cashier cage to cash in my chips as Ms. FUBU lingered behind me in an attempt to get my attention. Something must be wrong back home because it's late and Lauren's number keeps popping up on my caller ID. It's one-thirty in Vegas and three-thirty in Chicago. I decided to return the call.

"Hello," Lauren said, answering the phone on the first ring.

"What's up La-La?"

"Has Julian contacted you?" she asked in a stern and proper tone.

"No," I snapped back. "Why?"

"We had to put Mama back in the hospital today!"

"What happened?" I asked, leaning up against a wall to gather myself.

"She had another asthma attack early this afternoon and she's been asking for you all evening, Kendall! Where are you?"

"I'm in Vegas," I answered. "I'll be home tomorrow."

"Well you need to get here as soon as possible," she warned with the intensity of a schoolteacher scolding a room full of bad students.

"I'll be there tomorrow!" I shouted defensively. I understood Lauren being frustrated, but right now, I'm pissed off at Julian for not calling to let me know about Mama's condition.

"Well I hope so," she countered.

"How is she?"

"She's stable, but she's still in intensive care at Roseland Hospital. Mama asked Julian to call you and let you know," she said in a whimpering voice that suggested she was trying to keep from crying.

"Let Mama know I'll be there tomorrow when I get back in town."

"Kendall, you need to tell us when you're leaving town. Anything can happen."

"I'm sorry La-La," I replied. "I promise I'll be there tomorrow."

"Okay Kendall."

I hung up the phone and placed it back into my right pocket. I stood near the cashier cages and tried to gather my thoughts. It was difficult. The loud noises coming from the gambling machines made it hard to concentrate. Mama's health changes so quickly. One moment she's doing fine and the next moment she's sick and being rushed to the hospital.

I love Mama, but I can't do a damn thing for her while I'm here in Vegas. Julian and Lauren act like I don't love Mama because I'm not around as much as they want me to be. Fuck them.

I rubbed my hand across my face and took a deep breath. Since I got out here everything had been going my way. I won money on the fight; handled my business with Hector; and had even been lucky playing the slot machines and roulette.

Well since I'm going home tomorrow, I might as well enjoy my last night here. I beckoned for Ms. FUBU to come my way. Maybe I'll take her up to my room and hit her jackpot.

3

LAUREN

I'm glad it's Friday. Putting out fires at work and running back and forth to the hospital to see Mama all week has me feeling exhausted. I'm glad I decided to take a half day so I can have more time to take care of some of my business. I feel so behind on my responsibilities. I need to pay some bills, do laundry, and go grocery shopping. My refrigerator is so empty that if I open the door and say something, I'll probably hear an echo. And I still have some clothes that I need to get out of the cleaners. Where does the time go?

Instead of running errands for myself or going straight home to get some rest, I promised Mama I would stop by the hospital and bring her some fresh clothes, just in case she's discharged over the weekend. She's been in the hospital for over a week now, and is extremely anxious to go home since she's finally out of ICU. I'm sure being in the hospital, for weeks at a time, gets a bit old after a while.

I hate coming to see Mama when she's in this hospital because this area is so dangerous and the security isn't very good. I'm always worried about getting robbed or someone breaking into my car. That's why I prefer to come during the day instead of at night.

The desk attendant in the lobby smiled and gazed into my dark brown eyes.

He greeted me in a deep, gravelly voice. "Hello."

"Hello," I responded with an alluring smile. "I'm here to see Hope Collins in room 238."

"Here you are ma'am," he said, still smiling and gazing into my eyes with a look of both admiration and intimidation, handing me a visitor's pass to stick to my tight-fitting, knit sweater. I thanked him and walked away. Down the long corridor I went. His window of opportunity was closed, but I could still feel his eyes probing my body from head to toe. And I was making it a point to giving him something he could remember me by.

Freshly braided cornrows rested neatly down the arch of my back as I distanced myself from my new admirer. Short, swift steps made my legs strut lovely and my hips sway heavenly. A mini-skirt and a pair of pumps can take me a long way. I had to thank God and Mama for my eye catching traits.

A family photo album showed Mama in her youth as a vivacious woman; sexy, sassy and strong. She looked happy then. Maybe that's because Daddy was in the pictures also. Many of the photos were taken shortly after they were married, but before my birth; most of them view Julian as a toddler and Kendall as an infant. Maybe I was just a thought at the time. I was supposed to be Daddy's little girl, but I didn't see many pictures of me being cradled in my father's arms. I was abandoned.

I rode the elevator to the second floor and passed the nurse's station on my way to Mama's room. I walked through the doors and heard her cheering on Judge Mathis and praising him for laying down the law to a trouble-making teenager.

"You tell him Judge," she cheered. "He talkin' like he done lost his damn mind!"

"Is the Judge setting him straight, Ma?" I asked, as I approached the bed.

"You know he is!" she declared. "That's why I like him: He don't waste no time setting folks straight," she said, reaching out her left hand to touch mine. "I like all the judges, but Judge Mathis is my favorite."

"I like him, too!" I agreed, taking a seat next to the bed. "So how are you feeling today, Ma?"

"So-so," she answered, rolling her eyes.

"Has your doctor been in here today?"

She made a face and waved him off. "He stopped in here for a little while."

"What did he say?"

"He said since I had pneumonia, they wanna make sure my lungs are clear before letting me go home." She shook her head in resignation. "I'm tired of this hospital, but it ain't no sense in me going home if I'm gonna keep coming back. I'd rather just stay here 'til I get well."

"Well you look better and sound better," I said, in an attempt to lift Mama's spirits. "You had so much fluid in your body last week, I could hear you rattling when you talked."

"Yeah . . . I guess that was the pneumonia you heard."

"I see your ankles aren't swollen anymore."

"I know."

"I read on the internet that swelling in the ankles or hands are one of the symptoms of people suffering from congestive heart failure."

"Oh yeah?"

"Umm hmm," I replied. "I read quite a bit about your condition."

"That internet has a lot of good information on it huh?"

"Yes Mama."

"You know, La-La, you were always very inquisitive and smart. Your brothers are smart, too, but you were always very observant and paid close attention to stuff."

I smiled. In my quiet moments I wonder what will happen to me and my two brothers once Mama is gone. Her blood runs through our veins, her spirit saturates our souls. Our seeds are planted in identical soil. The roots of three siblings surge through the same tree, but our branches stretch out individually and waywardly; each of us reaching for our own space in the sky, but falling way short of heaven. We've yielded a mixed bag of fruit. Some sweet, some sour, and some rotten to the core.

My oldest brother, Julian, is a Mama's boy. He's a good guy with a warm heart who has always tried to play by the rules. I feel for him. Unfortunately, he's too nice and the cold world we live in devours men like him everyday. It even carries over into his dating life and the pseudo, upper echelon women he's trying to hang out with. Most of them are semi-pro gold diggers who could give less than a damn about how sweet he is and how much he loves his mother. He's too busy trying to do the right thing, and they're too busy trying to get in his pockets. Some of these women out here are probably waiting in line to run over him.

Meanwhile, women seem to be waiting in line to be run over by Kendall. He was afforded that luxury at an early age in life because he doesn't give a damn. Kendall's primary concern is Kendall. I remember back in the day, my grade school girlfriends would come over, supposedly, so we could study together and do homework, but they were really trying to study Kendall. We were in junior high, but they were working the game already. They played the role to the hilt and accepted tutoring from Julian, but Kendall was the teacher they were trying to get lessons from. It was so typical. Julian, the good kid would come in the house like a hero to save the day, while Kendall, the devious kid was lurking outside waiting to reap all the rewards. Kendall always marched to the beat of his own drum. Julian worried about what people thought. Kendall could care less. I love my brothers, flaws and all.

I hate seeing my mother suffer like this. It makes me feel helpless and awkward. Mama needs me right now, but it seems like the closer I get to the situation, the more stressed out I become. Guilt takes over my mind when I'm not around to help, but I'm totally overwhelmed when I am. It makes me realize how limited my power is. I hate not having control. Sometimes the anguish makes me wish I could get in my car and just drive far away from it all.

"So what you got planned for tonight, La-La?" Mama asked, interrupting the thoughts flowing through my head.

"I don't know," I replied, covering my mouth to yawn. "I'm in the mood to go home and go to sleep. I may go to the office for a few hours tomorrow morning."

"Girl you need to go out and have some fun and stop working so damn hard."

"Ma . . ."

"Ma nothing," she mocked, cutting me off before I could finish my sentence. "La-La, I understand you being ambitious and all, but you need to think about more than just that damn job. That company is going to be there with or without you."

"I know Ma."

"You better enjoy your life La-La while you're young and still able to do the stuff you like to do. Believe me, you'll be old before you know it. You ain't gonna be able to switch around in short skirts and high heels for the rest of your life."

I rolled my eyes at Mama and shook my head. I didn't come here for this nonsense and wasn't in the mood to hear it either.

"Girl, don't look at me in that tone of voice!" she warned.

The Spoken Word Café was a convenient place for me to hang out on a Saturday night and unwind after another trying work week. Located in the up and coming area known as Bronzeville, the Spoken Word Café is about a five minute drive from my condo in Hyde Park. It was nice because I was able to get out on the town without having to go too far from home.

Back in the forties and fifties, Bronzeville was home to the city's burgeoning blues and jazz scene with an array of artists around every corner eager to perform and perfect their craft. On par with the renaissance taking place in New York City's Harlem, Bronzeville was Chicago's Black Metropolis, and a historic district. Unfortunately, a recession, crime, drugs and despair caused the foundation of the community to crumble during the sixties and seventies, becoming a mere shadow of its former self. By the time the eighties rolled around, the community was considered the low end and one of the worst places to live on the south side.

Fortunately, the area is making a strong comeback, with several new facilities opening to bring life back to a community yearning to be revived. The corner of 47th & King Drive seemed to be the intersection of entertainment and the soul of the area's new tradition. The new Harold Washington Cultural Center sits on the southeast corner of the street and is named after Chicago's first black mayor. The Harold Washington Cultural Center had recently opened, and was already hosting concerts featuring some of the brightest up and coming artists of R&B and hip-hop.

The Spoken Word Café is located directly across the street from the Harold Washington Cultural Center, on the northeast corner of 47th Street, and is giving writers and poets a stage in Bronzeville the way in which it had done for Richard Wright and Gwendolyn Brooks years ago. In addition, the popular Afrocentric Bookstore had recently moved from its former downtown location to its new home on the corner also. It's nice to see black businesses thriving again in our community.

I entered the Spoken Word Café and gave the lady at the door a crisp ten dollar bill. I quickly scanned the laid back crowd of the cozy club. The atmosphere embraced the intimacy of an oversized living room, complete with big chairs, a sofa, and a fireplace. There's also a small stage for the band, The House of Twang, to keep the crowd grooving to a fusion of jazz and funk.

I got in a short line along the left side of the club and tried to make a decision on what I wanted to drink. I spoke to the cashier and decided to order a vanilla latte. While waiting for my latte, I surveyed the room for a seat. There were a few seats available near the front, but I preferred to sit in the back and observe. Besides, I didn't want to be an unwilling subject for someone's material.

Saturday is open mic night at the Spoken Word and every week poets yearn for an opportunity to step to the stage and shoot off a few blazing verses. I kept a journal and wrote some poetry when I was younger, but I didn't have the spirit to speak my thoughts in this type of setting. My words might be too tame for this audience. I'll probably get booed off the stage for speaking proper and annunciating my words too clearly. The poets lighting up the stage were spitting fire and coming with the heat!

A light skinned brother by the name of Red Storm attacked the mic with an oral onslaught of thunder and rage. He verbalized the struggles of a black man trying to stay out of the system designed to keep him down, while attempting to survive on the streets at the same time. His rhymes told a graphic story about pressures of trying to avoid drugs and violence, with shady cops looking for another brother to beat down. The wrath of Red Storm's verses captured the soul of the attentive audience and unlocked the prisons of our mind.

Somehow we need to unite and understand how much brothers and sisters really need each another.

I sipped on some of my vanilla latte and took a deep breath to gather myself. The intense Red Storm had finally passed over. That brother rhymed with passion.

A brief intermission allowed people to stretch their legs, socialize, get more refreshments and listen to The House of Twang, while more poets signed up for the second set. I sat there alone and continued to observe the crowd. I could tell a lot of the people in attendance were regulars. Most of the folks were dressed in comfortable attire with several sisters sporting head wraps and big afros. It's obvious how influential the neo-soul movement is because a lot of ladies are working the Angie Stone, Erykah Badu, Jill Scott vibe to the max.

I finished the rest of my latte. The taste was sweet, but not nearly as yummy as the tall, dark skinned brother walking my way.

"Are you gonna sit back here in the Rosa Parks seats or are you gonna move closer to the front?" he said, wearing a navy linen pants and shirt outfit, navy dress sandals, and a navy Movado watch. He looked good, but I remained coy, admiring his outfit from head to toe. Nice shoes.

"I'll stay here," I said. "I like being able to sit back and watch from a distance."

He extended his hand and introduced himself. "My name is Andre."

He gently massaged my fingers. "Hi Andre," I replied. "My name is Lauren."

"So are you gonna grace the stage with your presence Lauren?" he asked, taking a seat in the empty folding chair next to me. I didn't invite him to sit down, but I liked his aggressive attitude.

I shook my head. "No thanks," I responded, realizing my latte was all gone. "Who knows, maybe I'll consider it at some point in the future. What about you?"

"Yeah I got a few thoughts flowing in my head."

"Just a few?" I joked.

"Oh . . . I see you're a witty sista with jokey jokes," he replied with a smile.

"Yeah just a few," I blushed.

"Okay then Ms. Lauren," he laughed. "I'll remember that."

"So do you have a cool stage name also, Andre?" I asked as the house lights were turned down and people returned to their seats after the brief intermission.

"Yep."

"What is it?"

"You'll hear it when they call my name," he replied, with an air of confidence.

"Excuse me!"

He laughed and looked at me with sincere eyes. "I wanna talk to you, but I don't wanna be disruptive and disrespectful to the people on the stage. Can I talk with you later before you leave?"

"I'll be here," I confessed, inhaling the fragrance of his cologne and his dark brown skin tone. They were intoxicating.

"Maybe we can exchange information?"

"That'll be fine," I reassured.

"Cool. Well, I'll talk to you later then."

"Okay."

"Nice meeting you Lauren."

"Nice meeting you also, Andre," I replied with a flirtatious smile, displaying a full set of pearly white teeth. I took a good look at Andre's body as he walked away from me and received a vicious stare from a lady with a big Angela Davis afro. She seemed like she wanted to protest my conversation with Andre, and appeared to be on the verge of starting a revolution. I just hope her revolution isn't televised because the first thing she needs to do is comb her hair.

The host cracked a few jokes and invited the next poet to come to the stage.

"The next brotha I wanna bring to the stage has been flowin' strong up in here on the regular for some time now. Y'all know he gon' come wit' a vibe y'all can feel for real. Ladies if you love chocolate, then y'all definitely gon' love Mr. Hershey. Come on up here, brotha. Show some love for Andre Evans aka Mr. Hershey."

I grinned deviously. "Mr. Hershey, huh?"

I smiled and watched Andre as he walked to the stage and grabbed the mic from the host. I admired him from the back of the room and felt a moistness trickling between my thighs. Andre is eye candy for days. I'll end up going to the hospital for diabetes if I mess around with all that chocolate. I just hope Mr. Hershey is packed with a lot of nuts.

4

JULIAN

Good news, Mama is going to be released from the hospital today. I don't have any court appearances or real estate closings to handle, so I was counting on a relatively quiet day at the office anyway. The phones at my law firm are ringing off the hook, but fortunately today I don't have any pressing issues on my calendar. Since this is the case, I'm able to make time to pick up Mama from the hospital without having to rearrange my schedule.

This time Mama's hospitalization has lasted more than two weeks, with her making two separate trips to ICU because of asthma attacks and breathing problems occurring during the middle of the night. It's frustrating to see Mama get her hopes up about going home, only then to experience a setback the night before being released.

It's been draining for me as well. I went to visit Mama every evening and had also gone by the house on a regular basis to look over things and check the mail. I was managing my house, Mama's house, and trying to run a law practice, all at the same time. People think it's easier for me because I'm my own boss, but when I'm not taking care of my business, I'm not making any money. Sometimes all the running around has me not knowing whether I am coming or going.

Mama was sitting in a chair instead of resting in bed when I entered the room. She was watching *The Price is Right* and trying to make a bid on a new living room set.

"There's my son!" she shouted with excitement.

"Hi Ma," I replied, greeting her with a kiss on the cheek. "Are you ready to go home yet or are you staying here?"

"Go home!" she shouted with the energy of a contestant greeting Bob Barker.

"I know that's right," I agreed. "You've been in here a long time."

As Mama gathered all of her belongings and made a final bid on the showcase showdown, a petite, bespectacled nurse entered the room to say goodbye.

"I heard you're leaving us today, Ms. Collins," she said with a big grin.

"You heard right, sweetie," Mama replied. "You heard right."

"Well, I'll miss you, but I'm glad to hear you're finally going home."

"Me too, sweetie, me too," Mama said, using her cane to beckon the nurse to come closer to where I was standing. "This is the son I been bragging about. Julian this is Vanessa. She has really looked after me since I been here."

I extended my hand to Vanessa. "So you've been looking after my mother, huh?"

"Yes I have," she answered in a raspy voice that failed to match her youthful appearance. She appeared to be in her mid to late twenties, but her disposition seemed older and wiser. Vanessa is small in stature, much slimmer and plainer looking than the ladies I'm usually attracted to, but she possessed a wholesome, innocent girl next door kind of appeal.

"I really appreciate you caring for my mom."

Vanessa smiled. "Your mom is a wonderful lady. She reminds me of my mom."

Mama interjected. "You two are probably around the same age and might have a lot in common," taking the opportunity to use some of her matchmaking skills. "He's a very busy attorney, but he always finds time to look after his old Mama," she continued, giving

Vanessa tidbits of information about me while blowing sunshine up my butt. "Whenever I need something, I know I can call on Julian and he will be there to help. A lot of children don't have time when their parents get up in age, but Julian always makes time for me. I'm proud of him. And I love him dearly."

"God is going to bless you for being there for your mom the way you have."

I blushed. "He already has."

Mama may have been laying it on thick to impress Vanessa, but her comments regarding my dedication are accurate. I make sacrifices, considerably more than either of my two siblings. Kendall is always in and out of town, living the lifestyle of an illegal big shot. He's angry because I didn't call him and let him know Mama had been rushed to the hospital. As it turned out, he was in Vegas and wouldn't have been able to do anything anyway. He should've at least let us know he was going to be out of the state as he puts it, doin' business. He's doing business in more towns than Wal-Mart.

Meanwhile, Lauren makes a celebrity appearance like a diva in search of the spotlight and good publicity. Trying to avoid the situation is perhaps my sister's way of dealing with Mama's deteriorating health, but right now, all of us need to step up and do a little more to make things easier for Mama.

"Vanessa, what time do you get off tonight?" Mama inquired.

"I'm here until seven o'clock," she answered. "I'm working twelve hours today."

"Julian give Vanessa one of your business cards," Mama ordered boldly. "Who knows, she or someone she knows may need some legal advice one day." Mama was calling plays in the huddle and throwing touchdown passes like an All-Pro quarterback. She was happy to be going home and was putting on a MVP caliber performance in trying to set me up with Nurse Vanessa.

I felt good when I woke up this morning. Knowing Mama got out of the hospital yesterday is a major relief to my spirit. I didn't even go into the office yesterday after taking Mama to the house. Instead, I went to Blockbuster to rent some DVDs and spent the afternoon and evening watching movies and listening to some jazz. I needed some time for myself, and yesterday I was able to accomplish that. It was a very relaxing Monday. I guess that's why I feel so refreshed and recharged this morning. Everyone needs a mental health day every now and then.

My law practice has been keeping me extremely busy lately. Most of the emphasis has been in the area of real estate. I process mortgage loan applications and occasionally take clients to look at buildings, houses and condos. I'm also doing a lot of real estate closings which makes the end of the month very active yet stressful for me. The money is easy so I'm not complaining.

The smooth saxophone sounds of Boney James accompanied me as I moved at a snail's pace along the Dan Ryan Expressway. As usual, rush hour traffic was sluggish and irritating, but Boney's horn was stirring and invigorating. I changed lanes to find a quicker pace, but my thoughts steered in the direction of Vanessa and the way Mama had driven home the point of us getting to know each other. It seemed as though Mama wasn't going to put on the brakes until she made sure Vanessa and I had exchanged phone numbers. I was kind of embarrassed by how quickly Mama made her move to set us up, but Vanessa seemed to take it all in stride and went with the flow. I don't want to appear too anxious so I'll probably call later this week. Maybe we can go out to dinner or catch a movie.

Once I made it downtown, I stopped in Starbucks to get a cup of coffee. There's a Starbucks on almost every corner in the Loop these days. As usual, the line is long with people trying to get an extra boost to start the work day; paying way too much for a cup of coffee. Most of them seemed pressed for time, but I felt relaxed and was enjoying the breeze coming in from outside.

Early autumn is my favorite time of the year; the air is crisp, but the temperature is not too hot or too cold. This would've been a good day to get out and take an early morning jog; I need to get more exercise and keep my weight in check so I don't have to go out and buy new clothes. I enjoy dressing up and putting on my nice suits when the weather is mild and breezy like it is today. The look of a classy, well-tailored suit and a colorful tie always brightened my mood and put more pep in my step. A positive vibe flowed through me with a magnetic energy that captured the attention of an attractive woman standing in line behind me.

I paid for my coffee and strolled toward the exit with confidence. The woman in line was looking in my direction and smiling. My instincts encouraged me to wait. She paid the cashier and came my way.

"I love your tie," she complimented me.

I blushed. "Thanks," I said, holding the door open for her to pass through in front of me. Doing this gave me the opportunity to get a better look at her figure while being a gentleman at the same time.

"A lot of guys wouldn't have the confidence to wear a pink tie, but you're definitely pulling it off without a doubt," she said with a warm smile and cheerful eyes.

"Well, I'm glad it got your attention in a positive way," I stated modestly. "By the way, my name is Julian."

"My name is Annette."

"Nice to meet you," I said, with a shy grin.

Annette's personality is bubbly and contagious, and matches the enthusiasm I have for the morning. My work week is definitely starting off on a bright note because Annette is voluptuous, vivacious and has booty for days! It almost made me wonder if Annette was the leader of the Disciples or Vice Lords or maybe the Crips or Bloods because she has a gang of ass following her around. Damn girl!

"You work in the area?" she asked.

"Yes. I'm at 200 South Wacker."

"You're close by," she stated. "I'm in the Sears Tower."

"Oh you're right across the street!"

"Yes sir."

"Since you're across the street, maybe we can get together and have lunch soon?" I asked, taking a look at her hands and noticed she isn't wearing an engagement or wedding ring.

"That would be great," she replied jubilantly. "I love to eat."

I laughed. "Most women do."

I walked Annette over to the Sears Tower and swapped phone numbers. My confidence seemed as though it was at an all time high. Yesterday, I met and exchanged phone numbers with Vanessa and today I meet Annette. With me, its feast or famine; I'm either meeting women at every turn, or I'm striking out and not meeting anyone to hang out with. I want to ride this momentum out as long as possible.

Some of my acquaintances have used the Internet to meet people, but I'm still reluctant to taking the approach of finding a soul mate on line, even though some people have success with it. A lady I went to college with actually met her future husband on the Internet. They had somehow managed to meet each other and maintain a long distance relationship with her living in the Midwest, and the guy residing in Maryland. He proposed and she decided to move there to become his wife.

On the other hand, I know of men and women who met folks on line who turned out to be downright crazy. No cyber romance for me. I want to meet my potential soul mate face to face.

One time I even let a buddy of mine talk me into checking out a speed dating gathering at the Ramada Inn in Hyde Park. I think there were about fifteen men and fifteen women on hand trying their luck at this new dating strategy. Before the session started, we all had to put our personal information on an index card. Next, all the men and women were seated at a table across from each other and tried to get to know each other within three minutes. After the three minutes were up, we moved on to the next person. At the end of the night, we gave our index card to the moderator of the forum so that she could pass our information along to the person we were interested in or who was interested in us.

Two women sought to get to know me better. One piqued my interest slightly, the other didn't do it for me at all, but I was polite and contacted both of them.

Stephanie's sexy figure turned me on, but her excessive use of makeup turned me off. Her foundation looked like it had been caked on and made her face look heavy and spooky. She put it on thick. We went out a couple of times and had some fun. Our first date was for dinner at the Chicago Firehouse; it was a fire station converted into an upscale restaurant. The food was average, but the conversation was good. It was cool because Stephanie and I split the bill 50/50; that was a pleasant surprise.

We got together again about a month later and saw a movie near her home in Addison. She was cool to have as a friend, but I wasn't really attracted to her physically. The heavy make up made me feel like I was dating Space Ghost, and I wasn't thrilled about driving all the way out to the west suburbs every time I wanted to see her either.

Lola, the other lady expressing interest in me, baited me into a date by challenging me to a game of air-hockey. We agreed to meet each other at Odyssey Fun World in south suburban Tinley Park. The two of us played a variety of arcade and video games with the victor talking a lot of crap to the loser. It was good clean fun. There weren't any fireworks exploding between us, but it was an enjoyable Friday night. The speed dating scene was okay, but it seemed strained and made me feel like a failure if I didn't come away from the event with the phone number to someone I really wanted to go out with. I'd rather for romance to happen naturally and unexpectedly. That's why meeting Vanessa and Annette seemed so right. We were at the right place at the right time.

I ran to catch an open elevator and rode to the 10th floor. I was all set to have a productive day. Since I took off yesterday, I figured I would have a lot of phone calls to return and emails to read and respond to.

I stepped off the elevator with the same confident stride I had when I walked from Starbucks with Annette. Unfortunately, the pep was taken out of my step the moment I reached the office and found the door already open.

My office was a mess and looked like a tornado had touched down and destroyed the place. File cabinets were open and confidential documents were scattered all over my desk and floor. My computer was gone.

The Starbucks cup and briefcase I was carrying fell from my hands and hit the floor. Fresh, black coffee splashed all over my clothes and shoes. My hands trembled with terror and anxiety, and my heart raced with rage and confusion. I wondered why this would happen to me. My office was completely ransacked. Oh my God! Oh my God!

5

KENDALL

Instead of parking my Cadillac Escalade on the street out front, I parked in the alley and walked quietly through the backyard I grew up in. As a child, neighbors usually had seen or heard me running back and forth, playing in the yard, but now I didn't want anyone seeing or hearing me doing anything. I always tried to operate under the radar, especially after being caught earlier in my life when I was young and reckless.

At age fifteen I was arrested for burglarizing a house a few blocks away with some guys in the neighborhood. We used to pass the house every morning on the way to school and would see the family leave around the same time each day. The man of the house would say good morning as he carried his briefcase and walked with his small daughter to the car. We spoke back, pretending to be friendly, but our plan was to get in his house and still his shit.

One day, we decided to cut class and scheme on how we wanted to break in the house and find out what was on the inside. I was a little apprehensive at first, but a couple of hits off a joint and a healthy swig of MD 20/20 calmed my nerves and gave me the courage I needed to pull off my first heist. It's amazing how a bottle of cheap wine can give a person the balls to do damn near anything. We were wild and out of control.

The man of the house must have been a gadget freak because the basement was loaded with electronic stuff; just perfect for the music lover. He had two Kenwood turntables, a Pioneer dual cassette player, a Pioneer equalizer, and a pair of compact Bose speakers, with an album collection large enough to open his very own record shop. Motown was everywhere. It was unbelievable considering all we had to listen to music on at home was an antique hi-fi with a needle that scratched most of our records.

A nosy next door neighbor heard us rummaging through stuff in the basement and called the police. Two squad cars caught us coming out of the house carrying a television set and some stereo equipment. The same mad-dog wine that had given me the guts to break in the house was now taking them away and had me throwing up in the front yard. Cops were hollering and blue lights were flashing all around us. I was scared to death and feeling sick as a dog. Dark red wine stains were all over my white gym shoes.

The victim of our stupidity must have been a man of God because he refused to allow the court to go hard on us. The guy actually pleaded on our behalf. He viewed us as young men in need of a second chance in life, and didn't want us to be scarred emotionally and psychologically by becoming prisoners of the system at such a young age. I was a young man without a father. We got probation. I remember hearing Mama thanking God after the judge decided to give me probation instead of sending me to a juvenile detention center.

Instead of ringing the bell, I used my side door key to enter the house. I walked softly up the steps to the kitchen and saw Mama asleep from the entrance leading to the living room. She was resting comfortably on the brown sofa and didn't hear me come in. The large oxygen tank next to the couch hummed and pumped air into Mama's nostrils to allow her to breathe easier. The house resembled a hospital ward with machines, canes and medicine taking up space in the living room. Mama was resting peacefully, so I decided not to wake her.

I sat down in the tan recliner several feet away from Mama on the couch. I pulled the lever on the right side of the chair and allowed my body to stretch out and my feet to be lifted from the ground. The back of my head creased the supple fabric as I began to sink into a zone of comfort. It felt good. Being in the house was allowing me to rest easier. Rest isn't something I get a lot of. The business I'm in forces me to always stay on my toes. Letting my guard down at the wrong time can get me killed.

The house hasn't undergone many changes since my childhood. The walls in the living and dining rooms are still tan, the carpet is still green, and family portraits and graduation photos still take up residence over the seldom used fireplace. The pictures on the mantle of me with my siblings during our school years made me reminisce of years gone by.

I remembered how Julian and I used to playfully wrestle each other until one of us starting winning and made the other mad. Suddenly, we were no longer playing, we were fighting for real. Those developments usually provoked Lauren to run and tell. And that usually forced Mama to get the belt and go ballistic. While Julian was sniffling and wiping his eyes in the corner, I was choking back the tears and screaming "I won't do it no more" to keep Mama from knocking me into the middle of next week as she often promised. Once I recovered, I thought of a way to pay Lauren back for going to Mama. La-La was always a little rat, telling Mama everything.

As we got older, Mama made Julian and I take La-La with us when we went out on recreational activities. We liked hanging out at amusement parks and attending school basketball and football games. La-La was there to be Mama's roving reporter, her eyes and ears. She did her part and threw blocks to keep Julian and me from trying to score touchdowns with girls after the game. To her disappointment, things changed after she started getting the attention of boys and wanted to date. That's when I altered my role as big brother and became a father figure, enforcer and full-time bodyguard. When teenage boys called the house or walked La-La home from school, I approached them and threatened them with bodily harm, warning them to never call or visit again! La-La got mad because she liked the attention. She always liked the attention. Now I was the one doing the blocking. I knew I would pay her back and even the score one day.

My trip down memory lane was cut short by a loud cough from Mama. It snapped me back to the realties of the present. Life seemed so simple then, the stakes weren't as high. Everything now seems to be a matter of life and death.

I expected the coughing to wake Mama, but she continued to sleep. She still didn't know her middle child was in the house. I reached into my pocket and pulled out a thick envelope with MAMA written on it. Inside were crisp hundred dollar bills wrapped in a piece of paper with my name on it. Mama was on a lot of prescription medications that I knew Medicare wasn't paying for. It was my way of trying to help out, it was the only way I knew how. I put the envelope on the couch next to her and left the house as quietly as I had entered. Mama never knew her dark angel had been watching over her. If she asks me about the money, I'll just say I won it in Las Vegas playing craps.

Being an entrepreneur in my endeavor meant always paying tribute to those in higher positions. I was never an official member of any gang or organization, but have friends who are. Many of them are childhood buddies who have been through the fire and burned by life. Life on the streets had made them cold and hard. The gang affiliations are all some of them have ever known; a family to those who'd been abandoned and lost. Now they belonged to something.

Today, a couple of those childhood friends are apart of the higher-ups. They have influence in the hood and help make decisions. Their influences and decisions allowed me to have an enterprise without being a blip on the radar. And they're able to wrap their arms around me and protect me if I need it.

Most people considered me a drug dealer, but in a lot of ways, I was a franchisee. The higher-ups had given me a franchise to run and I planned on running it with the skill of a chief executive officer operating a fortune 500 corporation. The higher-ups loved me because I was a good earner.

Customer service representative was the title I gave to crew members working under my wings. They interacted with our clients in the hood and tried to satisfy their needs. It's all about supply and demand. Customers demanded, and my representatives and I supplied.

Most of the guys on the street were juvenile young guns trying to come up in a blaze of glory, hoping to live long enough to tell their story. They're all attracted to the flash and the cash. They want easy money, flashy cars, expensive jewelry, and fast women. Many of them grew up in homes more dangerous and volatile than what they're experiencing on the corners for me. They distrust the world. A lot of them want to belong to something. I allowed that to happen when they came under my wings.

The beginning of the month is important because that's when folks get government checks, and have money to blow on drugs. An elimination period occurred each month for members working in my crew. On the first three days of the month, all profits belonged to me. Each day had its own significance. Day one was set aside for the higher-ups and allowed me to meet my financial obligations to them at the end of the month. Day two was set aside for me; dues must be paid by crewmembers in order to work under my wing; it makes them a member of a union. Day three was set aside for legal fees and money we used to pay off cops. Beginning on day four, they were allowed to retain some of the profits. It was like starting a new job and having to go through a probation period every month. All of my service representatives have goals to meet. And their activities are watched.

Supervisors are like team captains and monitor the activities of the service reps working the streets. They're my buffers and keep me insulated from the day to day action taking place in the trenches. Most of them are in their late teens or early twenties and have been in the game long enough to know how it should be played. Supervisors provide the reps with coaching and discipline. To keep morale high and loyalty intact, they are encouraged to reward reps with gifts for achieving monthly quotas. Stuff like leather jackets, gym shoes, velour warm-up suits and sports uniforms are all proven performance incentives. The young ones are hungry for the sizzle of the steak.

When necessary, supervisors are responsible for reprimanding and punishing the younger members of the crew. Situations should be resolved before escalating to a crisis condition. These problems usually arise out of greed and kids trying to come up in the game too fast. Crisis conditions have to be kept in check because they could possibly draw attention from the higher-ups or the police.

If a problem got too big for the supervisors, they reported it to Ray. That wasn't a good thing, because Raymond McNeal, known by some as Dirty Ray, is a no nonsense type of guy and a brute force to be reckoned with. Ray is a robust guy, who walks slowly and speaks in a calm drawl that could become loud and crazed if provoked. He wears fancy sweaters and lots of jewelry. He has a hustler's rhythm.

Ray and I grew up together. He was one of the participants with me in the failed burglary that occurred in my teens. Being put on probation by the judge caused me to cut back on some of my illegal activities and be more careful, but being let off the hook made Ray bolder and more reckless. This character flaw eventually caused him to be put on lockdown for a six-year prison stint in Western Illinois for armed robbery, aggravated assault and grand theft. Ray is my enforcer and right hand man. We are a partnership and split everything 50/50. I'm the brain, he's the brawn.

6

LAUREN

Weekends always go so fast. I had planned on getting some rest Saturday, but I ended up running errands and doing some grocery shopping for Mama. She has a refrigerator and deep freezer full of food, but insists on sending me to the store to buy items just because they're on sale. Saturday, she sent me to three different stores; bacon was on sale at one store, toilet paper and paper towels were on sale at another, and I went to a third store to get chicken wings and ground beef. I hate grocery shopping on Saturdays because the stores are crowded and the lines are long.

By the time I returned to my condo, I was exhausted. I turned the ringer off my phone and was in bed before ten o'clock. Andre, the guy I met at the Spoken Word Café last week, called to see if I was interested in going out, but I just wasn't in the mood to do anything. I needed to rest and catch up on some sleep. He appears to be a pretty cool guy, so I am looking forward to going out with him soon. It seems like he's eager to impress me. We'll see. Between dealing with Mama and my job, my schedule is always so tight. I hardly have time for myself.

Now here I am, back in the office, trying to start another work week.

Monday mornings are always crazy and today is proving to be no exception. I've been in my office since seven o'clock and I can tell I'm going to be in for a long day and stressful week. Being the director of a customer call center for a health insurance company is very demanding. My staff is comprised of 75 client representatives, trained to answer incoming telephone calls from customers covered under our group insurance plan through their employer. I also manage three supervisors, who are responsible for monitoring calls and providing assistance to their respective teams.

I looked at the electronic board in my office and shook my head. It's only a few minutes after nine, but my adherence numbers for the day are already a disaster. The company executives looked at adherence numbers to see how many calls we answered and how long our customers had to wait. Our adherence objective is 92%. In my opinion, the goal is unrealistic, but it's the objective the executive officers set and want met. They are the big shots making the rules, but I'm the one managing the reps on the phones taking abuse from abrasive customers. There is no way we will be able to meet that goal today.

My boss will be looking to me for answers. I have 120 callers waiting on hold in queue, 65 reps taking calls and answering questions, and no other reps available. The longer my reps stay on the phone with a member, the longer the callers in queue have to wait. Client reps are trained to answer a lot of calls and assist members quickly and efficiently, but some calls aren't that simple. It's almost as if they're expected to serve two masters.

The customer call center hours are from seven-thirty to five-thirty. The start time for client representatives are staggered on fifteen minute increments. Our schedule allowed for five people to be off today, so I still should have five more reps available to take calls. From my computer, I'm able to monitor which reps are logged in taking calls and which reps are in an unavailable mode, not allowing any calls to come through to their line. It's frustrating because it's usually the same employees breaking the rules all the time. I logged on to the phone center database and entered the code 7245, and listened in on line as one of my employees, Regina Coleman, engaged in dialogue with her son.

"Dammit, Jamal, I told you I ain't buying you no more video games. You damn kids act like I got money coming outta my ass!

I just bought you a Madden Football game two weeks ago. I can't afford to buy them damn games every other week. You got enough football and basketball games already. I paid almost fifty dollars a piece for them damn games."

"But Mama," he interrupted. "I'm not talkin' 'bout that kinda game."

"What you talkin' 'bout then, Jamal?" she snapped.

"I'm talkin' 'bout the Grand Theft Auto game," he replied.

I can't believe my ears. I have almost 150 calls waiting in queue, and she's on the phone arguing with what sounded like an eleven or twelve-year-old kid about a video game for PlayStation 2. Jesus Christ. I wonder how many games she'll be able to buy if I free up her future and have her visiting the unemployment line. I took a sip from my bottled water and massaged my temples. It's too early for a headache. I continued to listen to Regina Coleman fuss at Jamal.

"Grand what?" she asked.

"It's called Grand Theft Auto, Mama," he advised.

"Dammit, Jamal," she countered. "I don't care if it's called Grand Theft or Petty Theft," she snarled. "You ain't gettin' it."

"Dag, Mama," he pouted.

"Don't dag me, boy," she warned. "I'll beat yo' black ass. Who you think you talkin' that dag Mama shit to? I let you stay home from school 'cuz you said you was sick. Hell, if you feel well enough to play a video game, then you well enough to take yo' ass to school. You getting D's and F's, and want to stay home and play video games. You know what Jamal? I'm gonna take that damn PlayStation out of your room the moment I get home."

"But Mama," he countered, trying to defend himself.

"But my ass," she scolded. "We'll finish this when I get home."

"But Mama," he repeated.

"What Jamal?" she asked, getting more agitated. "Don't you know I'm at work?"

"Is Daddy gonna come get me this weekend and let me spend the night?"

"I don't know, Jamal."

"He promised he would come this weekend, since he didn't come last week."

"We'll see, Jamal."

"He promised, Mama."

"I said we'll see, Jamal," Regina responded gently. "Something may come up with your father, and I don't want you to be disappointed."

"He never keeps his promise."

Regina and Jamal had been on the phone for over ten minutes. During the lengthy conversation, I had made up my mind to have Maryann, her immediate supervisor, fire her. Regina is probably going to go home after work and punish Jamal for failing in school and begging for a new video game. She didn't realize Jamal's statements about his father had caused me to have a change of heart. If their conversation had ended thirty seconds earlier, she would've been looking for a new job.

Fortunately, for her, listening to Jamal ask about seeing his father, and hearing the disappointment in his voice after not seeing him last weekend, took me down the road to my past when I was around his age.

I used to see father's walking their daughter's to school, and wonder why it couldn't be me. School was exciting and fun for me. I always got A's and B's and was usually on the honor roll. In second grade, my grades were so good, the principal promoted me to third grade. I felt proud being able to say I made a double.

Sometimes I got jealous seeing the relationship some of my girlfriends had with their fathers, especially my childhood friend, Keisha Johnson. Keisha was an only child and the apple of her father's eye. Occasionally Mama would allow me to spend the night at the Johnson house on the weekend. Mr. Johnson would take us to the movies, order us pizza and bring us candy to munch on. Sometimes he used to bring us large, round pieces of peanut brittle. He used to have to make Keisha and I stop eating candy because he was afraid we would get sick.

I remember being around seven or eight and going to the Halsted Drive-in with Keisha and her parents. It was my first time going to see a movie outside. Mrs. Johnson made sure we were dressed in our pajamas and tucked comfortably in the backseat while Mr. Johnson went to the concession stand to get us snacks. I think Keisha and I were sound asleep before Mr. Johnson even got back with the goodies. Those were great childhood moments for me.

When I was in fourth grade, I participated in a school play in the assembly hall. The auditorium was full of parents, teachers and students. After the play ended, I looked on as fathers greeted their daughters with fresh flowers and proud faces. I didn't receive any flowers that day and saw no proud fatherly face. My father was never able to teach me how to ride a bike, take me to ballet lessons, pick me up from school or see how pretty I looked when I went on my senior prom. I wish my father had been there to see me graduate number one in my class and hear my high school valedictorian speech. I wonder how proud he would've been to see me attend Loyola University on a full academic scholarship, and later obtain a Master's degree from Northwestern University.

There are always studies about how the lack of a father figure has effected the youth of black America. We hear about how much a young boy needs a male role model to learn how to be a man. I wonder how differently my brothers would've been if we had a dominant male figure in the house. Someone should do a study on how the absence of a father figure has impacted the development of the black woman. I would be more than willing to contribute my thoughts.

7

JULIAN

"What's wrong, Julian?" Mama asked, as we rode in silence to the doctor's office.

"Nothing, Ma," I lied.

"You haven't said two words since we left the house," she added.

"I'm okay."

"You sure?" she asked. "You know I can tell when something is wrong."

I faked a smile. "I'm fine, Ma."

"Well you know you can talk to your Mama about anything," she assured.

"I know, Ma," I said, wishing I really could tell her about the anguish dominating my thoughts over the last week. I haven't been able to eat or sleep. My clothes are feeling big on me because I've lost eleven pounds since I started dealing with this mess. Every time I close my eyes, I see my ransacked office. I try to picture the authorities going through my cabinets and seizing my files, leaving folders and paper everywhere.

Among the papers cluttered on my desk, was a search warrant, allowing the FBI and the Cook County Sheriff's office to confiscate confidential, client information. I'm afraid to conduct business and know I'm living under constant surveillance. My life has been drastically altered, and I wonder if it will ever be the same again.

"Did you call Vanessa?" Mama asked, once again breaking the silence.

"We talked over the weekend," I answered.

"Are you gonna take her out?"

"I don't know," I answered, hesitantly. "Maybe."

"Maybe?" Mama shot back. "What else you got goin' on?"

"I don't know, Ma!" I hollered. "I got other things on my mind right now!"

"Well excuse me!" she said with a tone of surprise.

"I'm sorry, Ma," I apologized, tapping her gently on the left hand. "I didn't mean to disrespect you. I didn't get a lot of sleep last night, so I feel a little tired and crabby."

"I understand."

I drove into the handicapped parking space, and helped Mama out of the car. I put the portable oxygen tank over her right shoulder, and gave her a brown cane so she could maintain her balance.

A full-figured receptionist buzzed the door, allowing us to enter the doctor's office. I wrote Mama's name on the sign-in sheet while she went to sit down. We had only walked about thirty yards from the car to the office, but Mama was already experiencing shortness of breath. Mama is okay as long as she stays in bed and rests, but simply walking from one room of the house to another caused extreme wheezing. It's hard seeing my mother in this condition.

Mama was always a hardworking woman. In the spring, she looked forward to planting seeds in the garden and growing vegetables. By summer, the backyard would be full of tomatoes, cucumbers, greens and other fresh produce. She also took pride in keeping a clean house, and made us mop, vacuum and dust on a regular basis. Now even performing minor activities had become a major chore. I took a seat next to Mama and waited, hoping her name would be called soon.

The waiting area is full of patients, mostly edgy, senior citizens, anxious to be called next by the doctor's assistant. Failing health makes a lot of seniors grumpy and difficult to be around, but Mama seems to take it all in stride and doesn't complain much. I notice an elderly couple seated in the corner with wrinkles of impatience making lines on their foreheads. The gray-haired gentleman looks at his watch and shakes his head, while the lady mumbles a few unchristian words and taps her cane on the floor. They have major attitudes as well as their health issues.

Mama's appointment was for eleven-fifteen, but as usual, the doctor appeared to be way behind schedule. Mama sensed me getting restless. It's almost noon.

"Julian, do you have some errands you need to run?"

I shrugged. "I guess."

"Ain't no sense in you waiting around here if you got something else to do."

"I'll stay with you, Ma," I said begrudgingly.

"Baby, go on and take care of your business," she said.

"Are you sure?"

"Yeah," she responded. "Boy, it ain't no telling how long I might be waiting."

"Okay."

I rush out of the medical facility to call my friend, Steven Strong, on my cell phone. Steve and I were in law school together. He's someone I can confide in. I'm praying he'll be available for lunch because I really need someone to talk to. Trying to carry this dilemma around is eating me up on the inside.

My call to Steve's cell phone went directly to his voicemail. About ten minutes passed before he returned my call. He was just leaving court, and had a couple of hours to spare before meeting with a client. We agreed to meet at Leona's Restaurant in Hyde Park.

Steve's Nissan Maxima was parked in a diagonal space in front of the restaurant when I arrived. Seeing his car brought a smile to my face, something I hadn't done much of in recent days. Steve has a law office in the South Loop. He specialized in personal injury cases, but had also handled some real estate transactions and criminal cases as well. Steve is married with two small children.

We greet each other by the entrance and make small talk as we wait to be seated by the hostess. A large lunchtime crowd is still being served, so we had to wait a few minutes before finally getting a booth in the no smoking section of the restaurant.

"So how are you holding up, Julian?" he asks with a look of concern.

"I'm hanging."

"I read about your problem in the newsletter."

"You did?" I ask, feeling embarrassed by the situation.

"I wanted to talk to you, but I wanted to wait until you came to me with it."

"Steve, this situation has me all messed up."

Our conversation is interrupted when a young waiter comes to our booth to take our order. Steve orders catfish and fries. I'm not really hungry, but I order a salad and a club sandwich. I need to try to eat something. We wait for the waiter to leave the table and move beyond hearing distance before we resume our conversation.

I continue. "Man, I've hardly slept since this stuff happened."

"What's happening with your clients?"

"Basically, I've pushed everything back and informed my clients I had to handle a family emergency. I just need some time to regroup. I haven't been able to concentrate and have gotten behind on a lot of my cases. Man, Steve, this has been a very humbling experience. I wouldn't wish this on my worst enemy. Man, it's a shame what they did to my office. They took practically all my files, my computers; and my phones are tapped. They even tapped my phone lines at home."

"You need to get a support team together."

"Steve. . ." I hesitated.

"Julian, you need some people in the law community, family and friends to rally around you and provide support when it comes time to deal with this mess."

We halt our conversation as the waiter returns to the table. The waiter places the food in front of us and asks if we need anything else. Steve and I hold hands as he blesses the food. He finishes saying grace and immediately takes a bite out of his catfish. I sip on my water and nibble on my sandwich. Steve swallows a piece of fish and continues to give me insight to what I may have to deal with in the near future.

"Julian, if the authorities are coming at you this hard, they must be after one of your clients in a big way."

"No kidding," I respond, nibbling on my food. I don't even have an appetite.

"Julian, that's what the Racketeering Influenced Corruption Act is all about."

"Damn, Steve," I sigh with fear. "RICO is some Mafia type of shit."

"I know," he agrees. "They can't reach the gangsters, so they chase the trails."

"I can't believe I spent four years in law school, reading boring ass cases, with school loans up the kazoo, to possibly get disbarred and convicted of racketeering."

"That's why we have to be very careful who we accept as clients."

I take another sip of water. I feel sick to my stomach.

Steve continues. "That's why I'm trying to get to the bench."

"Are you trying to become a judge?"

"Yes indeed. I got a family at home. I want to spend more time with my kids, plus I'm tired of chasing money. Folks come to us for representation and then we have to chase them around the world to get paid. Julian I have tens of thousands of dollars out there in uncollected fees."

Steve sips on some water and continues.

"Julian, check this out: I was at a social function a couple of weeks ago and ran across a client I assisted with a legal matter a few months ago. As soon as I said hello, she started whining and heeing and hawing about how she's struggling financially and needs to get some things in order so she can pay me. She can't find the money to pay me, but she can strut around town in a mink coat and a pair of ostrich boots. Julian, I was ready to snatch that coat off her ass and take it home to my wife."

"I know what you mean."

"Do you have any idea who the authorities may be looking for?" Steve asks.

A million thoughts enter my mind. "I'm afraid to even think about it."

I answered Mama's phone call from the doctor's office. It was almost two o'clock. She had been there almost three hours. I said goodbye to Steve and thanked him for lunch. We promised to keep in touch; with him agreeing to help me in any way he could. I appreciated his support.

I helped Mama get settled into my car and strapped the seat belt around her shoulder and waist. She looked eager to return to the comforts of home.

"So what did the doctor say?"

"Nothing I didn't already know."

"What's that?"

"My lungs are weak, and that I might not be able to stand another asthma attack."

"When does the doctor want to see you again?"

"The middle of next month," she answered. "Can you bring me?"

"I'll see."

"Did you get a chance to finish your errands?"

"I had lunch with a buddy I went to law school with."

"Did the two of you have a good time?"

"Yes," I lied. "He was telling me about some challenges he's having at work."

"He's having problems on the job?"

"Yes."

Mama waved her hand. "These jobs will kill you and ask you why you died."

That comment made me laugh. "You're about right."

"Oh yeah, I need to get three prescriptions filled."

"Three?"

"Umm hmm," she nodded. "One of them is medicine for my heart."

"This doctor sure has you on a lot of different medications."

"Doctors don't give you anything to cure you, son," Mama reasoned. "They just give you enough to keep you alive and coming back for more medicine. Everybody got a racket these days."

"That's about the size of it," I nodded in agreement. "Everyone has a racket."

"I'm tired of taking all this mess, too," she groaned. "I'm taking pills around the clock. I wake up taking pills and go to sleep taking pills."

"I know," I replied. "The prescriptions are probably very expensive, too."

"I got the money to pay for them," she bragged.

"Oh yeah?" I asked, curiously, knowing Medicare didn't pay for prescriptions.

"Kendall gave me money to pay for my medicine."

Now my stomach is really in knots. I should have Mama put in a prescription for me also. Since Kendall is busy playing Robin Hood, maybe his money can pay for my medicine as well. I feel sick!

8

KENDALL

 I could hear the sound of music bumping even before reaching the door of the club. Heavy bass lines banged loud enough to damn near knock a hole in the walls. The rhythmic verses of R&B and hip-hop filtered the air with sex as musical artists bragged about wearing Rolex watches and driving fancy cars. I entered the doors and saw Big D. standing nearby; he's the beefy bouncer, in charge of keeping the atmosphere controlled and the chaos light. I gave Big D. a hug and a handshake.

 Club Antonio, located just east of I-57 in the south suburbs, is a nice, secluded lounge for men to unwind and fantasize. If you didn't know what you were looking for, you would drive by here and never look back. It's a spot for guys to get their drink on and escape from reality for a little while. Men sit on stools and stand around the bar; guzzling down mixed drinks and beer, as the clock slowly approaches midnight. It's eleven-thirty. Just thirty minutes before show time.

 Thursday nights are cool because people are in a weekend mode, but usually lack the aggressiveness and unruliness of a Friday or Saturday night crowd. The odds aren't as great for a lot of nonsense to jump off. As the clock ticks towards midnight, eager men pay off liquor tabs and tip the bartender. I chill in the corner and take it all in.

Three guys entered the lounge with puzzled expressions on their faces. The confused gaze in their eyes hinted they weren't sure if they had come to the right place or not. They're looking for something else, but don't have the courage to ask. They appear to be in their early twenties. I watched as two of them surveyed the surroundings, while the other dangled his keys impatiently. Finally, the one with the keys shrugged his shoulders and shook his head. I checked my watch. Now it's eleven-fifty. They mumbled a few more words to each other and then decided to leave. I laughed to myself. They shouldn't have made their move so soon. It's about to get wild in here.

At midnight, a door behind the bar opened. Rick, a suburban cop, stood in the entrance and watched as a cashier seated at a small table collected fifteen dollars from each customer passing through. I remained in the corner chilling. I held a glass of rum and Coke and observed the money changing hands. I stirred my drink with a small, black straw and took a sip. The cold, intoxicating fluid soaked my tongue. It was strong; I tasted more rum than Coke. To my delight, loud mouth Sharon was behind the bar pouring stiff drinks. A couple of cocktails like this and I'll be good to go for real. I let the liquor trickle down my throat and approached Rick at the door behind the bar.

"What up K?" he said, greeting me with a hug and a handshake.

"I can't call it, Rick," I replied. "How's it looking tonight?"

"Everything is straight."

"That's what I wanna hear," I responded, pounding his fist with appreciation.

"Niggas been rolling up in here since about ten-thirty."

I laughed. "See that's what I'm talkin' 'bout."

"Yeah we looking good tonight," he added. "Brothers are up in here drooling."

"I can tell."

"Man, K, there's a tall light-skinned babe in there that's totally off the hook!"

"Sounds like she got your attention?" I asked, noticing Rick's enthusiasm.

"I'm a short brother, so my eyes can't help but stare directly at her chest."

"You a fool," I laughed. Rick is more excited than some of the patrons.

"They were aimed right at me," he said, looking like he was ready to be breastfed.

"She sounds lethal."

"K, this babe has some of the biggest jugs I've ever seen in my life."

I grinned, but remained silent.

"K, this chick has enough cleavage to hide the weapons of mass destruction."

I laughed. "I guess the government didn't look there."

"I guess not," Rick agreed. "But I'll be more than happy to look for 'em."

"The way you act, they seem like weapons of mass distraction."

"No shit."

I touched fist with Rick and entered the large room. I made eye contact with a couple of regulars and gave a nod before retreating to a spot against the wall. Rap lyrics from Nelly's "Tip Drill" rebounded in the air as anxious men situated themselves at tables and in chairs close to the stage. Everyone wants to have a good view. Perverted smiles and lustful eyes filled the banquet room in a matter of moments. Another off duty cop in attendance got on stage and grabbed the microphone, cautioning liquored up patrons to stay under control. He made it clear that anyone refusing to play by the rules will be arrested. What he really meant was violators will be taken out back and given a brutal fuckin' beat down.

After the warning from law enforcement was given, scantily clad women patrolled the stage one at a time in sexy outfits and platform stilettos from *Hos R Us*, jiggling and bouncing to the beat of the music. The MC introduced each dancer one by one.

Several strip clubs occupy the south suburbs. Some establishments are very visible and did advertisements on certain radio stations and newspapers. The restrictions of zoning laws, and the inability to pay off some politicians, made exotic dance clubs less appealing in the city. Most of the clubs in the suburbs have total nudity and serve alcohol. The women in the more visible clubs are a mixture of all races and backgrounds soliciting lap dances to earn a living. It's like a rainbow coalition of strippers, united with a common goal of getting paid. A topless dance is ten dollars; totally nude dances are twenty. Women can tease, but men can't touch. That's how it works at the more legitimate clubs. However, Club Antonio is underground and operates on an entirely different level.

Club Antonio was more than a strip club, it's a borderline brothel. Dancers took turns sashaying back and forth across the stage. They slid down silver poles and shook their assets to the rhythm of a hardcore beat. They advertised on stage, but made their money by working the crowd. Guys moved quickly to the back of the club in a make shift area known as the barbershop. For one dollar, men were able to bury their heads inside the thighs of a female participant for a quick facial. I laughed and watched guys munch between the legs of complete strangers. That's some wild and sexually dangerous shit right there. Some of those kitchens are probably nasty enough to be shut down by a health inspector. Niggas be eating from the wrong tables.

Not all of the women participated, but a lot of them did, and thoroughly enjoyed it. Some of them actually moaned and groaned as men took turns getting a little something to nibble on. Bouncers stood close by and controlled the sexual buffet line. Many of the men were greedy and wanted to stay at the table of erotica too long. They were munching as if they had been suffering from famine in Africa.

The deejay introduced the next dancer. Horny, intoxicated men roared as Cookie strutted across the stage, bouncing and jiggling in a special way. The honey toned, dancer, appeared to be about five-nine or five-ten, but the clear, stiletto platforms made her over six feet tall. She wore a red thong with a red bra that was being stretched to the max. Red and white, candy cane stockings stopped just above her knees, and a white garter belt held a wad of money on her left thigh.

Men howled, and shouts of damn, flooded the room when Cookie removed her bra and flung it across the stage. With juicy areoles and ripe nipples, the bouncing Cookie probably had enough milk in her breast to feed a small country in the motherland. She was giving the term *Got Milk* a whole new meaning. I looked to my right and saw Rick's mouth watering. He looked like one of those starving Ethiopian kids from the Sally Strothers commercial. Guys were hoping to nibble on a piece of Cookie in the barber shop, but she wasn't serving.

They say crime doesn't pay, but it pays for my lavish home in the south suburbs. I live in an upscale community and have doctors, lawyers, entrepreneurs and ball players as neighbors. I'm a long way from the south side streets on which I make my money. If I were an entertainer or athlete, my house would probably be featured on MTV Cribs. Four bedrooms and three bathrooms were just some of the features providing comfort in the place I call home.

Ivory, Italian leather furniture, silk trees and a fireplace decorated a sunken living room I rarely used. One of my bedrooms had been converted into an office; complete with a computer, bookcases, and a twelve inch globe, sitting on a three foot stand. A Sony 50" plasma television rested on the wall of my family room. My home theatre system and extensive bootleg DVD collection made going to the show unnecessary. Hell, sometimes, I got movies before they even reached the theatres.

Three big screen televisions anchored the wall in my basement. I had almost as many big screens in my crib as the nearby Cineplex. During football season, my Direct TV NFL package allowed me to watch three games at once. I also had an eight foot, cherry wood, pool table. Guys love hanging out in the basement.

Upstairs, my master bedroom was bigger than some folks' apartment; spacious enough to contain a flat screen television, a leather sofa and a cocktail table. The long corridor exiting the room led to two walk-in closets and a master bathroom featuring a Jacuzzi. Women love this room. I love this house.

Years ago, I found four abandoned buildings and purchased them. I turned two of them into barber shops and converted the other two into hand carwashes. These businesses are perfect for me because the IRS cannot monitor my profits as easily. They're excellent fronts and gave me legitimate places to hide my money.

Customers pay in cash and receipts are nonexistent. Cash comes in, cash goes out. Since the barber shops and car washes are registered in my name, it allowed me to purchase my house in my name as well. I'm an entrepreneur. A lot of guys in this game have to buy houses and cars in the names of relatives and girlfriends because they show no other legal means of producing income.

And then some of the players in the game are just plain stupid. They're nineteen and twenty-year-old guys out here with a fleet of cars. These kids are driving Navigators on Monday, Benzes on Tuesday, and Jaguars on Wednesday. Five-O pull these guys over and inspect cars having about ten thousand dollars worth of stereo equipment blasting out of the windows and seven grand worth of rims spinning on the tires.

Some of these guys are not even old enough to buy liquor yet, but they're riding around town in fifty thousand dollar vehicles with porno DVDs like *Booty Talk* being shown in the backseat, even though there aren't any passengers in the truck with them. That shit is just plain stupid! When the cops ask whose vehicle it is, they say it belongs to their mother. At least I can pull out the registration and prove the vehicle belongs to me. I can't imagine my mom rolling around the streets of Chicago in a Cadillac Escalade sitting on twenty-four-inch rims, listening to 50 Cent and G-Unit with a DVD featuring Janet Jacme fucking on screen for her viewing pleasure.

I took a hot shower in the master bedroom and slid into a pair of silk pajamas. I took a seat on the leather sofa and rolled a couple of joints. The clock on the wall was approaching three. I turned on the television and started scanning the channels on cable. As usual, infomercials for growing hair, losing weight and buying real estate with no money down were dominating the late night airways.

The batteries of my remote control were losing power because of the constant channel surfing I was doing. I kept flipping until I got to BET and tuned into an episode of UnCut. I watched some of the raunchiest music videos ever made. The videos were so explicit that the program came with a disclaimer stating it may be inappropriate for viewers under the age of seventeen. It was as if the rappers had taken a video camera into a strip club and shot a music video. I was on the verge of throwing dollar bills at the television set. I felt like I had never left Club Antonio.

I was all prepared to kick back and relax. I fired up a joint and watched the video hootchies shake it fast on my big screen. I took a long pull off the joint and let the smoke flow freely into my nostrils. The elevator of my mind was going to a higher floor.

All of a sudden, the sound of the doorbell disturbed my groove and lowered my high. I grabbed a gun from under my pillow and checked the clip. I put on the robe that matched my pajamas and walked down the spiral staircase to open the door. I was able to see the silhouette of a female through the stained glass window. A long legged treat with a bright smile greeted me.

"Hi Kendall," she said, dressed in a long, black leather coat.

"Come on in," I said, kissing my tall, tantalizing guest on the lips.

"Are you glad to see me?" she asked, opening her coat to expose her red lingerie.

"I'm always glad to see you, Cookie," I replied with a huge grin. I thought about Rick and the other guys at the club. I bet they would love to be standing in my slippers right now.

It's bedtime. And I'm going to enjoy my milk and Cookie.

9

LAUREN

    Instead of hitting the pavement for an early Saturday morning jog, my feet are dangling in the air with my toes curling towards the ceiling fan. I'm nibbling on Andre's earlobes and gripping the muscles of his back. It's only eight-fifteen, but Mr. Hershey has already spent much of the morning dipping his long, hard, chocolate bar deep into my creamy center. Lust juice is dripping down my thighs and my sweet La-La pastry is oozing with sugar.

    Andre continues to dig deep, stirring my hot coffee in a slow, circular motion. His long spoon is tapping all the corners of my cup, suggesting I'm good to the last drop. My nails dig in and grip the crease of his back. I moan loudly and let myself go. Andre grabs my hands from his back and uses my wrists to pin me to the bed. He's enjoying it. Now his strokes are fast and hard. I can feel my body bubbling from within, I'm on the verge of erupting with hot lava. The earth is shaking, my pelvis is quaking, and my legs are trembling in the air from the aftershock. Damn, I can't stop my thighs from twitching. I keep waiting for Mr. Hershey to sprinkle his warm nuts inside me, but he doesn't. Damn he has a lot of stamina.

    "See, I told you I was gonna take care of you didn't I?" Andre gloats.

    I mumble between deep breaths. "Umm hmm."

"Yeah I know," he laughs, pulling his manhood out of me to take a look at his work. He's admiring his rock hard tool in the way a painter appreciates the brush he strokes the canvas with. "My job is to make sure you never get the short end of the stick."

"Believe me," I moan. "That's not the short end of the stick I'm feeling."

"Turn over, Lauren," he orders confidently.

"Okay," I agree without a second thought.

Andre was aggressive. I knew it was only a matter of time before he would have me flat on my back with my legs in the air, or sprawled across a floor on my hands and knees. Since meeting him at the Spoken Word Café a couple of months ago, I knew I wanted to give him a piece of my La-La cream pie, but he was going to have work for it and pay for it.

I was used to dating doctors, lawyers, and many other high achieving professional men, so I was accustomed to white collar guys with nice homes, fancy cars, and major credit cards, allowing them to wine and dine me at some of the city's most elegant restaurants. Andre held down a blue collar job with the Chicago Transit Authority, but was doing his best to impress me, so I decided to sit back and enjoy the free ride.

On our first date, Andre had taken me to a restaurant located on Chicago's Gold Coast. The owners had renovated a mansion into an upscale steak and seafood eatery. Opulent chandeliers and cozy fireplaces provided an elegant ambiance to each of the restaurant's ample dining rooms. White linen cloths covered each table. The attentive wait staff, dressed in white jackets, used a staggered service approach to make sure our glasses were filled with water and kept fresh baskets of bread at our reach. It was impressive. I had never heard of the place. We were a long way from Red Lobster.

While I perused the menu looking for something to catch my eye and appetite, Andre's focus was on me and the form fitting, black dress hugging my body tight. My four inch black pumps with the strap around the ankles gave me added power and confidence. I was attracted to him, and even though I hadn't had sex in several months, I was determined to keep my thighs closed and my feet planted firmly on the ground.

We enjoyed a light conversation with Andre telling me all the things he enjoyed doing. Both white collar and blue collar men are always trying to impress me with how much culture they have and how different they are from everyone else. Yeah right. It's kind of funny watching men working hard to stay on their best behavior. Most of them try to say all the right things and don't want to use profanity or let their real personalities come to the surface. I threw a few saucy lines to Andre about sex to see if I could make him expose his true intentions. He ignored the bait.

When it came time to order our meals, I asked Andre if it would be okay if I ordered the lobster. By asking, I allowed him the opportunity to say no. The price wasn't even listed on the menu, so I knew it wasn't cheap. Declining my request would've given him the appearance of a frugal gourmet trying to get served from the wrong kitchen. He said yes. Of course he said yes. Besides, I was looking very edible and scrumptious as well and knew he didn't want to make any mistakes. They say all the right things. Men afraid of making a mistake give women like me all the power.

After dinner, we went to the third floor of the mansion and listened to some jazz while sipping on a few overpriced cocktails. The drinks relaxed us and made us laugh. Now, Andre was cracking jokes instead of trying to show me how smart he was. We were having fun. The musical trio; a keyboardist, a saxophonist and a drummer kept the upbeat audience in a festive mood. Andre even put a tip in the glass bowl sitting on a table near the keyboard player. It was nice.

The ride home on Lake Shore Drive was soothing and sensual. It seemed like Andre had orchestrated the evening by having a CD full of romantic music playing in the background as he drove me home. I smiled on the inside as Andre made subtle attempts to rub my left hand as he hummed along to the music. I used that same hand to cover my mouth and pretended to cough. I even cleared my throat and said excuse me for added effect. After faking a cough, I folded my arms across my breast and continued to enjoy the ride.

Andre seemed a little disappointed by my lack of affection, but remained a gentleman. When we got to my place, he opened the passenger door for me and walked me to the entrance of my condo. I could tell he wanted to end the night with a passionate kiss. Nope.

I don't think so. Instead, he got a real nice church hug; all shoulders and arms, with enough room between us to allow a choir full of midgets to run through. He reminded me of Charlie Brown as he walked back to his car, kicking rocks with his head down. I laughed myself to sleep that night.

The other dates we shared were also nice, even though they were less extravagant. We went to a jazz club, saw a couple of movies, and took walks downtown and on the lakefront.   Andre had been very patient in dealing with me. I admired him for taking the time in trying to get to know me. He made an effort to court me and took me places. I appreciated that.

Some guys think a date is coming over to my condo and watching HBO. They want to prop their corn chip, smelling feet up on my cocktail table and wear out the batteries on my remote control flipping through cable channels. Get real. Many of them come with lame excuses about why we shouldn't go out on Friday or Saturday night, but want to come over to my place on Sundays to check out the latest episode of *The Sopranos*. I don't think so. I'd rather be at home by myself watching a movie on Lifetime.

I was attracted to Andre the moment I laid eyes on him at the Spoken Word. By observing the ladies in the crowd that night, I knew I wasn't the only one vying for his attention. I figured it was only a matter of time before Andre stepped up his game and became more aggressive in trying to initiate some type of physical contact with me. We had gone out several times, but I had never invited him inside my condo. I could see the fire in his eyes when he came over to visit for the first time last night.

The night had started innocently, with us sipping on a bottle of Beringers White Zinfandel as soft music played in the background. We lounged on the carpet of my living room floor with a game of Monopoly stoking our competitive fires. I always want to win.

As I continued to move around the Monopoly board in my silver boot creating wealth, the look in Andre's eyes said he was ready to pass GO. His little dog was ready to land on my Community Chest. He wanted to collect a piece of booty instead of a piece of property. Two more red hotels became a part of my possession. I laughed and raised my arms in the air victoriously. My ego was getting big.

Andre laughed too, because the little dog in his pants was getting big also and was ready to take a bite out of me.

Andre pushed the board aside and threw the play money into the air. He grabbed me by the arm and signaled the game was over. He leaned back on the carpet and pulled me on top of him. Excitement and wine were taking control. I parted my lips and allowed my tongue to taste the White Zinfandel on his tongue. We'd kissed before, but nothing like this. This time it was passionate. It was heated.

His strong hands explored the crease of my back and curves of my hips. My breathing got heavier as I felt the stiffness in his pants. He rolled over on me and started grinding his lower torso. I could feel the inside of my jogging pants getting wet. I gripped his legs with my feet and gyrated with him in unison. He pressed hard while nibbling on my ears and neck. Andre was excited. Somehow his hands managed to get under my T-shirt and began caressing my breast. He unhooked my bra and allowed my C cups to roam free. I was bubbling over and was too hot to stop him.

Now, here I am, the morning after, sprawled across the bed, with an arch in my back and my booty in the air because Andre wants to get me from behind.

"Who's winnin' the game, now?" he asked, slapping me on the butt.

"You are," I replied.

"Be more specific, La-La!" he snapped, spanking me like a naughty girl. "You are who?" he demanded, totally taking control of the situation. "Who's winnin' now?"

"Mr. Hershey is!" I hollered.

"Yeah that's right, that's right," he agreed with laughter. "That's what I'm talkin' 'bout." He was playing games with my mind and my body.

I had won most of the fake money last night playing Monopoly, but if I had a dollar for every time Andre had slapped me on the ass over the last several hours, I would almost be able to retire and move to an island.

To be honest, I was turned on by the way he took charge in the bedroom last night. That's why I let him spend the night and was anxious to give him some more juice this morning. Andre enjoyed talking dirty and I loved it. I was able to be the freak I am, and he was able to feel like he was freeing me of my sexual inhibitions. If I got too wild, I could always blame it on him. He was aggressive. The bedroom is no place to be passive and scared.

Suddenly, the phone on the nightstand rang. I wanted to ignore it. My body tensed up, but Andre kept stroking. Every time I stretched my arms to try to answer the phone, Andre altered his position and kept the sex alive. It felt too good to stop, but I wanted to see the name on the caller ID. He grabbed me by the ankles and pulled me away from reaching the phone. He was a wild man.

"Answer the phone, La-La," Andre teased. "Tell 'em you're having sex."

"Damn!"

"Answer the phone, La-La," he said, talking cocky and swinging a big stick.

"What are you doing to me, Dre?" I asked, in a state of heated passion. My head was ringing louder than the cordless phone on the nightstand. The name on receiver showed Hope Collins and the number at the house.

"Damn, Mama!" I hollered. I adjusted my body and slid into a more comfortable fetal position. Andre made the adjustment with me and never lost his stroke. Where did he learn this?

"Answer the phone, La-La," Andre said, thoroughly enjoying the moment.

"Hi Mama," I said, finally answering the phone on the fourth ring.

Mama didn't even say hello. "La-La, you said you were gonna take me to get my hair done," sounding somewhat impatient. "Were you busy La-La? Did you forget?"

"I didn't forget," I mumbled, as Andre continued to work his magic on me. "I just had a real long night. That's all. I'll be there to pick you up."

"Are you sure, you'll be here on time?"

"I'm coming, Ma," I whispered, savoring Andre's sweet strokes.

Last night was fun, but when it comes to sex, I'm definitely a morning person. Starting my day with sex was better than a hearty breakfast any day of the week. Andre snickered and made wisecracks softly in the background as I tried to complete my conversation with Mama.

"Tell her, you're on your way, La-La," he mused.

Mama continued to ramble on. "Well my appointment is at ten o'clock and I don't wanna be late."

"I'll be there on time," I responded, trying to control the activity taking place between my legs and the two conversations flowing simultaneously into my ears. My head was ringing. The dirtier Andre talked, the wetter I got.

Andre chided in. "Tell her you're having a long morning also."

Mama continued. "Alright then because Lisa gonna be waiting on me."

"I'm coming!" I shouted. "I promise you, Ma, I'm coming!" A climatic sensation took control over me. I hung up the phone and threw it across the room. My body was shaking, and I gripped my pillow to hold on. I could feel Andre's body jolt and jerk as he climaxed into a pulsating frenzy. Mr. Hershey was packed with a lot of nuts. Damn that was good!

10

MAMA

"Lord thank You for letting me live to see one more day. It's your will Lord to have me still on the side of the living. Awake, in my bed, Father, not a hospital bed. Thank You for keeping me closed in my right mind. Lord You could have made me senile, given me Alzheimers or made me, just plain crazy, but You didn't. Lord, Jesus, I thank You. I might not have all my health and strength, but I thank You for what I have. Father, God You know I'm in the twilight of my life. And I've seen some good days and some bad days. Lord I just wanna say thank You."

    I finished my prayers and braced myself on the side of the bed. My body don't ache like some folks my age, but I'm tired all the time. It don't take much for me to get out of breath and start wheezing. I just don't have much energy anymore. I try not to complain and take it one day at a time. Lord give me this day.

    It's still early, but I need to get up and eat breakfast, so I can take my pills. I'm on all kinda pills: heart pills, sleeping pills, water pills and blood pressure pills. They ain't no good for me, and it seems like they all have some kinda side effects. I found out the inhaler I use for my asthma is a steroid. It makes me feel better sometimes, but it also leaves me feeling bloated and all puffed up. These damn medicines fix one thing and hurt another. My body is just breaking down. Medicare gave me a oxygen tank to use to help me breathe a little better.

I got situated on the side of the bed and reached for the brown cane dangling on the rail. The kitchen ain't that far away, but it seems like a journey to me these days. I rocked my body on the side of the bed 'til I got the strength to get up. The cane in my right hand supported my stiff knees. Slowly, I made my way to the kitchen, using my left hand to get more support from furniture and walls. I plopped my weary body down in a chair near the refrigerator. I'm outta breath already.

I opened the refrigerator door, looking to find some food I had a taste for, but really didn't see anything I wanted. I hate not having things in the house that I like to eat. I'm not used to running out of stuff. Since I don't drive anymore, and can't get around like I used to, I have to depend on Julian, Kendall and La-La to run errands and do my shopping. Them kids don't know a damn thing about shopping. They get the wrong stuff and usually pay too much. I'm used to catching sales and stocking up so that I always have everything I need.

Lord knows I don't wanna be a burden to my children. They got their own lives to live. I hope they live to get old, then, they'll see what it's like not being able to do the things they're used to doing. I don't blame them for my illness, but I'm sure a lot of my sickness is probably due to me worrying about them. As a mother, I want the best for my three children, but at this point, all I can do is pray. I did the best I could raising them all alone. I hadn't counted on being a single parent.

I opened the oven door and checked the four strips of bacon sizzling on the inside; the toaster on the counter next to the stove warmed two slices of raisin bread. I sat down at the kitchen table and looked through the window. The trees were bare, and leaves needed to be raked. Witnessing the change of season made me think about how far God has brought me.

Warm raisin bread popped up from the toaster and distracted my attention from the weather outside. I like my bacon crisp, so I let it sizzle in the oven a little while longer. I let a couple of minutes pass before pulling the hot pan from the oven and sitting it on top of the stove. Hot grease continued to pop. I got a plate from one of the cabinets and covered it with a paper towel. I put the bacon on the plate and covered it with another paper towel to absorb some of the grease. I poured the grease from the pan into a jar that I kept on back of the stove. The bacon was able to cool off a little while I went back to the refrigerator to get a bottle of orange juice. I'm about to run out of juice soon. I'll have to get Julian or Lauren to go by the store and pick up some more.

I munched on a piece of bacon and gazed out the window. I'm in the winter of my life right now; my days are getting shorter. I've done my time; I have only a few hours left on this earth. The last several decades didn't exactly go the way I had planned.

Forty years ago, I was a pint-sized, dynamo with massive talent. God had blessed me with a booming, harmonious voice that made folks sin on Saturday night and repent on Sunday morning. From my lips, the blues of despair and verses of love gone wrong, flowed through smoke filled nightclubs; from my heart, the gospel of hope and better days ahead, roared from the spirit-filled choir of a Baptist church. I had the power in my voice to make people wanna laugh and party on Saturday and wanna cry and pray on Sunday.

Singing in the choir one Sunday morning was where I first laid eyes on Kenny. It was January, 1965; the second Sunday of the New Year. It was a long time ago, but I remember it like it was yesterday. Pastor James Humphrey opened the doors of the New Calvary Baptist Church and Kenny walked down the aisle.

He introduced himself as Kendall Collins, and said he wanted to join church with Christian experience and become a member of the Usher Board. Shouts of thank you Jesus and amen filled the tiny, storefront church. Pastor Humphrey shook Kenny's hand and asked the congregation to accept Brother Collins as a new member of New Calvary. Kenny was a fine specimen. He was tall and had an engaging smile that offset rugged good looks.

Women dominated the congregation at New Calvary and most of us were very excited about seeing a new man join the church. It was about twelve degrees outside, but some of the women in the congregation were hotter than a ram in a burning bush. They were having their own private summers and were waving fans frantically to cool themselves off. Some of the holy and horny women looked as if they were ready to shout and pass out. And Kenny hadn't even laid hands on them or touched the hem of their garments yet.

A month of Sundays had passed before Kenny approached me at a church tea. He raved about the power of my voice and called me a little songbird. I complimented him on being an active new member and admired him for his enthusiasm in serving God. He showed dedication and seemed excited about establishing a firm relationship with the Lord. I liked him and he liked me.

Nine months later, Kenny and I were married. Pastor Humphrey performed the ceremony with a small gathering of family and friends in attendance. I was happy and excited about being Mrs. Kendall Collins. Kenny was anxious to start a family, but for me, conceiving a child and carrying it the full term was proving to be a difficult task and was putting a strain on our marriage. In four years, I'd suffered two miscarriages.

When I found out I was pregnant a third time, I was afraid to tell anyone because I didn't want to build expectations and let people down, especially Kenny. By then, my dream of getting some kind of record deal was on the back burner. I still loved to sing, but I didn't mind putting my ambitions on the shelf to become a loving wife and a good mother.

Kenny was making good money working at General Motors and soon had saved a down payment for us to move into this house. By the time Julian was born, we were on top of the world. God was blessing us.

Kenny stood at the altar looking peacock proud and hallelujah happy when Julian got christened by Pastor Humphrey at New Calvary. We were an attractive young couple in the church and appeared to have a bright future ahead of us. He had become president of the Usher Board and I was singing and leading songs in the choir. I was so in love. Most of the ladies in the church were happy for me, but I could tell some were jealous. They were coveting my husband.

My pregnancy with Kendall was much more difficult. I had to stay off my feet and spent most of the last trimester on bed rest. I was having the same problems I had experienced during my previous miscarriages. My body was tired and my mood was edgy. Kenny was less loving and supportive this time around. He still seemed happy, but sometimes looked as though he was overwhelmed and in over his head. Julian had just learned to walk and was getting into everything not nailed down. I lacked the energy to chase him around the house. Looking back, sometimes I wonder how my frame of mind during that pregnancy influenced the spirit and attitude of my unborn child.

Kenny and I were relieved when the doctors delivered our second son without any complications. He was healthy and showed signs of being a fighter. We named him Kendall Lamar Collins Jr. Early on I could tell Julian was gonna be my baby and Kendall Jr. was gonna be a chip off the old block.

With a wife, a toddler and an infant to feed, Kenny was a bit subdued when he learned I was pregnant again. The look of love was starting to disappear from his eyes. It seemed as though our growing family and all its responsibilities had stripped him of the excitement he once had. The enthusiastic man I had fallen in love with just a few years ago, was now just a distant figment of my imagination. I still loved him, but he wasn't the same man anymore.

When I was pregnant with Julian, he used to rush home from work to be with me and watch over me. He wanted to rub my stomach and massage my swollen feet. His eyes were warm and caring then. However, seeing me barefoot and pregnant again had turned his once warm eyes into a cold stare. It was a look of disdain. The shapely body that used to turn him on was long gone. I no longer triggered excitement in his loins anymore. I was never able to lose the weight I gained while carrying Julian. As my weight increased, my self esteem decreased. I didn't recognize Kenny anymore and I didn't recognize myself anymore either.

Kenny was no where to be found when I went into labor with Lauren. That hurt me deeply. He showed up at the hospital the next day with a bouquet of flowers and a couple of balloons. A smile of guilt ushered him into the room. He came in with a weak apology and an empty promise to do better. The kiss he planted on my forehead lacked passion. I don't think I ever forgave him for that.

The glass of orange juice helped me swallow the small tablet I took daily for my heart. It was supposed to keep me from having an attack in the future, but failed to heal the damage already done. They say only time can mend a broken heart, but sometimes time ain't even long enough. A lot of years have come and gone since then, but my mind still looks back on those days and wonder. I can still remember the sound of the doorbell ringing in my ear; it changed my life forever.

I was in a bad mood that Saturday afternoon. Kenny had left home on Friday night, leaving me alone with three, small kids. He didn't come home Friday night. I was angry and worried. It was time for me to give him a piece of my mind. Finally, I had gotten fed up with his gambling and staying out all night. To make matters worse, women were calling and hanging up. I still loved him, but I was ready to leave. I was trying to put up a good front for family, friends and people at church, but by this time, I was tired of pretending.

I remember the day vividly. It was July 1, 1978. The weather was sunny and pleasant. I had the front door open so that a cool breeze could air out the stuffiness in the house. Julian liked sports and was watching the Cubs play on channel 9. The radio in the kitchen was tuned to WBMX and was playing Rick James' "You & I" in constant rotation. Kendall was showing signs of a rebellious trait and was racing a *Hot Wheels* toy car on tables and chairs. La-La was discovering the art of running, but was still messing in her diapers. I was changing her for what seemed the umpteenth time when the doorbell rang.

Two police officers were standing on the front porch. I opened the screen door with Lauren in my arms and Kendall Jr. holding me around the leg. One of the officers asked me if I knew anyone by the name of Kendall Collins. I nodded my head and told them he's my husband. Right away I asked about Kendall's whereabouts. They showed me a picture of Kenny and informed me his body was in the Cook County morgue.

My world stopped.

My body started trembling and I held La-La tighter than I ever had before. I was rocking her, but trying to console myself. The officers said Kenny and a woman by the name of Barbara Dixon had been shot and killed in a motel parking lot. I was in a daze.

Barbara Dixon was a member of New Calvary and sang with me in the choir. Her estranged husband, Robert Dixon had been arrested and was being charged with first degree murder. He knew about the affair and had used a friend's car to follow her to the Dunes Motel on Stony Island to meet Kenny. Robert Dixon was waiting in the parking lot of the motel while my husband and his wife rendezvoused in Room 26. Dixon watched them leave the room hand in hand. He jumped out of the car and fired five shots from a .38 caliber gun. Three bullets hit Kenny in the chest. Barbara was struck twice in the head at close range.

I knew Kenny was cheating on me, but I never thought it would've been with a person I sat next to every Sunday in church. Barbara and I used to greet each other with a hug and kiss every Sunday morning. In the choir, we sang songs from the same hymn book. I shared *my Bible with that woman!* We had even held hands and prayed with each other during alter call. She used to give Julian and Kendall candy and even cradled a new born Lauren in her arms. And on top of all of that, she was sleeping with my husband. That woman and I served God together. I thought she was my friend.

Kenny and Barbara died instantly. A part of me died also, although my death has been a slow one. The lives of Julian, Kendall and Lauren were changed forever on that day as well, but at the time, they were still too young to realize it.

11

JULIAN

The Cook County States Attorney's Office said I had clients accused of money laundering and property flipping schemes. Since I was the attorney of record on several of the property deals, the Cook County States Attorney's Office had gotten a search warrant for my files. Because of this, I was constantly attending hearings and filing motions to quash the search warrant so that I could have my computers and files returned to my office.

The States Attorney's Office had crippled me. I had gone out and bought a new computer, but it still took a lot of time trying to reproduce certain documents. As an attorney, people were always coming to me to get legal counseling, but now I needed someone to lean on for a change. I was hoping an evening with Annette would allow me an opportunity to escape for a little while.

Because of all the craziness occurring in my life, I was excited about getting a chance to see Annette again. So much had taken place since we met in a nearby Starbucks a few weeks ago. Dealing with legal matters consumed a lot of my time, and being a single parent occupied much of Annette's. We had talked on the phone on a couple of occasions, but our conversations always seemed to get interrupted by this or that. On two occasions we were supposed to get together, but each time she called to cancel at the last minute, saying something had come up. It seemed as though planning an outing with her would always be a challenge. I found it frustrating.

Annette and I agreed to meet each other in the lobby of the Sears Tower. She gets off work at five; our dinner reservations are for six. Since 9-11, being in the lobby of the Sears Tower seemed like going through airport security. Identification monitors checked the name and photo of all employees attempting to gain access to the building elevators. Surveillance machines scan all bags and briefcases.

I kill time by waiting in the corner by the payphones and watch people eager to end the workday exit the elevators. It's an excellent place to sightsee. A lot of lovely ladies work in the Sears Tower.

I had gone home earlier to change clothes and had ample time to properly dress for the big evening. First I freshened up with a hot, lathery shower; then I shampooed my short, black hair and applied a conditioner with a fresh scent. I felt good, looked great, and smelled even better.

Desiring to be immaculately attired had caused me to vacillate repeatedly over which suit or blazer to wear. After surveying a rack of famous designers, I had finally decided on a navy Sean John six-button, double-breasted, pinstriped suit, which I accessorized with a crisp white shirt, accented by monogrammed sleeves and cufflinks; a navy and white polka dot power tie completed my look.

The fragrance oozing from my neck and wrist was a combination of elegance and erotica. I was smooth and ready to strut around town in a pair of black Cole Hahn shoes that glared with intensity from an impeccable spit shine. It was my Dapper Dan, savoir-faire is everywhere attire. When it comes to clothes, I can dress with the best of them. I was ready for a night of fun, and was hoping for big things from Annette. It was almost five o'clock and I was ready to make my move.

I spotted Annette the moment the elevator door opened. She looked good and was dressed fittingly for a chilly, overcast evening in December. Annette was pretty in pink, in a three-quarters length, wool coat and matching colored hat that complimented each other perfectly. She possessed a Jackie-O type of elegance. A burgundy leather skirt and a pair of knee high burgundy boots helped to complete her stylish ensemble. Annette had my attention immediately and dollar bills were already jumping around in my pocket eager to be spent. We made eye contact and she came over to greet me with the same bubbly energy she had the day we met. Annette and I shared a hug.

"It's good to see you again," I said, observing her round face and bright eyes.

"Finally," she replied.

"Tell me about it."

"I'm sorry," she stated with an apologetic look in her eyes. "I just been dealing with a lot of stuff lately," she continued, shaking her head. "Sometimes things get crazy, but I don't wanna talk about that now. It's good to get off work and unwind for a while."

"I know that's right."

Annette and I made small talk as we walked to the Union Station garage to get my car. I was able to relate to what she said about things in life getting crazy. I was still feeling stressed out about my own stuff.

We rode the elevator in Union Station to the third floor. I used the remote control on my key ring to deactivate the alarm and unlock the doors of my shiny, black Infiniti G35 Coupe. I opened the passenger door and helped Annette get in. A single, peach rose rested on the tan leather seat. Annette picked up the rose and smelled it.

"Is this for me?" she asked.

"Yes," I answered with a smile, feeling good about the thoughtful gesture.

"Thank you," she smiled. "You're so sweet."

"Do you like roses?" I asked.

"Of course," she said, twisting her mouth in a pouting smirk. "Don't all women?"

"I'm glad to hear that," I grinned, setting up my next move to make a good impression on Annette. I opened the trunk and reached for a plastic box containing a dozen peach roses and handed them to her.

"Julian . . . you didn't have to do this," she declared with a look of surprise.

"I know," I said with a sly grin. "There's no sense in that rose being all alone."

"Wow. Thank you!"

"You're welcome."

"What does a peach colored rose mean?"

"It means desire, anticipation and optimism for the future."

"That sounds good," she said, and once again inhaled the fresh scent.

I parked in front of the Catch 35 Seafood Restaurant and received a ticket from the valet. The upscale eatery located on downtown's west Wacker Drive was popular with seafood lovers and restaurant critics throughout the Chicago metropolitan area. The restaurant featured an extensive menu and a variety of seafood specials daily. One of the cool things about it was all the seafood selections can be observed from a display case. A pianist tapped melodious keys and entertained patrons with live jazz. It's a real classy place and Annette seemed impressed.

We were on time for our reservation and the host sat us right away. Annette excused herself and went to the restroom to wash her hands. Like always, that vicious gang of ass followed her, inflicting men with whiplash with every step she took. Damn, she looked good in that leather skirt and boots.

The waiter came to take our orders shortly after Annette returned from the ladies room. We perused the menu and discussed what we thought might satisfy our hunger. Annette deliberated over several seafood dishes, whereas I made up my mind quickly and ordered the pan seared Creole seasoned salmon. In the meantime, an indecisive Annette continued to study the menu with the fervor of a marine biologist. She was beginning to test my patience as she grilled the waiter about how the meals were prepared and served. Come on already.

"Can I have the oven baked Pacific shrimp served without the crabmeat stuffing?"

"No ma'am," answered the waiter.

"The grilled Florida Grouper sounds good."

"That's a popular choice," replied the waiter with a smile. "It's prepared with lemon caper butter that really accents the taste and brings the flavor out."

"How is the blackened Block Island swordfish?" she asked.

"What is she, a deep sea fisher or something?" I wondered to myself.

The waiter gave a fake smile. "It's delicious. Our blackened Block Island swordfish is seasoned with roasted red pepper and a chipotle sauce that gives it spice."

"I just can't make up my mind," she said, shaking her head. "There are so many choices that it's hard for me to decide. They all sound so good."

"I can come back later if you like?"

"Oh . . .," she said hesitantly. "I guess I'll have the grilled Atlantic salmon."

"Are you sure?" he asked.

"Yes . . . I'm sure."

I smiled. It's about damn time. I take her to a seafood restaurant and all of a sudden she becomes a mermaid, asking more questions than Jacque Cousteau. You just can't give some women too many choices. Next time I'll take her to Popeye's and let her order some chicken wings. She'll probably be in line all day trying to decide between spicy and mild. Annette had gotten on my nerves and the waiter's. He's earning his tip.

"I'll be back shortly with your drinks," the waiter replied, taking the menus.

"Thank you," we responded in unison.

The conversation flowed easily between Annette and me. She's witty and seems to enjoy a good laugh. We were on the subject of relationships when the waiter returned with our meals. Annette extended her hands to me so I could bless the food before eating. After a brief prayer, I said amen and reluctantly let go of her small hands. Her fingers were soft and gentle to touch. Freshly, manicured nails were covered with clear polish. Annette possessed a quiet sex appeal and appeared to be a lot of fun to be around. I needed some fun in my life right now.

A humming sound interrupted our conversation. Annette checked her purse and found her cell phone vibrating non-stop inside. She looked at the number and placed the phone back in her purse. We resumed our conversation.

"So Mr. Collins, do you have anyone you're seeing seriously at this time?"

"No."

"That's surprising," she replied, with a smirk suggesting she didn't believe me.

"Why do you say that?" I asked.

"You seem to be a brother with a lot going on. You have a professional career, you're handsome and well groomed, you're funny, and most of all: you seem to be a God fearing man."

"Well . . . thank you," I blushed. "I try my best."

"You're welcome."

"I guess my timing has been off lately. Sometimes I meet women interested in me, but I'm not feeling them on that kind of level, or maybe I like them, but they don't like me. You know . . . It's tough out here these days. The new millennium is fierce."

Annette laughed. "You're right about that."

"What about you?"

"I'm in the process of trying to end a relationship," she admitted with her head down, looking at her food instead of me. "I've been dating this guy for a couple of years, but things just aren't right."

"Why not?" I asked.

"Well . . .," she hesitated. "I just found out recently that he's still married. He's separated from his wife, but he's still legally married. Also, he's almost fifteen years older than me and I want to be with someone closer to my own age."

"That means he must be in his mid-thirties because you look like you just went on prom and graduated from high school a couple of weeks ago," I charmed.

"You better watch out," she blushed. "Flattery might get you everywhere," she flirted. "Actually, I just turned thirty-two in November, but I appreciate the compliment."

"You're welcome," I said and took a sip of wine. "So what are you going to do about the relationship with the guy you're dating?"

Annette made a face and rolled her eyes. "I want to break things off because I've felt differently ever since I've learned he's still married. I've been trying to distance myself from him, but he won't let me go. He says he needs me and wants us to work things out."

I heard the cell phone vibrating again inside her purse.

"Someone is really trying to get in touch with you," I said, becoming somewhat annoyed and wondering why she just didn't cut the phone off, but also remembering she has a child who may need to get in contact with her.

"It can wait," she replied, rolling her eyes with a slight smile parting her lips.

"Are you sure?" I asked.

She sighed. "I've been avoiding his phone calls all day and now he's wondering where I'm at. Good for him. Now he has something to think about. He's probably mad because he doesn't know where I am or who I'm with."

"Oh really!" I sniped, feeling very uncomfortable with this situation.

"Yeah," she smiled. "He's still married, but he wants to keep tabs on me and worry about my whereabouts. He's probably jealous and wondering why I haven't made it home from work yet. He knows where I park my car in the morning when I can catch the train downtown. He got a wife, but still trying to be possessive with me."

I was no longer enjoying my time with Annette. Our conversation was laced with too much drama. Finally, Annette turned the phone off after hearing it vibrate in her purse for a third time. I really don't have time for a drama queen, with a stalker boyfriend, who should be old enough to know better. I'm not saying her boyfriend was right or wrong, but I understood.

He's an older man, in his late forties, who was being twisted and hung out to drip dry by a fresh piece of juicy booty. Annette has a voluptuous body and magnetic sex appeal, and he's drawn to her and can't pull away. She's his fountain of youth. Refreshing and overflowing with enough vitality to quench his sexual thirst. For him, Annette's middle name might as well be Viagra.

Furthermore, I could tell Annette loved the attention and the fuss he was making over her. She was eating it up, and he was offering her seconds. I could hear my instincts telling me to run before it's too late. There's no sense in me getting hoodwinked by a big butt and a smile. Run Julian, run.

Where's the waiter?

Check please!

12

KENDALL

Instead of driving out to my house in the south suburbs last night, I chilled out at my apartment in the hood and stayed close to the action. The two flat building in the middle of 108th street keeps me in the trenches near the battlefield. One block over on Michigan, buses and cars travel down the heart of a community known as Roseland. Because of its reputation for murder, mayhem and madness, a lot of people refer to this area as the wild hundreds. It's almost three o'clock in the morning, but the people living in this part of town rarely close their eyes on nightfall. This is where I make my money.

The heroin flowing through the streets of Chicago comes from Southeast and Southwest Asia, South America and Mexico with traffickers using everything from commercial airlines and cargo trucks to transport drugs into the United States. Some couriers use secret book compartments, hollowed out shoes, and even put drugs up their ass to get past customs. Many others even hire young women and use infants as props while concealing drugs in cans of baby formula.

Chicago has long been the Midwestern drug hub allowing all kinds of illegal narcotics to make its way through our town and surrounding suburbs. Chi-Town also serves as the distribution point for all drugs en route to neighboring states such as Iowa, Wisconsin, Indiana and Missouri. Crack, cocaine and marijuana are responsible for destroying the foundation of inner-cities across the United States, but heroin, in its various forms, devastate the community like no other drug.

Prepping the product for the street is a tedious process. Recently I'd received a shipment of drugs from my Las Vegas buddy, Hector, and was getting ready for the street market. I spent hours packaging white heroin into small rectangles of aluminum foil. On special occasions, I wrap heroin in tiny glassine bags and stamp them with the brand name TNT. It's the trademark I use to let customers know they're buying some very potent shit. My goal was to blow their heads off and have them staggering back for more. And they always did.

Heroin bags sell for ten dollars a pop. I'm making a nice piece of loot out here on the south side, but nothing close to the money being made by the hustlers on the west side. They have a great location and a clientele with more disposable income. Because of these factors, the west side is the main site in Chicago for open-air heroin sales. Dealers out west are able to set up one stop shopping spots near the Eisenhower Expressway.

Their prime location allows them to provide curb service to affluent white customers coming in from the western suburbs. Out west, some buyers make purchases in the morning on their way to work, some buy packages during lunch, and others do their buying on the way home after leaving white collar jobs in the Loop. The convenient shopping allows users to exit the expressway to make purchases quickly without having to venture off into dangerous, unknown areas. Within minutes, they're back on I-290 and headed in the direction of their destination. Money is being made around the clock.

To a certain extent, the west side dealers prefer white customers because they know their sole purpose for getting off the expressway is to purchase heroin. Also, many white customers make bulk purchases and buy $150 to $200 worth of heroin to take back to their friends in the suburbs. On the other hand, my clients are residents of the area, who beg and steal money to get a quick fix. I'm about a mile and a half from the expressway, so white folks are less enthusiastic about venturing off into my hood. As a matter of fact, a lot of black folks aren't eager about wandering into certain pockets of the wild hundreds either.

I fixed a few more heroin packets and glanced at the time on my Rolex watch. It was almost seven o'clock. I had been up all night and was feeling a bit tired. I got up from the table in the kitchen where I prepared the drugs and walked to the living room. I yawned and looked outside. The sun was making a lazy attempt of peeking through the clouds. It appeared as though we were in for another chilly, overcast day. It's still winter time, so as long as the weather stayed dry, it's cool with me.

Drug addicts aren't discouraged by weather conditions. They have to have it winter, spring, summer and fall. They come to get their fix in rain, sleet or snow, and when the temperature is 100 degrees or 10 below zero. Dope fiends hit the streets earlier than the mailman. I looked on and saw my regular clients walking down the street to approach one of my guys on the block.

Albert is the first customer I see. He's a lanky, light-skinned man in his mid fifties, but looks like he's about ten or fifteen years older. He's rail thin and stands about six feet tall. Albert possesses a sneaky grin that sometimes opens to display a mouth full of gaps where teeth used to be. The whites of his eyes are covered with a permanent, drug induced haze. He used to be a sharp dresser who took pride in his appearance, but now he walked through the neighborhood in dingy clothes and run down shoes with holes in them. He's raggedy and tore up from the floor up.

I yawned again and watched closely as Albert tried to make a deal with Rodney, one of my guys on the street. Since I was on the second floor with the window closed, I couldn't tell what words were being exchanged, but I could see Rodney shaking his head repeatedly as Albert flailed his arms trying to make a point. I increased my vision with a pair of binoculars and got a closer look at the action. I figured Albert was broke and was trying to cut some kind of deal. He scratched his face and his body fidgeted in uncontrollable movements. Albert was going through withdrawals and was in desperate need of a fix. Looking at him from the living room window almost made me start itching.

Albert reached into his pocket and pulled out a watch and gave it to Rodney. Typical Albert; he had probably stolen the watch from a relative's house. Rodney gave Albert a dime bag worth of heroin and sent him on his way.

After Albert left, a lady by the name of Rochelle approached Rodney. She was just another female in a long line of women being turned out by the streets. She was very short and thin. Her light brown skin was full of enough blotches to keep a dermatologist in business for life. An oversized, auburn colored wig covered most of her forehead and slightly shielded her eyes. It was too late for Rochelle to try to conceal her identity. She had run through too many streets, and too many guys on the streets had run through her. Rochelle had a reputation for literally sucking a gang of dicks to get drugs. Guys in the hood referred to Rochelle as Roblow and described getting oral sex as Ro-jobs instead of blow jobs. I let her blow me a couple of times just for the hell of it. She was pretty good since she doesn't have a lot of teeth in her mouth.

Rochelle was a favorite in the hood for guys looking for oral sex, but she definitely wasn't popular with residents in the area who had been foolish enough to believe her lies. She was an expert at preying on caring citizens for money and using small children as bait to pull at their heart strings. One of Rochelle's schemes was to ring the doorbells of people living in the neighborhood to ask for money to take the small child she was carrying to the emergency room for medical attention. Seeing Rochelle with a supposedly sick toddler made sympathetic folks reach into their pockets and shell out ten or twenty dollars so she could get a cab to get to the hospital. Eventually the folks in the neighborhood caught on to Rochelle's plan. The hospital was right around the corner, and I was the doctor she was coming to see.

Rochelle is in her mid-thirties and is already a grandmother. She hasn't raised her own children, and isn't in a great position to provide sound advice to her grandkids either. She's too busy giving Ro-jobs to bake cookies and help with homework. Rochelle's mom is growing old and weary worrying about Rochelle, her grandchildren and now her great grandchildren.

I smelled the aroma of hot pancakes and bacon cooking in the kitchen the moment I entered the house from the side door. Usually, I'm able to sneak into the house while Mama is still asleep, but this time, she was sitting on a stool near the sink washing some dishes.

"You were expecting to tip in here on me again, huh?" Mama asked.

"Not really," I answered, not sure where our interaction will lead me.

"You want something to eat?" she asked, never taking her attention away from the dishes in the sink to look me in the eye.

"Ahh . . .,"

"Now Kendall you know you wanna eat," she snapped, interrupting me before I could finish my sentence. "So I don't know why you trying to pretend like you not hungry. Boy sit down and eat," she ordered.

I obeyed my mother. I sat down at the kitchen table and tried to gauge her mood. Mama has a poker face. She isn't frowning or smiling. Her words aren't harsh, but not affectionate either. I can't tell if she's glad to see me or is just relieved to know I'm alive. I'm not sure if Mama wants to wrap her arms around me and hug me, or slap the shit out of me.

"So where you been?" she asked. "I haven't seen you in a while."

"Just here and there," I answered vaguely.

"You been back to Vegas?"

"No."

The television is on and turned up loud. I shifted my attention to the contestants on *The Price is Right*, spinning the wheel to qualify for the showcase showdown. Mama put a plate in front of me and looked at me through troubled eyes. I put my head down and allowed the aroma of the hot pancakes to flow through my nostrils. I buttered the pancakes and cut them into neat, little squares and poured the syrup. A smile formed on my face after taking the first bite. Mmm good!

"These pancakes are delicious, Ma."

"Thanks," she mumbled.

"Mama, you could've opened a pancake house and made a lot of money," I joked in an attempt to lighten the mood and cut through some of the tension.

"Umm hmm," she mumbled. "So what you been doing with yourself, Kendall?"

"Ain't nothing going on, Ma," I responded, feeling very uncomfortable with Mama's interrogation as I bit into another section of pancakes. This is the reason why I don't come around more often. The tension here in the kitchen is thicker than the syrup I'm pouring over my pancakes.

After devouring several stacks of pancakes and four strips of bacon, I rinsed off my plate and washed the remaining dishes in the sink. Mama took a seat at the table and sipped on a glass of orange juice. I focused my attention on the conclusion of *The Price is Right*. There were no winners in the showcase showdown because both contestants had gone over with their respective bids.

I heard Mama take her last gulp from the glass and placed it on the table. She cleared her throat, but never said a word. Her eyes were burning a hole into the back of my head as she used her arms to elevate herself from the table. Mama reached for her cane and walked slowly to her bedroom. The long cord attached to the oxygen tank followed her along the way as she used the walls and furniture to balance her short steps. She climbed into bed and turned on the television in the room with a remote control located on a portable table. I could hear the channels changing rapidly until Mama reached a station broadcasting the news.

While Mama rested in bed, I cleaned up the kitchen and did a few chores around the house. I mopped the kitchen and bathroom floors and vacuumed the carpet in the living room and dining room. I don't come around much so I was trying to do as much as I could to offset my guilt. I walked to the bedroom to thank Mama for breakfast and to let her know I was about to leave.

"Ma I'm about to go," I said, leaning down so she could kiss me on the cheek. She gave me a light peck, but didn't say anything. I stood up straight and looked down over her frail body. Mama stared at me, but still didn't say anything. The silence was killing me. I turned and walked away.

"Kendall," she whispered, as I exited the room.
I turned around and came back. "Yes Ma."
"I pray to God . . . you don't break my heart."

13

LAUREN

"Are you okay, La-La?" Andre asked, as he reached for my left hand. He has been around me long enough now to sense my uneasiness.

"I'm fine," I lied. I was biting my lower lip and rubbing my hands on my thighs.

"You sure?" he asked, with a lighthearted smile.

"Yes," I nodded.

"You haven't had much to say since I picked you up," he said, grabbing my hand.

"I guess I'm kind of in a quiet mood today," I responded with a fake smile.

"We all have our quiet moments."

"Umm hmm," I replied, still biting nervously on my bottom lip.

Andre hummed along, accompanying Alexander O'Neal and Cherelle as they belted out the soulful lyrics to "Everything I Miss at Home" with passion. I looked out of the passenger window aimlessly, as Andre focused on the road leading us to the house he grew up in. It was time for me to meet the parents. I had reservations about it. The thought of it had me worried about breaking out in hives. I didn't want things to move too quickly.

Meeting the family sometimes creates false expectations and puts pressure on relationships. A couple can be in the early stages of dating, but before long, relatives are trying to plan weddings and wondering how the kids will look. They rush the relationship more than the people involved.

A few years ago, I dated this guy named David whose uncle always asked him at family gatherings when he was going to be able to eat some cake. I never understood what he was talking about until David explained his uncle was actually asking for some wedding cake. The old man was already a diabetic. He didn't need any cake.

I must admit, having Andre in my life over the last few months has been a blessing. He's constantly showering me with gifts and tokens of affection. Andre likes to send cute email cards to me at work to brighten my day and let me know he's thinking about me. He's very thoughtful. Last week, a delivery man came to the office with two dozen, long stemmed roses with baby's breath and a vase to put them in. Colleagues and a few bold client reps were coming from every direction to get in my business. They were asking who the roses were from, and if they could read the card. I enjoyed the attention; especially making the female haters in the office jealous. Nosy heifers.

People say I'm observant and pay attention to detail, but Andre has proven to be one of the most attentive men I've ever met. He seems to remember everything about me and the things we've done. One night, while relaxing in bed, Andre recalled our first seven dates in chronological order. He remembered the places we went, the outfits I wore, and the things we did. His memory was remarkable and scary.

Andre's parents, William and Bertha Evans live in a Georgian style home, located on Chicago's far south side. The house rests on the corner and overlooks a portion of expressway which merges the Dan Ryan into the Bishop Ford; a picturesque view of traffic flowing into the city or out to the south suburbs.

Andre held my hand as we walked up the steps and opened the unlocked door.

"Hi everybody!" he shouted, as we entered the house.

"Well it's about time!" shouted a female voice from the nearby kitchen. The house wasn't very large, but it provided a warm atmosphere.

"He usually gets here later than this," said another female voice, chiming in. "He must be trying to make a good impression."

Most of the people on hand to celebrate Granddaddy Evans' eighty-eighth birthday were women. They're in the kitchen preparing food, while several men sat in a family room at the back of the house and watched a football game on a big screen television. As Andre assisted me in removing my leather coat, a short, stout woman came and greeted me.

"Mama, this is my friend, Lauren."

"Hi Lauren," she said, greeting me with a warm embrace and pleasant smile. "Make yourself at home."

"Thank you, ma'am."

"You're welcome, dear," she replied. She seemed surprised by my politeness and display of respect in referring to her as ma'am.

I relaxed a little.

Andre led me to the kitchen and introduced me to the voices I heard earlier.

"Lauren, these are my two older sisters, Carol and Charlotte."

"Hey Lauren," Charlotte said, with an engaging smile.

"I hope you're hungry," Carol added. "We have plenty of food." Carol is shorter than Charlotte and seems a bit more reserved, but appeared to be friendly and eager to use any opportunity to tease her younger brother. Just from what I could sense while being in the kitchen with them; Charlotte is the sister with the bubblier personality and Carol is the wisecracking, sarcastic sister always making smart comments.

"We have to cook so much food because Mama always gives Andre extra food to take home so he can eat for the next three weeks," Carol joked with a sneaky smirk.

"See if he brought his Tupperware?" Charlotte asked with a hearty laugh.

"Yeah yeah," Andre replied, waving them off.

Andre led me into the dining room, adjacent to the kitchen, to meet his aunts, Lillian and Ernestine. I assumed they're aunts on his father's side because they didn't greet me with the warmth I felt when I met his mother. They're tall, regal looking women, with caramel colored skin and short gray afros. I bet the dignified divas were real show stoppers back in their youth, and probably still turn a few heads on the senior circuit these days.

I could feel them sizing me up and looking right through me; almost as if they were visualizing themselves when they were my age. Skepticism is etched all over their faces. My instincts are talking to me. Suddenly, I'm nervous again and biting my lower lip. I hope I don't start breaking out in hives. Inside, I'm begging for Andre to get me out of this room. Please save me. Telepathy must have occurred because he heard me. I could feel the gray-haired haters watching me as we made our way to the family room where the men watched football.

Being around men helped me to relax and regroup. Andre's father towered over me when he stood up to say hello.

"It's a pleasure meeting you, Lauren," he said, extending his large hand.

"It's nice meeting you, also," I replied, observing the striking resemblance between Andre and his father. Height appeared to be a dominant trait on the paternal side of the family. Mr. Evans looked as though he exercised regularly, and was probably better fit than men half his age. His rich dark, chocolate skin glistened under the ceiling lights. Those strong characteristics were passed down from father to son.

As Andre returned to the kitchen to get beverages from the refrigerator, Mr. Evans introduced me to the other three males in the room. Alvin and Calvin, the twenty-something twins, seated on the couch, are sons of Carol. Ben, the older man, seated in a recliner with a beer in his hand, is Andre's uncle, and the husband to one of the evil divas. I can't tell the identical twins apart, but one of them got up from the couch and offered me a seat. I sat on the tan, leather sofa and asked the score of the game to make conversation.

Touchdowns, kickoffs, tackles and rushing yards no longer seemed important to the men in the room. My heavenly hips had caused them to fumble their attention and intercepted their thrill for the game. They looked like eager fans ready to give Andre a high five and a pat on the back for making a great catch.

Andre hollered from the kitchen. "La-La, do you want something to drink?"

"Did he call you, La-La? Did he call you La-La?" Uncle Ben asked with sheer excitement and enthusiasm, rising up in his chair like a crazed fan about to do the wave.

"Yes sir," I answered, trying to remain polite without bursting out in laughter.

"You mean La-La like that old Delfonics song?" he asked. Then all of sudden he started singing. "La la la la la la la la la la means I love you . . . oh baby please now!"

"The Del who?" asked one of the twins, not familiar with the old school song.

"Oh hell nah!" Charlotte yelled from the kitchen. "No he ain't tryin' to sing."

"A man with too much to drink might try any damn thing!" snapped Ernestine.

Uncle Ben is drunk and making a fool out of himself; Andre is embarrassed; Mr. Evans is amused; Mrs. Evans is baffled; Carol and Charlotte are snickering in the kitchen; the evil divas are fuming in the dining room; and the twins are laughing so hard that tears are rolling down their cheeks. And now I'm hungry.

"Yo Uncle Ben, sing that song one more time," laughed one of the twins.

"Calvin quit messin' with Ben," Carol ordered. "Go upstairs and wake granddaddy up. It's time for us to eat dinner." Calvin walked up the steps leading to the bedroom with his shoulders still shaking up and down. He was hunched over with laughter and looked like he was about to go into convulsions. Meanwhile, Alvin was still on the couch, drying his eyes with his Allen Iverson jersey.

I hope the food is as good as the entertainment.

Granddaddy Evans used a cane to make his way down the stairs to the dining room. Alvin and Calvin worked together in helping him to sit down in a chair at the head of the table. He's tall, but age and fragile bones has shortened his height and caused him to walk bent over. Granddaddy's complexion is a shade lighter than

Andre's, closer to the caramel tone shared by the evil divas, Lillian and Ernestine. He's in his late eighties, but a full coat of white hair still covered his head. Small hearing aids rested in both ears. His long fingers trembled as he gathered himself in the chair.

    The Evans clan gathered around the dining room table and waited patiently as Granddaddy Evans said grace. With one of the twin's two-year-old baby daughter in attendance, Granddaddy Evans was preparing to lead five generations in prayer. Five generations. We stood hand in hand around the table as the feeble family patriarch blessed the food and thanked God for surrounding him with generations of family and being able to live another year. He prayed for a long time, but no one seemed to mind. I put my head down and closed my eyes. Tears were welling up under my eyelids. I grasped Andre's hand tightly and allowed his fingers to intertwine with mine.

    I was apprehensive when Andre came to pick me up, but now I'm jealous. I've never experienced family life like this. Five generations are breaking bread together on a Sunday afternoon. A lot of history is represented in this room. God, I have no idea what this is like. I don't have my father; my mother is ill; and my siblings and I are going our separate ways. Lyrics from Alexander O'Neal and Cherelle started playing again in my head. Everything I Miss at Home.

14

JULIAN

    Excitement and anticipation dominated my thoughts after I ended my long distance conversation with my good friend, Leonard. He had called to give me the weather forecast for northeastern Florida. Being able to escape a Chicago winter for a few days is always nice, so it's a blessing having friends living in milder climates. The fifty degree temperatures were cooler than what I wanted, but still more inviting than the thirty degree temperatures here. I was looking forward to getting away for a little while and relaxing my mind.

    My trip to Florida comes with an extra bonus this year because Jacksonville is hosting the Super Bowl. The New England Patriots are set to battle the Philadelphia Eagles in the big game. And Leonard had managed to get tickets. Life doesn't get much better than this.

    I had a busy day ahead so I tried to get off to an early start. I paid some bills on line, dropped off a premium check at State Farm for my auto insurance, took a payment to the cable company, and made it to the barbershop for my nine-thirty appointment. My barber, Gerald, had the chair waiting for me when I arrived and was able to take his time in providing me with a neat cut and a trimmed goatee. I examined my fresh look in the mirror and tipped Gerald a few extra dollars. By ten-thirty, I was on my way to the house to spend some time with Mama before leaving for Jacksonville in the afternoon.

I retrieved my luggage from the baggage claim area and looked around for Leonard. My flight was supposed to arrive in Jacksonville at seven-thirty, but we were about fifteen minutes ahead of schedule. JAX is busier than usual because of the festivities taking place in the city, but the atmosphere still reminds me of a relaxing day at the mall instead of a frantic day in an airport. Even during Super Bowl week, O'Hare or Midway on a calm day is still more hectic than JAX could ever be. The pace is slow and tranquil. I'm in the state of Florida, but Jacksonville is a long way from Miami in both distance and activity.

"Julian! Julian!"

My lips formed into a smile. It's been over a year since I'd seen my buddy, Leonard. So much has happened in our lives since we last stood face to face. I sized him up quickly and went to greet him with a hug. His short, stocky frame appeared lighter and less energetic. I can tell he has lost weight. Sophisticated, designer frames covered what seemed like lonely and weary eyes. The smile on his face appeared somewhat strained.

"Leonard, it's good to see you," I said, gripping my friend in a bear hug.

"It's good to be seen," he quipped. "It's good to be seen alive."

"I know that's right," I agreed. I unzipped the heavy, brown leather jacket I had on and allowed my body to cool off a little. Night had fallen upon Jacksonville, but the temperature was still in the upper fifties. Leonard and I made small talk as we walked through the parking lot of JAX looking for his car. We searched the pavement on two floors in an attempt to find his vehicle. Frustration was marked by the wrinkles on Leonard's forehead; drops of sweat begin to form on the top of his shaven head.

"I can't believe this," he mumbled under his breath. "Where did I park my car?"

I continued to follow him around the massive parking lot, but kept my comments to myself. Leonard is a person who takes pride in being in control, always making sure each *I* is dotted and every *T* is crossed. That isn't the case right now. He is extremely flustered.

"There my baby is," he said, pressing his key chain to deactivate the alarm. "Julian . . . Cynthia got my head all twisted up," he admitted as he opened the trunk to his burgundy Toyota Camry and placed my luggage inside. "Man, I keep asking myself why in the hell did I sell my house and move down here in the first place."

"I guess love made you do it," I replied.

"Yeah and love can make a man do some real fucked up shit."

"This is true."

In no time, Leonard was navigating the lanes of the expressway, allowing me an opportunity to inhale the city's landscape and bask in the serenity coming from the Atlantic Ocean.

"Julian, I gave up a lot coming down here."

"Yeah you did," I nodded, still taking in a view of the aquatic scenery.

"My parents died and left me with a house that was already paid for. I left friends and people who've been in my life for years to move down here. Hell, I left my daughter Lynette in Chicago. She's grown and in her last year of college now, but I miss her. We communicate via email and phone calls once a week, but it's not like me being there for her. I have a few friends here, but I don't have you, Miguel and Chuck around like I did when I was in the Chicago. I gave up a whole lot!"

"So what is Cynthia saying now?" I asked.

Leonard pounded his hand on the steering wheel. "That bitch had the nerve to say Jacksonville isn't big enough for the both of us and that if I stay here, she might move back to Dallas."

"Say what?"

"Yep," he confessed, his eyes were getting wide with anger.

"What about her family?"

"Please," he replied, shaking his head. "Cynthia doesn't have any loyalty to anyone, Julian. When things get tough, she bails out. Her mom is up in age and is worried Cynthia may leave Jacksonville again because that's the kind of shit she does. She wants to run away from every fuckin' thing."

"That's a shame."

"Julian, I blew it because I put her on a pedestal. I can't blame anybody but myself. She was my dream girl. For fifteen years, I worshipped her from afar." He continued. "Remember, how I used to always refer to her as the one who got away?"

"I sure do."

"We met years ago when I was on the road doing advertising for Rolling Stone Magazine. We dated briefly and had good chemistry. Even when I stopped traveling to that area of the country, we always stayed in touch, but distance kept us apart. She dated guys and got engaged a couple of times, and I dated other women and eventually met Veronica. But when it came to Cynthia, I always lived with wondering what if."

"Things happened real fast between you guys."

"Man, she called me one day and said she wanted to come to Chicago for the weekend to visit me."

"I remember."

"Julian, she came to Chicago and turned my world upside down. I was vulnerable at the time because my mother had just died a few months earlier and I had recently broken up with Veronica. Man, I was ripe for the picking. She came up on the weekend of Valentine's Day and gave me some of the best loving I'd had in years. Julian, she straight broke me off! One night after making love, she went in the bedroom where my mother used to sleep and found my mom's wedding dress tucked away in a closet. Man, I don't even know how she found the dress."

I remained silent and shook my head in amazement as Leonard told the story.

"I hadn't really felt like going through all of Mom's clothes, so a lot of dresses and clothes were still in the house. Somehow, Cynthia stumbled across the wedding dress and tried it on. Julian, I was in the basement basking in the afterglow of making love and she came downstairs with my mother's wedding dress on. Man, I was totally fucked up after that. Cynthia and my mom wore the same size. Before the weekend was over, we were talking about getting married and I was planning on moving to Florida."

"Damn, that's some unbelievable shit," I said, shaking my head. "Leonard, I was absolutely shocked when you called and told me you were getting married."

"Bottom line was, she wanted to get married first before getting pregnant. That's what it was all about. She wanted to have a baby. Cynthia was close to forty and had never been married and wanted to be a mother. But being a southern girl with southern values, she didn't want to have a baby out of wedlock, so she rushed me into marriage. My nose was wide open, so I agreed to everything. Besides I was ready to get married again and start over."

"Leonard, women are capable of saying and doing some unbelievable things."

"It's amazing," Leonard grinned, shaking his head in disbelief. "The tripped out part is, I thought dealing with women would be easier as we got older, but I think I'm even more confused now. Man, we can't live with 'em and we can't kill 'em."

"Not unless you're O.J."

We both laughed.

"Man, I wish I had followed my father's advice years ago," Leonard continued.

"What was that?"

"My father was on his death bed at Mercy Hospital and told me never to put all of my eggs in one basket when it came to a woman. My father said women are too fickle and wishy washy, and that they can turn on your ass in a heartbeat. One moment you're big daddy and the man and the next moment you ain't shit."

"And that's probably on a good day," I added with a laugh.

"Julian, I love my mother, may her soul rest in peace. I miss her dearly and think about her everyday, but my father was talking from experience. That was my mother, but she was still a woman."

"I hear you."

"Man it's a blessing having a wonderful woman in our life, but damn they can create a lot of confusion and make shit complicated sometimes."

"Tell me about it."

"So how are the ladies treating you, Julian?" Leonard asked.

"The way your father said: fickle and wishy washy," I confessed. "Leonard, I meet these chicks who want me to wine and dine them and jump through a bunch of hoops. Women are always asking where they can find a good man, or where are the good brothers, but I'm trying to find out where I can find a good woman. Sometimes I get very lonely, but often it's easier to be alone, then to have to deal with some of that nonsense that comes into play when I'm in a relationship."

"I don't think some of these women really know what they want."

"A lot of them want an image," I reasoned. "Some of these women want guys with the perfect looks, job, home and car, and all the extra amenities that come with it."

"And you still better get first row tickets to concerts and plays."

"Plus they want you to be able to defend their honor and kick some ass if something crazy jumps off while the two of you are out for an evening on the town," I added. "And later on you have to be the sensitive type and recite your favorite poem while playing the piano at the bar to appeal to their romantic side."

"Dude, trying to defend some of these chicks will get you killed."

"That's funny."

"That wouldn't be funny," Leonard shook his head. "That would be fucked up."

Both of us enjoyed a hearty laugh. Being with Leonard reminded me of old times. We've always been able to laugh and discuss matters near and dear to our heart without feeling like our manhood would be questioned. He is a true friend, a brother. I can share with him the thoughts and fears I have that I would be ashamed to share with anyone else. I'm blessed to have a buddy like Leonard in my life. My bond with him is stronger than the bond I have with my own brother.

"Man, I guess we've all been guilty of making some bad decisions," I admitted. "I know I've met some nice women and let them slide by instead of really going after them the way I should have; I just wasn't feeling them on that level. Some of them I could've really taken advantage of, but that's just not me. I was probably too busy concerning myself with the shape of their hips and the fullness of their lips."

"There has to always be some kind of physical attraction first," Leonard reasoned. "It's not like we're gonna spot a lady walking through the mall and marvel at how lovely her personality is."

"Yeah, but sometimes I wonder if I spend too much time looking at the outer shell instead of the person on the inside. Maybe I've been too picky also and don't always know what I want either. I can only blame myself for that."

"That's not your fault, Julian."

"Well whose fault is it then?" I asked.

"It's your dick's fault," Leonard laughed. "You can't let your dick have too much power and make decisions on your behalf."

"I guess your dick encouraged you to move all the way down here to boring ass Jacksonville, huh," I joked.

"Yeah, no shit."

Unincorporated land and aquatic beauty surrounds the city some refer to as southern Georgia. The waterfront home that should've been shared by husband and wife is instead the quaint quarters of a reluctant bachelor. Cynthia had found the place for them while Leonard was still in Chicago preparing for relocation. Located in the community of Arlington, the three bedroom apartment, with the living room view of the Intracoastal Waterway was supposed to be the place they called home.

It never worked out like that.

Before Leonard was able to finalize the sale of his house and move to Florida, Cynthia was announcing a change of heart. For her, getting married was now a bad idea. Leonard thought they would be able to resolve their issues once they were together in Florida. Unfortunately, man and wife never lived under the same roof.

A nighttime chill enveloped the Friday evening sky. Football fans and tourists paraded through the damp streets of downtown Jacksonville in jackets and hats representing their favorite teams. The crowd of pedestrians and cars made the area congested and tough to maneuver. Finding a parking space was difficult, but we got lucky when Leonard saw a driver in a mini-van pulling out of a spot next to a meter. We saluted the accomplishment by touching fists. He was happy to do what seemed to be impossible. We were only a short walk from the Landing.

The Jacksonville Landing reminds me of Navy Pier in Chicago. It's a cool place to grab a bite to eat while enjoying the outdoors near the water. Finally, Leonard is smiling and having fun. Seeing him happy brings a grin to my face. He's taking pride in being able to show off the city he now calls home. The Super Bowl is only two days away and Jacksonville is getting primed for its time to shine. A herd of international media is on hand and using the Landing as its headquarters to focus its spotlight on the shores of a big country town.

Jacksonville will probably never see this much excitement again. And even though Super Sunday is approaching, there still aren't a lot of activities for tourists. Leonard told me about the challenges the city had in trying to provide lodging for the wave of visitors invading the city for the first time. There definitely didn't seem to be a lot for blacks to do either. It's a nice place to visit, but I wouldn't want to live down here. From what I've seen thus far, I would be bored to death living here.

Both of us were hungry, so we decided to stop in Hooters to get something to eat. Leonard munched on wings. They looked too greasy for me, so I ate a burger instead. He was finally having a good time and seemed as though he didn't have a care in the world. Leonard flirted with the Hooter girls and peppered them with lines spicier than the sauce on the hot wings. He was in rare form. The spicy wings probably would upset his sensitive, ulcer plagued stomach, but I wasn't going to ruin his moment. I allowed my buddy to reminisce and hold court.

Leonard was traveling down memory lane and was laughing about all the freaks he had screwed back in Chicago. Having worked in advertising for years, Leonard took pride in being able to influence people to get whatever he wanted when he wanted it. Leonard could overcome a woman's objections long enough until they just seemed to give in. He didn't blow ladies away with his appearance, but he made up for it with charm and confidence. Leonard went after women with the tenacity of a used car salesman on a mission to make a quota. He was never intimidated by the word no.

Leonard sucked on hot wings and conversed with one of the Hooter girls as patrons at nearby tables laughed and guzzled down glasses of beer. The crowd was festive and talk of the Super Bowl was flooding the air. Suddenly, Leonard's mood changed. His eyes got big and his face became flush. He pounded his fist on the table with the force that caused our plates and glasses to rattle. It startled me and even interrupted the boisterous group of guys frolicking at the table next to us.

"What is that bitch doing up in here!" he shouted.

I turned around and saw Cynthia being seated at a booth with a middle-aged white man. Before I could turn my attention back to Leonard, he was out of his chair and headed in their direction.

Lights, camera, action! Leonard was ready to make a scene.

"Leonard! Leonard!" I shouted twice, trying to get his attention before he did something stupid, but my words fell on deaf, unresponsive ears. He was zoned out and locked in on a target with the focus of a cheetah chasing one gazelle. Leonard shouted profanities at the white guy who was making a valiant attempt to defend Cynthia's honor.

Cynthia stood up with a few choice words, and Leonard shoved a basket of greasy hot wings in her face.

I can't believe this is happening. The media is here from all over the world! We're going to be on the news because my buddy is assaulting patrons in Hooters with a basket of greasy hot wings. Damn! He's shoving food into a woman's face! What kind of James Cagney bullshit is this? Only Leonard could do something so bizarre and dramatic.

The security staff on the Landing escorted Leonard and I out of the restaurant. I pulled two of the officers to the side and explained the situation. I guess they weren't in the mood to deal with a lot of nonsense and unnecessary paperwork because they agreed to give Leonard a break. Thank God. It was embarrassing. I promised to get Leonard away from the Landing as soon as possible.

One of the officers tried to remain stoic, but the other showed signs of a suppressed smile. Cynthia's a southern belle, and Leonard frankly didn't give a damn. She's a woman who always made a conscious effort of following the appropriate etiquette in a restaurant. However, she didn't look very sophisticated with a face full of oily barbecue sauce dripping from her eyebrows and nose. Cynthia even had sauce splattered on her hair weave. It was unbeweavable!

My buddy was a basket case. His mind was occupied with anger, pain and loneliness. During the ride back to his home, I tried to be a good friend by listening and allowing him to vent. My eyes focused on the shores of the Atlantic as an ocean of thoughts swam through my mind. I was truly at a loss for words. Leonard took deep breaths and tried to compose himself; he was drowning in a sea of love and there wasn't a life preserver big enough to save him.

    I had come down to Florida to get away from my problems at home, but it seemed as though Leonard needed me more than I needed him. Perhaps Cynthia was right; Jacksonville may not be big enough for the both of them.

15

KENDALL

I heard the sound of Ray's booming, bass voice, barking out violence the moment I entered the back door of the cleaners. McNeal's Dry Cleaners was open for business Monday through Saturday, but Sunday was the day in which we held meetings and really cleaned things up.

"Beat the shit outta him!" Ray ordered. "Teach his young punk ass a lesson."

Two teenage boys are carrying out Ray's orders. The victim of the beating is a puny kid with ashy skin. He's a member of our crew and sells drugs for us on one of the corners in the area. Tight-fisted youths punched the small kid in the face and kicked him in the stomach with their black boots. I watched the young victim moan and curl up in a fetal position. He coughed and clutched his stomach. Blood trickled from his nose and mouth. He never cried and looked as though he was accustomed to taking beatings.

I walked over to Ray and whispered in his ear. "What's going on?"

"Nothing much, K," he answered nonchalantly. "We just need to put this little nigga in his place that's all."

"What happened?" I asked, as the tiny youngster coughed up blood on the floor.

"His little ass keeps on breaking the rules," Ray snapped.

"What he do?" I asked.

"He trying to stash money and won't follow our rules regarding the elimination period at the beginning of the month."

"You're kidding me, right?" I asked, but I wasn't surprised.

"Hell nah!"

"How old is he?"

"Ten," Ray answered.

"Ten," I echoed. "And he's already stashing money?"

"The game is getting younger and more fierce, K."

"No kidding."

"And these little niggas are fearless."

"These young guns are much wilder than we ever were, Ray."

"Yeah, but if they continue to fuck up, I'm gonna continue to make sure they get the shit beat out of their young asses. Kendall, I'm not gonna let any of these young boys mess our game up. Fuck that shit!"

"I hear you," I replied as I observed the young kids in attendance.

Ray owns the cleaners, but spends little time here. Two of his younger brothers are responsible for cleaning clothes and running the day to day operations. For Ray, it's just another way to hide money. He also owns an automotive accessory shop that sells car alarms and rims. Ray spends more time at the cleaners on Sunday than any other day of the week.

We usually have meetings with the crew every Sunday afternoon to make sure everything is going smoothly. I like running an efficient operation, and our meeting time gives us the opportunity to keep the crew unified and enforce discipline on those who get out of line.

There are approximately twenty crew members on hand, most of them, hard-looking teenagers, dressed in baggy jeans and hooded sweat shirts, along with Eskimo coats and skull caps to endure the winter chill on the corners and shield their identity.

Instead of being in church on Sunday, they're being steamed and starched by an angry Ray McNeal. To me, he's just Ray being Ray, but for the young guys being scolded, he's a very dangerous individual, with a violent, hair-trigger temper. Ray was preaching a satanic sermon on the importance of tithing to the higher-ups. Some of the young ones stood with disobedient scowls on their faces. They were trying to act tough under pressure, but I could see the fear in their eyes. This wasn't some grammar school detention class. These kids were playing a grown-ups game of life with deadly consequences. Ray was serious about everything he said. They leaned up against the walls and around the ironing equipment, listening to Ray, the enforcer, shout out more orders.

"You little niggas need to realize the importance of honoring our rules for the elimination period. Y'all need to understand the big fuckin' picture! You young muthafuckas need to know that we gotta pay lawyer fees, bond and court costs with that fuckin' money! We use that loot to pay for summer picnics and reward y'all with new fly ass gear and shit. This shit pays for y'all guns. We also use that money to pay off dirty muthafuckin' cops and keep them off y'all black asses!" Ray shouted as he marched around the small space in the back of the cleaners, wearing a black leather jacket and a matching leather cap turned backwards.

I observed the faces of the fearful faithful, and listened closely as Ray continued his verbal assault. He paced back and forth with rage in his eyes. Spit doused the flames of each one of his fiery words. His voice was volcanic and angry. He looked deranged and ready to erupt. Some of the young ones had never seen this tirade before. A few of the older guys who had been around for a while knew it wasn't just some riot act. Ray is crazy.

Ray walked over to the kid who had just gotten beat up and snatched him from against the wall. He grabbed him by the throat and slung him across the room like a rag doll. Ray then walked over to where the kid was sprawled on the floor and kicked him again in his stomach. The kid moaned and groaned as Ray stood with his foot planted on the small boy's head, still barking vicious instructions. His voice got louder and his tone became more frightening. Ray had everyone's undivided attention now.

"It takes money to keep this here shit flowing tight and right! We got expenses too! After the elimination period is over, you can sell drugs for some profit. Y'all need to understand that shit! And for you little niggas who don't get the point, I'm gonna guarantee you an intense, fuckin' beat down, just like the one this little nigga Smiley just got. Take a look at this little muthafucka over here! Look at him! Don't you see my foot on this little nigga's head? I could smash his fuckin' brains out right now. I ain't standing for none of this shit! Y'all can fuck wit' me if you want to and I'll use one of them fuckin' pressing machines to put a nice, hot crease in your black ass. I'll have folks making funeral arrangements for you punk muthafuckas! Meeting adjourned! Now get the fuck outta here!" Ray shouted, taking his foot off of Smiley's head.

One by one, they filed out of the back door of the cleaners. Two of the other young teenagers helped Smiley to his feet and ushered him out the door. Once again, they were ready to hit the streets and assume their positions. Some were couriers who moved drugs and guns. Others acted as look-outs who watched and protected our businesses, giving warnings when the police patrolled the area. It was important for Ray to make an example out of Smiley. They figured if he was cruel enough to step on the head of a ten-year-old kid, then he would have no problem killing one of the older guys.

"Rodney!" I shouted, getting the attention of one of the crew members. He stopped at the door and turned to look in my direction. He froze like a deer staring into headlights of a car being driven by the devil. And after what he had just witnessed, he probably wasn't sure what the hell we had in store for him.

"Get over here!" I shouted, pointing and beckoning for him to come to me. He ran over to me with nervousness in his eyes and sweat beading on his forehead. His Adam's apple looked ripe enough for me to snatch it out of his throat.

"You want me, K?" he asked.

"Yeah I want you," I snapped. "Why you think I called you?"

He shook his head and mumbled. "I don't know."

"You know Ray and I been watching you, don't you?"

"...Yeah," he answered, hesitantly.

"And we gonna keep our eye on you."

He nodded his head and swallowed hard, taking a deep breath.

"Have you been holding out on us, Rodney?" I asked.

"No, K," he answered.

"Don't lie to me, nigga!" I yelled.

"I'm not lying," he replied, shifting his weight from one leg to the other.

"You wanna fuck us around, don't you?"

"I been straight K," he pleaded. "I swear. I been straight wit' you guys."

I looked over at Ray. "What should we do, Ray?"

Ray laughed. "Since we're in the cleaners, we can always starch his ass."

"Yeah we can let one of the pressing machines down on his ass."

"I think that's a good idea," Ray agreed.

"Me too," I said. "I'm tired of these little niggas trying to steal our grip."

"K, let's just get this shit finished, so we can go dump his ass," Ray suggested. "Besides I'm hungry and wanna go get something to eat. Let's do this shit in a hurry."

"I'm game," I said with a sinister grin. "Get on your knees, Rodney."

Tears started flowing from Rodney's eyes as he bent down first on his right knee and then his left. Ray and I stood over the sixteen-year-old kid with scowls on our faces.

"I promise, K I been on the up and up since day one."

"I know," I responded with a grin. "That's why we need to take care of you."

"Get up little nigga," Ray joked with a hearty laugh. "We just fuckin' wit' you."

"Keep on handling your business, Rodney," I said, handing him ten crisp one hundred dollar bills. "You cool with us, dude. And as long as you stay cool and play by the rules, we won't have any problems down the road. Are we clear on that?"

Rodney nodded frantically and smiled. "Thanks K."

"Thanks K?" Ray teased. "What about me? You got a few Benjamins and you say fuck me, huh? What's up with that, Rodney? What's that all about?"

"Ah ah ah," he stuttered. "I'm sorry, Ray."

"Ah ah ah, stop stuttering and get the fuck outta here," Ray mocked with a robust laugh. "Before I take that money back."

Rodney ran out the door and left Ray and I laughing our guts out. It was a cruel psychological game to play on a sixteen-year-old, but sometimes it had to be done. We needed kids like Rodney and Smiley to help distribute our product. They were helping us rake in about $10,000 a day.

Ray and I had a problem to take care of; it was just one of those things that occur when supplying customers with products to keep their bad habits in check. This time, we were dealing with a very popular radio personality with loyal listeners tuning into his show daily. Everyday, Keith Porter concluded his time on the air by encouraging his listening audience to keep God in and drugs out. The folks in radio land would've been shocked to know Mr. Porter, the popular personality with the positive perspective, was a pipe smoking drug addict living life on the down low.

I nearly died laughing every time I heard female callers praising Keith for being such an influential presence in the community and a role model for young brothers to emulate. I damn near totaled my Escalade listening to that shit on the radio one afternoon because Keith and his El DeBarge looking lover had just come and copped some coke from us the day before.

The bottom line is, I don't give a fuck how popular Keith is as a radio personality. I'm gonna make sure he pays us the money he owes; even if it means we gotta beat the shit out of him and his boy toy, and let the world know he's sucking dicks and packing fudge. And if Keith gives us a problem, everyone on the FM dial will know he's taking more packages to the rear than a delivery man. Bitch ass nigga.

Ray and I waited for Keith's radio shift to end and watched him leave the station in his red Corvette with his faithful companion by his side. We trailed them all the way to Keith's high-rise apartment in Lake Meadows, scheming on a tactic to get into his unit. In some ways, I felt like one of those private investigators on the show *Cheaters* setting a trap to catch our target in a compromising position. And we set his ass up perfectly.

Earlier on the radio, Keith told listeners about how anxious he was to celebrate his thirty-fourth birthday in a couple of days. Since

Keith's big day was approaching, we decided to buy some roses and balloons from a nearby gift shop. We told the security guard at the front desk that we worked with Keith at the radio station, bribed him with a couple of CDs, and told him we would get him some concert tickets if he let us up to Keith's apartment unannounced.

When we got to Keith's corner apartment on the fourteenth floor, Ray knocked on the door and used the roses and balloons to conceal his identity and hide his gun. I waited behind Ray with a gun in my hand and a duffel bag on my shoulder. Keith, like an idiot, thought we were loving fans and opened the door to accept his gift.

Surprise!

Ray and I rushed into the apartment with nine millimeters loaded and ready to fire. I hit Keith's frightful friend in the face with the butt of my gun and sent him reeling on the living room floor.

"What's this all about?" Keith yelled, as his friend wiped the blood from his nose.

"You know what this is about!" I hollered. "You owe us money."

"Dammit, Keith, pay them!" screamed the boyfriend in a high-pitched voice.

"Shut the fuck up!" I shouted, pointing the gun in his bloody face. "And take your clothes off before I put a bullet in your head."

"Why?" he whined. "Keith what's going on here?"

"Keith, tell your cute boyfriend to shut the fuck up!" Ray barked.

"Do what they say, Marvin," Keith pleaded.

"I want both of you to take your clothes off!" I ordered loudly.

"I don't understand what you mean," Keith replied, as sweat dripped profusely from his receding hairline.

"Don't worry," I laughed. "You will soon."

"Man, this shit is unnecessary," Keith complained, as he rose up from the couch.

"Sit your punk ass down!" Ray shouted, striking Keith in the face with the barrel of the gun. "Now take off your clothes before we cancel your radio show."

"Keith, let's just do what they say," Marvin suggested in a whimpering tone.

Under The Same Roof

"Yeah Keith, just do what we say," I mocked.

As Keith and Marvin reluctantly removed articles of clothing, I went on a private tour of the three bedroom apartment that overlooked King Drive and featured a beautiful view of the downtown skyline. This is nice. Shit, with his job and status, living in a pussy palace like this, I would be fuckin' chicks named Marva instead guys like Marvin. While Ray kept a gun on them and forced them to strip, I looked at celebrity photos on his wall and saw him posing with famous people from all over the world. Also on the wall, was the NAB Marconi Radio Award proclaiming Keith as a distinguished on-air personality.

Everyone knew of Keith's accomplishments on the radio, his voice was famous. Now, our goal was to establish him as an on-camera personality as well and allow more people to see his face if necessary. Ray walked over to the sofa where the partially nude duo sat and ordered them to perform oral sex on each other.

"Why are y'all doing this shit, Kendall?"

"You one of those people who need motivation to pay," I snickered. "So we're making sure you have it."

"And if you ask another fuckin' question, I'll blow Marvin's brains out," Ray sniped.

"Come on now, Ray," I teased. "Why you gotta blow him?"

"Ha, ha, ha," Ray laughed. "You a fool."

"That was funny shit, huh?"

Ray and I were laughing are asses off, but Keith and Marvin weren't. The distressed duo looked as if they wanted to protest, but the nine-millimeter in Ray's hand made protesting unwise and had a major influence in coercing them to follow our orders.

As one of Chicago's most favorite radio personalities found himself in a compromising, position, I was all set to film the event with a Sony camcorder. This is some disgusting shit. However, filming this X-rated affair wasn't about Ray and me getting our rocks off. This was all about blackmail and extortion, and having a little leverage in the future.

Maybe now Keith will be more motivated to pay his drug debt on time. Stupid muthafucka. He's getting just what he deserves for misleading his listeners and pretending to be the perfect role model.

Maybe if he had stopped snorting drugs and misleading people on the radio, he wouldn't have gotten caught with his pants down.

16

LAUREN

Darkness is becoming light and a new morning is on the way. I glance over at the red numerals on the clock. Its 4:07. I want to close my eyes and get a few minutes of sleep, but I can't . . . I'm wide awake. Time is flying by. I've been staring at the ceiling most of the night with my mind taking on too many thoughts. Another busy week is just a few hours away. And thinking about all the activities scheduled for the days ahead has me edgy and restless.

At work, it seems as though we're having meetings just to have meetings. Conference calls from company headquarters are scheduled to dominate a day I already don't have enough time for. There are daily debates about which steps we need to take in order for us to achieve our latest objectives. All eyes are on me and my department.

Like many companies, the customer call center is a place of instability, where a revolving door of turnover ushers employees in and out. Because of the tension involved with answering a large volume of calls and dealing with demanding customers, reps are constantly quitting, forcing us to retrain replacements on a monthly basis. Therefore, almost a third of my staff has been in the position for less than six months. My department is expected to handle calls dealing with claim issues even though my representatives do not process claims. I've been trying to sell upper management on the idea of having all calls related to medical bills routed to the claims department.

Surviving in the workforce today is all about being able to multi-task. Since I'm the only African-American woman in middle management, the CEO and VPs are probably wondering if they can get me to stick a broom up my behind, so I can run errands and sweep the floor at the same time.

Dealing with pressure at work is one thing, but watching my mother age and become less independent adds considerably more anxiety to the moments of my day. I'm wrestling with the thought of moving back home or having Mama come live with me. I haven't lived with anyone since college, so just the thought of sharing my space smothers me. Relatives and friends with good intentions are always quick to give their opinion on what I should do, but they don't walk in my shoes; they don't even have to try on my shoes. My lifestyle would be the one stepped on, not theirs.

Living under the same roof with Mama would put her right in the middle of my life. After a long day at work, I'm too tired to walk into a house of questions about this and that. Some days I want to come home and just lounge around in my underwear the rest of the evening. I'm not accustomed to worrying about what I'm going to eat for dinner, or what I need to pick up on the way home. Sometimes all I want to do is munch on a bowl of dry Cheerios and go to bed.

I guess I've become too set in my ways and enjoy being able to do things when I want to do them. I like being my own boss and independence allows that. Living with Mama would strip me of my control and alter my routine. I love my mother, but I wouldn't want to resent her because of feeling pressured to do what some people think is the right thing to do. Then again, I would be tormented by guilt if something happened to her and I wasn't around to help.

For some reason, Mama was always more demanding of me than of my two older brothers. She catered to them, yet raised me to be independent. Mama always challenged me to dream big and to aim high. Never settle for less than what I felt I deserved.

My ambitious nature and never wanting to settle has also affected my love relationships as well. Andre has confessed his love for me. I returned the sentiment, but deep down I'm really not sure. I care about Andre a lot, but I'm beginning to wonder if we have the long term compatibility needed for our romance to survive. I'm always setting new goals and using my free time constructively. He seems to be content with driving a bus and just kicking it on his days off.

I'm thinking about going back to school to pursue a doctorate and perhaps starting a consulting firm, whereas he's satisfied with being a college dropout and bragging about having seniority on his job. We have fun together, but we want different things. The bedroom is where we're most compatible. I'm not sure if that is a good thing or a bad thing. Lord knows, if we weren't sexually compatible, he would've been gone a long time ago. Andre is very attentive and loving, but looking ahead, I wonder if that will be enough for the long haul. Sometimes I wonder if love is really enough.

Maybe I should put away my wish list. When I've gone out on dates with career oriented guys, many of them spent most of the evening bragging about how terrific they were and how much they had accomplished in their life. Some considered themselves God's gift to women and had their pick of the litter because they made a lot of money and had a bunch of educational letters behind their names. They looked good on paper, but most of them proved to be complete jerks. A lot of them were extremely self-centered and wanted women to be available to them at their beck and call. They expected women to cater to their every need and bow down at their feet to give them the praise, the honor and the glory. And then say Amen.

If sistas don't stroke their egos, then they'll probably find a woman of another race who will kiss their behinds because they have money. It's no longer good enough for some brothas to flaunt their success with a white woman on their arms, now they're chasing exotic beauties with Asian or Latin features. Looking as good as Halle Berry doesn't cut it anymore, now brothas want Lucy Liu or Eva Mendes.

On the flip side, men with less ambition have complained about me being a workaholic and too focused on my career to give my all to a relationship. Guys need to understand I have a stressful career which creates restraints on my time. They said I didn't know how to unwind and have fun. I don't want a man needing to have a monopoly on my attention. I need my space, so I don't need a clingy brother standing by the door when I go to use the bathroom, asking me if I'm okay just because he didn't hear me flush the toilet.

I remember one guy said I live to work instead of working to live. I didn't pay him any mind because he had probably just finished smoking a joint and thought he had become the world's latest philosopher. In fact, he should've been somewhere working so he could catch up on the child support payments for all his kids. He has too many kids and too much baby mama drama. Sometimes I wonder what made me consider going out with him anyway. It's probably because he had hazel eyes and a head full of curly hair. I guess sometimes I don't know what I want either.

The clock on the dresser displays the time. It's almost five o'clock. My mind is tired and my body is sluggish. I'm thinking about too much stuff. I raise my slender arms in the air and stretch. It's almost time to get up, so sleep is no longer an option. I cut the alarm off now because it's set to go off in about a half hour. I turn on a lamp and reach for the devotional materials on my nightstand; I need some kind of inspiration to get me going.

I opened my Bible and read a chapter in the book of Psalms. After that, I read a daily meditation from Iyanla Vanzant's book *Acts of Faith* and then got on my knees and prayed. I asked God to forgive me for my sins and to give me strength to tackle a day that shouldn't have even started for me yet. It's only five-thirty.

I walked into the bathroom and turned on the radio to hear the traffic and weather forecast for the day. As usual, Felicia Middlebrooks, the morning-drive anchor of WBBM-AM was providing the news in a voice full of vigor. I turned the bathtub faucet on and let the water get hot. Steam quickly fogged up the shower door and the vanity mirrors. I stuck my big toe under the faucet and quickly pulled it back. Ouch! The water was scalding. I turned on the cold water and adjusted the temperature to a more comfortable setting. My body was positioned under the shower head and anticipated the warm cascade to fall on my skin. It felt good.

The penetrating stream massaged the aching muscles of my neck and shoulder. I closed my eyes and sighed, pressing my hands firmly against the wall. Ooh. Tension had my body tied in knots. I'm under too much stress. I used my neck as a swivel and rotated my head, allowing the tingling sensation to trickle down the center of my back. I can sense my body changing. Time will not always be on my side.

Caressing and examining my torso in the shower made me wonder about the possibility of motherhood. Deep down, I have a lot of questions about it: Do I really want to give up my freedom? Do I have the maternal instincts needed to nurture a child 24/7? Would I be able to love enough or is my personality too detached? At the present time, I like being able to give children back to their mothers when I get tired of them. Am I really willing to make the sacrifices to be a good mother? I definitely wouldn't want to tackle parenthood as a single mother.

I saw how difficult it was for my mother raising three kids all alone. I guess that's why she's always so tough on me. She wants me to make the right choices and avoid the mistakes she made.

Mama was ambitious once, but she traded in her dreams to become a wife and a mother. She sacrificed her heart and soul while Daddy shared his sperm with other women. Mama was stuck at home raising the three of us, while he was off somewhere ejaculating his sticky goo into the womb of some horny hussy.

As we got older, Mama went out with a few men every now and then, but never got very close to them from what I could tell. Maybe she was afraid of getting hurt again and was trying to shield herself from more pain. Then again, perhaps she was worried about the challenges of having a strange man around impressionable young kids. I guess Mama was protecting all of us.

Besides, I'm not sure if I can even have children. I've never been pregnant. It's been years since I've taken birth control pills because I didn't like the side effects and the changes it had on my period. Initially, Andre was using condoms, but lately we've been having unprotected sex. I hated the feeling of rubbers sliding in and out of my body.

Also, Mama told me about the problems she suffered during her pregnancies and the miscarriages she had before finally giving birth to Julian. It makes me wonder if I'll suffer from the same problems.

Being in the health insurance industry, I'm constantly reading articles about young women having cysts on their ovaries or being diagnosed with ovarian cancer. It makes me wonder. At work, I've listened in on reps talking to frustrated women about whether or not In Vitro fertilizations are covered under their group health insurance plan. One time while monitoring a call, I actually heard a lady on the line crying hysterically because she wanted to have a baby. She said she wanted to have a child in order to feel like a complete woman because her husband wanted to have a family. Please! My body may be a little sore, but I'm still a complete woman! Child or no child!

I finished my shower and dried myself off in front of a full length mirror. It's not even six o'clock yet, and my mind has already worked overtime. I've spent the early hours of the morning worrying about Mama's health; trying to decide if I should move back home; if I'll have a long future with Andre; whether or not I want to have children one day; and how I can be more productive at work. My brain has been multi-tasking for the last three hours. Now I'm tired and sleepy. I wish I could go get back in bed.

Keep dreaming.

I have to get to the office for an eight o'clock meeting. The CEO and VPs will probably have some bright ideas on how I should do my job better. We'll see. They just better not ask me to run errands and sweep the floor at the same time.

17

JULIAN

    Cold butterflies floated freely within the walls of my stomach as I hurried anxiously through the busy intersection. My foot hit the curb as flashing hands signaled the traffic light's change from green to yellow to red. I took a deep breath and exhaled. The frigid weather caused the air from my mouth to form into a disappearing cloud. Once again, artic conditions are blanketing the city and have wind-chill factors dipping into negative numbers.
    Tiny pebbles of salt littered the pavement, deicing a walkway which had been pounded by more than a foot of snow over the past weekend. Unfortunately, frosty temperatures were predicted to linger in the forecast for the next several days. I raised the collar on my navy, wool overcoat and trotted up the steps leading to the Cook County Criminal Courthouse.
    I reached into the inside pocket of my suit jacket and pulled out my wallet. One of the guards at the entrance station acknowledged my court ID, and granted me access to the premises without being checked for weapons. People without a court pass have to go through the tedious process of emptying all their pockets, removing belts, watches, and any other type of metal object that might set off the alarm.
    For the most part, people entering this facility are either here to work, reporting for jury duty, the victim or defendant of some type

of crime, or are here to show support for a family member or friend. Located on the city's southwest side, the seven-story courthouse is the largest in Cook County, and the only one to handle criminal cases exclusively. It's known simply as "26th and California."

The location is also home to the Cook County Jail. Sitting on ninety-six acres of land, the single-site lockup serves as the largest pre-detention facilities in the United States; it also makes "26th and California" the new address for more than ten thousand defendants awaiting trials. Unfortunately, the incarceration of African-American men is the primary reason why jails are jam-packed. It's frightening to know African-Americans make up only 12% of the United States population, but account for 60% of the bodies behind bars. That alone makes it easy to understand why prison building is America's fastest growing industry.

It made my heart glad to see so many of my friends and colleagues seated in the courtroom when I arrived for my hearing. They had taken time out of their busy schedules to be here for me, and I wanted to show my appreciation by walking around the right side of the courtroom and greeting them. Having their support meant a lot to me.

My good friend, Steve Strong, was among those in attendance. Steve had promised to lend his support and had been there for me ever since we met for lunch and talked about putting together a team. Steve stood next to my attorney, Charles White. Since they're good friends, Steve encouraged Attorney White to take my case. Attorney White shook my hand and embraced me with encouraging words.

"How are you, Julian?" he asked.

"I'm a bit tired," I answered. "But I'm hanging."

"Don't worry, little brother," he said, patting me on the back with a massive hand. "Everything will work out alright."

This ordeal has made me weary, but I feel more confident since Attorney White is representing me. Standing six-foot-three and weighing close to three hundred pounds, White is an imposing figure with an ample knowledge of the law. As a prominent defense attorney, White has been involved in many high profile cases in Chicago and has a reputation for not being intimidated by prosecutors or judges.

He's also aware and very vocal about the racism taking place in the court system.

The first attorney I'd hired to represent me had been thoroughly bullied and disrespected by the States Attorney's Office. During one of the earlier hearings, they directed all of their comments and questions towards me as if my attorney wasn't even in the courtroom. They could never get away with trying to intimidate Attorney White because he didn't back down from anyone. Attorney White was usually the aggressor.

I huddled with my legal team and glanced across the aisle at the lawyers representing the States Attorney's Office. Gary Banks, the lead attorney, sat at the opposing table and smiled at me. His grin was devious and was contaminated with arrogance and bigotry. I was staring down the devil.

The presiding judge, the honorable Lewis H. Nathan entered the courtroom; his arrival brought an end to the staring contest between me and Attorney Banks. Nathan, a monotone speaking, bespectacled man, with an incomplete comb over, is the same judge who signed the search warrant allowing officers to seize all of my computers and files. His decision to permit the search warrant is what has put me in this predicament in the first place. Now I need him to quash the warrant so I can get all of my computers and files back.

Attorney White strutted across the room in a navy pinstripe suit and addressed the court with a blistering opening argument. He chastised the States Attorney's Office and accused them of being abusive, arrogant, and engaging in blatant misconduct.

"Your honor," Attorney White declared, pacing back and forth in front of the bench, near the prosecution's table. "The States Attorney's Office promised to provide an affidavit confirming all information gathered from Mr. Collins' office to remain confidential, and to return all evidence directly to the court. Your honor, we still have not received the affidavit we requested," Attorney White shouted in a booming voice. "This is ridiculous. The FBI promised delivery of all items, but there's still no chain of custody."

Judge Nathan sighed and leaned back in his chair, stretching his arms like an elementary school student eager to leave the classroom to take a recess. He seemed annoyed, but Attorney White was just getting started.

"Your honor, the States Attorney's Office didn't produce an affidavit. . . "

"Your honor," Attorney Banks interrupted. "We have an affidavit. May I present it to the court?" he asked.

Attorney Banks approached the bench and so did Attorney White.

"Judge Nathan," Attorney White said in a volcanic voice. "I would like to have a five minute recess to discuss the affidavit the States Attorney's Office has just produced."

Judge Nathan agreed to the request for the recess and Attorney White and his assistant left the courtroom while I remained at the table trying to gather my thoughts. I heard my supporters whispering comments amongst themselves, but I never turned around to acknowledge anything. My mind, body and soul are tired of battling, but having a tenacious attorney like Charles White made me want to keep fighting; especially since I'm able to see first hand how malicious the prosecution team could be in order to make a case, particularly against African-American defendants. They're ruthless.

Since this process began, I've learned of other African-American lawyers who have been harassed in the same way in which I was treated here. They have been violated and bullied also, but chose not to fight because of fear or other reasons. The Cook County States Attorney's Office is a formidable opponent. Nevertheless, I'm willing to battle to the final bell sounds. Besides, I've invested too much time and energy to quit now.

Attorney White reentered the courtroom and quickly resumed his attack on the States Attorney's Office after the court was called back into session.

"Your honor," Attorney White argued. "How can the States Attorney's Office stroll in here at the last minute and pull an affidavit out of the air like a band of magicians. Your honor, this is a court not a circus; we're here to support the facts, not to create an illusion. This is nothing more than a second hand affidavit; it wasn't even notarized. Your honor, this is another example of how this department has misled your court! We need a special prosecution and a special grand jury to take over this case because it's time for the States Attorney's Office to be held accountable for their blatant disrespect of the law. This is a terrible case! And the negligence must cease!"

I heard snickering from my supporters in the courtroom. Once again, Attorney White had produced a verbal assault on Judge Nathan's court and the States Attorney's Office. Since Nathan is the judge who approved of the search warrant allowing the FBI and the Cook County Sheriffs to enter my office and seize my equipment, it seemed like a huge conflict of interest to put him in the position to overturn his initial decision. I would feel much better if he removes himself from the case.

I watched Attorney Banks as he got up from his seat and looked at me with a satanic smile that sent chills down my spine. Attorney Banks is dapper and charismatic with aspirations of making a splash in the political arena. He's a ruthless prosecutor interested in taking all prisoners with power as his prize. His condescending demeanor reminded me of several of the hosts on the FOX Cable News Channel.

Attorney Banks is one of those guys who would probably pat a person on the back to befriend them while looking for the soft spot to insert the knife at the same time. He's an arrogant asshole who knows how to manipulate people and the system to his advantage. Guys like Attorney Banks are more dangerous than thugs on the street because they know the law and know how to abuse it.

In dramatic form, Attorney Banks threw his legal pad back on his table and came out firing like a gunslinger at high noon ready to take over the town. He wouldn't have any bullets left in the chamber when he finished shooting insults in my direction.

"Your honor, once again Attorney White is grandstanding and using his vicious rhetoric to bully the court. Attorney White has repeatedly marched in front of our table in an intimidating fashion while trying to negate the real reason we're here. Your honor, he's playing to the emotions of the people in attendance while failing to mention the fact that his client, Mr. Julian Collins has been the attorney of record on twenty-two fraudulent real estate closing transactions. Not one, not two, not three, but twenty-two fraudulent cases. Your honor, the court needs to know how a lawyer can be the attorney of record on twenty-two different fraudulent closings and not be linked to some kind of illegal activity," he charged, pausing for dramatic effect.

I looked on in disgust as Attorney Banks pranced around the courtroom laughing like a hungry hyena in search of his next prey. He had me in his sights and looked determined to clench his jaws on some dark meat. Attorney Banks stared in my direction and continued to chew me up and spit me out.

"Mr. Collins is representing clients who are flipping properties faster than they flip burgers at Burger King. Your honor, make no mistake, Mr. Collins is having it his way and he's living good in the process. Your honor I think it's about time we take a closer look at Mr. Julian Collins and find out how he really makes his money."

18

KENDALL

It's the first Sunday in March, but the unseasonably warm weather made it feel more like late April or early May. Mother Nature's unexpected spring break had folks engaging in activities rarely seen this time of year. The temperature had soared into the mid-sixties, but was predicted to fall back to the lower twenties by tomorrow morning. Adults washed their cars, kids rode their bikes, and people of all ages enjoyed the sunshine.

Unfortunately my world wasn't very bright right now. Difficult decisions were clouding my judgment and forcing me to view life from a darker perspective. I was hoping the drive into the city would clear my head and help me sort some things out. Instead of getting on the expressway, I took the streets. The first ten minutes of my drive was in silence, but the lack of noise drove me crazy. I put in a Jay-Z CD and let the hard knock rhymes thump inside my SUV to ride with me the rest of the way. Explicit lyrics flowed freely through the opened sunroof, making its presence known to the uncensored air. In the meantime, I hid behind tinted glass rolled down half way.

I cruised down 95th Street and got stopped at the railroad tracks near Trinity United Church of Christ; one of the city's largest churches. I shook my head in frustration, wondering why I came this way in the first place. 95th Street is always congested around this time on Sunday. I hate being caught by trains. People were leaving Trinity and were trying to get to their cars, but the slow moving freight train was delaying everyone's progress, including mine. I cut my engine off and waited impatiently.

My shiny, black Escalade and sparkling spinning rims got the attention of a young boy crossing the street with his mother and little sister. I turned my music down and rolled my windows all the way up, using my sunroof to get a cool breeze. The boy's innocent eyes looked in my direction and smiled. Dark tinted windows made me nothing more than a shadowy figure, but I saw him clearly. He appeared to be around ten years of age. The little boy was probably wishing he could grow up and drive a truck like mine, but right now, I was wishing I could be him, walking hand in hand with my mom and siblings again.

Seeing him with his mother and sister made me reminisce about going to church with Mama, Julian and La-La back in the day. Mama's heart was still at New Calvary, but hurt, embarrassment and disappointment had sent us to various churches seeking some kind of healing for our souls. I remember being at a new church one Sunday when I managed to catch the attention of a pretty girl with pigtails and barrettes sitting across the aisle. I was around eleven at the time and guessed she was about the same age. Our innocent eyes made contact with each other several times during service.

After the minister finished preaching, the deacons came down the aisles to serve communion to members sitting on each pew. All of us had been baptized, so when the tray of wine came my way, I picked up a glass and looked over in the direction of my new female admirer. I raised my glass up high and gave her a toast. Mama saw me and got mad as hell. She finished her communion and then reached across La-La and slapped the taste of out of my mouth. I was so embarrassed. I can still remember her grinding her teeth and calling me a little heathen.

Ray's white, convertible Jaguar was parked in the back of the cleaners when I arrived. I knocked on the door twice before entering. Ray was pacing next to dresses and slacks of customers with an open bottle of Hennessy in his hands; he was drinking cognac straight up. A scowl of danger was etched across his face. His eyes were red and his mouth was twisted with anger. He was intense. I could smell the scent of weed and alcohol on his breath when I greeted him with a hug.

"What up, Ray?"

"K, I had a funny feeling that little nigga Smiley was gonna cause us problems," he mumbled. "I just knew it dawg. I just knew it."

"Tell me again what the fuck happened Friday!" I shouted, rubbing my hand over my head. I heard about it on the news, but needed to hear it from Ray directly. "I need to try to grasp this shit."

"K, this little nigga been ditching school all year, but he decides to hang around the playground on Friday to be with his cousin. One of the older boys at the school sees Smiley and teases him about his face being ashy or some shit. Smiley gets pissed off and rushes the kid. The boy is bigger and knocks Smiley's little ass to the ground. Now Smiley is all salty and shit 'cuz the other kids on the playground are clowning him and shit. This little nigga goes and gets the gun we gave him and comes back to the school to get his revenge and shit when school ends for the day. K, this little nigga sees the boy from a distance and fires the gun three times into a crowd of kids."

"Fuck!" I shouted, rubbing my hand over my head again.

"He missed the boy he was shooting at, and ended up hitting a six-year-old, first grade girl. Kendall the little girl died early this morning."

"I know," I mumbled under my breath. "I know."

"Man this shit is all over the news."

"Damn!" I shouted. "This is fucked up!"

"K, we gotta find a way to calm this shit down."

"Ray, how the fuck can we calm this shit down now? We got Mayor Daley on the television, the alderman is on the radio, and that chick in the Sun-Times is writing articles and shit. How the fuck we gonna calm this shit down, when the whole fuckin' city of Chicago is in mourning over this little girl's death. Damn!"

Ray took another large gulp from his bottle of cognac and continued to pace back and forth around the cleaners, spilling liquor on clothes yet to be cleaned. His actions concerned me because he's too intoxicated to think rationally. Both of us needed to calm down and be composed when the rest of our crew arrived for our weekly meeting.

"This shit is gonna put unbelievable fuckin' heat on our ass, K. This shit is gonna send too much negative attention our way."

I didn't respond. I was trying to concentrate, but Ray's constant ranting had my mind moving in a thousand different directions.

Ray rambled on. "That crazy little nigga gonna go shoot into a fuckin' crowd with a school full of witnesses around. They knew it was his ass because they saw the argument between him and other dude earlier in the day. Man, this is straight fucked up. K, I should've smashed that little nigga's brains out when he got outta line a few weeks ago. But no, instead I took his age into consideration and gave his little ass a pass. If I had clipped him then we wouldn't be in this shit! Now we have to worry about the police and the higher-ups."

Time passed as Ray and I spent the remaining minutes gathering our collective thoughts. Alcohol and weed had him slurring over in a corner. Meanwhile I concerned myself with the mindset of crewmembers on their way to the cleaners. I also had images floating around in my own head.

My mind traveled back one hour in time and reminded me of the little boy I saw crossing the street with his mother and sister. He and Smiley looked to be around the same age, yet their worlds were about a million miles apart. The little boy I saw earlier had spent his Sunday morning in church with his mother and sister. I wondered if he had taken communion, and wondered if his mother was taking him and his sister out for dinner after church. He looked like a smart, well-mannered kid. Maybe he was going home to do some homework or play some video games. The weather was nice so maybe his mom will let him go outside and ride his bike with his little sister.

The conflicted thoughts of my mind returned to Smiley. Ray was only partially right on his assessment of Smiley. I'd heard through the neighborhood grapevine that his life has been troubled since the day he entered the world, and that he was headed in the wrong direction way before he reached us.

He was born Dwayne Patterson, but family members called him Smiley because of the innocent grin always seen on his face. Unfortunately, the little kid wasn't nearly as pleasant as his nickname suggested. The smile had been erased a long time ago. Like many kids on the streets, a hard life had caused him to grow up too fast. His mother, Darlene Patterson was a neighborhood slut who sold her body in the hood for crack.

Smiley's maternal grandmother had taken on the responsibility of trying to raise him and his siblings while Darlene continued to fuck strangers and pop out kids she was unable and unwilling to take care of. Grandma Patterson's fatal heart attack caused the Department of Children and Family Services to step in and place Smiley and his siblings in separate foster homes. While funeral arrangements were being made for Smiley's grandmother, his mother was being arrested again for prostitution. Darlene Patterson has been arrested more than twenty-five times.

It seemed as though Smiley had inherited his mother's mental damage as well as her problems with the law. Smiley hadn't even reached his teen years yet, but had already been arrested and convicted of several felonies, including armed robbery, burglary and grand theft. His short legs were barely long enough to reach the gas pedal, but he had already been arrested for stealing two cars.

Once again I thought about the little boy I saw earlier. It made me wonder about Smiley's whereabouts. I wanted to know where he was hiding and who he was with. Perhaps Smiley should've been in church also because he really needs a lot of prayer right now.

Heaven help him . . . Heaven help us all.

19

LAUREN

Hump day. Once I get past Wednesday I know I can make it through the rest of the work week because it's all down hill from here. Things have been crazy at the insurance company lately because of the restructuring taking place within the different departments. My objectives have been increased, and now my representatives have to answer more calls, but at least we're no longer required to deal with questions regarding claims.

Upper management finally realized the challenges the call center had in answering our customer's questions about claims since our area didn't process them. Todd LaDuke, the director of the claims department, isn't happy about the shift in duties, but he'll get over it. Maybe now he'll spend more time managing his department and less time outside taking smoke breaks.

Being in management is not all what it's cracked up to be. The fancy title of Director of Customer Service may look good on a resume, but having to manage others is more than a notion. A lot of people are lazy and just don't want to work. Many of them don't realize how blessed they are to have a job, especially since so many jobs are being outsourced over seas. I'm fearful because a lot of major insurance companies are sending customer service jobs over to India. These days if you call a Fortune 500 company for assistance, there's a good chance a rep by the name of Haseed will probably answer the line claiming to be Harry.

As tough as it is these days to keep a job, some of the people I'm managing will do and say just about anything to get out of doing theirs. I'm always on guard of people trying to manipulate the system. The employees who have been around for a while are especially tough because they're very creative and know all the tricks and rules in the company handbook. And if it isn't in the handbook, they're more than willing to lie to get extra time off.

I have one representative in the department who always gets sick while on her vacation. She'll have a week off and then come down with some kind of ailment before returning to work, forcing her to stay out for an additional week. She has a good relationship with her primary care physician, so she's always able to return to work with a note confirming she's been to the doctor. I want to fire her, but I'm in a bind because she's one of my best reps when it comes to servicing customers on the phone.

There are some people in my department who probably look forward to seeing their loved ones suffering from a serious illness, so they can take advantage of the Family and Medical Leave Act. FMLA allows an employee to take up to twelve weeks off to care for a family member. Or they can say they have to take a mother or father to the doctor and take the afternoon off. FMLA comes in handy for people eager to have a little time off, especially during the summer. Instead of taking a dying parent to dialysis treatment, they're gambling away the social security check at the riverboat casino or the racetrack.

Since most of our employees stare at computers and type all day, vision problems and carpal tunnel syndrome are always valid reasons for them to seek disability. Some have even gone on disability and used their free time to look for other jobs. One former employee went on disability and found a job in retail. I don't know what made her think no one would ever see her working the cash register in a department store on State Street. That wasn't very creative.

However, not long ago, I had a representative by the name of Deidre McMahon who came up with a stunt that stole the show. Deidre called the office one Monday morning crying, saying she needed to take some extended time off because she had to fly across the country to attend the funeral services for her brother. Like many companies, our policy is to allow an employee to take three days off for bereavement time for an immediate family member. However five days are given for services taking place out of state.

Deidre played it to the hilt. She came into the office acting brave, saying she was going to try her best to work through the day because she had some cases on her desk to complete. All day, Deidre sat at her work station sobbing, too distraught to take any calls. A photograph of her younger brother Darius in his Army uniform sat on her desk in plain view for everyone to see. In the meantime, sympathetic co-workers took up a collection for her and were making arrangements to have flowers sent to the funeral home for the services. There weren't many dry eyes in the office that day. The place was in such an emotional state that I almost had to go out and buy a box of tissue for myself.

Deidre left the office around noon with her eyes red from crying. They were probably tears of joy because she had gotten over two hundred dollars in bereavement money and had received an extra week of vacation in the process. One of the older ladies in the office had even pulled Deidre aside and prayed for her and her family.

It wasn't until several weeks later, that we learned the truth about Deidre and her brother Darius. She told us he had been killed by a roadside bomb during a second tour of duty in Iraq. Through choked up tears, she said her younger brother was just trying to do the right thing by serving his country in the aftermath of 9-11. In actuality, Darius was serving time in a downstate Illinois prison for killing a cashier after robbing a 7-Eleven. Ooh I couldn't wait to fire her lying ass!

Deidre did an incredible piece of acting and had even done research for the role. She had actually gone through the process of finding the name of a funeral parlor in Anaheim, California for us to send the flowers to. She was a real pro! Perhaps freeing up her future with the insurance company will allow her an opportunity to pursue a film career in Hollywood. She had reeled us all in. I had even gone in my purse to add ten dollars to the donation; ironically that's about how much it cost to get into the movies. Forget Denzel

Washington and Jamie Foxx. This deceitful chick cried better than Halle Berry at the Academy Awards.

And the Oscar goes to. . . Deidre McMahon for her heart-wrenching portrayal of the Scheming, Sad Sista in the tearjerker *Oh Lawd My Brotha Been Killed in Iraq!*

Even though my body is a little sore, I'm proud of myself for going back to the health club and getting in a strong workout. I hadn't exercised in a few weeks and my body was paying the price for its inactivity. Muscles that hadn't been used in a while had been stretched and pushed to the limit. Spending several minutes on the treadmill and taking a dip in the pool proved to be an excellent way for me to relieve stress and unwind.

Later, one of the guys, who I'd seen before, approached me and commented on not seeing me around the gym lately. He made subtle attempts to flirt, saying he missed me and wished he could *see more of me*, but I nipped the conversations in the bud faster than Barney Fife did on *The Andy Griffith Show*. For some, the gym has become a meeting place for men to show off their six-packs and women to display their assets while trying to get on the right track in the dating game. I was glad I had my MP3 player with me so I could tune it all out. My goal was to get in a good workout and go home. I'll probably call Andre to say goodnight.

I talked to Andre before leaving the office and let him know I was going to go to the gym for a little while before going home. Recently, he's been stressed out because the CTA has been threatening layoffs. Our schedules have been very hectic lately so we haven't seen each other as much as we used to. I miss him. Both of us made a promise to have a date this weekend and have a good time. We hadn't decided what we were going to do yet. I just wanted to be with him.

It was almost nine o'clock. My goal was to be home and in bed before ten. The parking lot was kind of dark, so I checked my purse to make sure I had my mace. I walked to my car quickly and noticed something sticking out from under the windshield wiper blade. I thought someone was passing out leaflets advertising a service or product, but noticed I didn't see anything on any of the other cars in the lot. As I got closer, I noticed it was a red envelope.

Once again, I looked around the parking lot to make sure I was safe. I deactivated the alarm to unlock my door and grabbed the envelope off the windshield. I got in the car and studied the envelope; it didn't have my name on it. Right away I wondered if it was from one of the guys I had seen earlier inside the health club trying to flirt with me. Enclosed was a card. I turned on the map light located on my rearview mirror and opened the card. A soft melody began playing. I held the card up to the light so I could read the words of the poem without straining my eyes too much. I recited the verses slowly and allowed the words to fall from my lips.

I WANT TO. . .

I want to study your mind as
I read the chapters in your book;
I want to explore your soul as
I focus to get a better look.

I want to learn your essence as
I admire your amazing grace;
I want to feel your spirit as
I caress you in a warm embrace.

I want to massage your body as
I try hard to ease your pain;
I want to weather your storm as
I shield you from the pouring rain.

I want to mend your heart as
I show you how much I care;
I want to earn your trust as
I will always be there.

I want to elevate your passion as
I lift you to an emotional high;
I want to cherish your existence as
I love you til the day I die.

Love

Andre

I batted my eyelids and tried to stop the tears from flowing. Wow! This is beautiful. I was about to put the card back in the envelope when I noticed something else inside. I pumped my fist in the air and let out a scream so loud that people in the parking lot were probably thinking I was being attacked in my car.

"Thank you, thank you, thank you, thank you, thank you!" I yelled. Enclosed was a ticket to see Jill Scott at the Chicago Theatre this weekend.

Andre has the other ticket. This explains why he was so insistent on knowing where I was going to be after work. He wanted to know where he could find my car. What a wonderful surprise!

Andre had me talking to myself.

"Ooh baby, you're going to get some rewards for this. I think I'll let you get some of your rewards tonight."

Lyrics from Jill Scott's live CD took me to a natural high as I danced and grooved through my condo. Jill's voice lifted my spirits and Mike Phillips' saxophone took me to new heights. Right now I don't have a care in the world. Ooh I'm so excited! Andre showed me how excited he was Wednesday night when I arrived at his home wearing a red, sheer chemise with a matching g-string and red, five-inch heels. As a matter of fact, Andre stayed excited for most of the evening. I guess he missed me as much as I missed him. He was making a strong point to show me the way he loves me. I got the point alright; I got the point all night long! You go Jill!

I heard the telephone ring and used the remote control to turn down the stereo. I looked at the caller ID and picked up the receiver on the second ring.

"Hi baby," I answered, seeing Andre's name and number on the display.

"Hey lovely La,"

"I was just thinking about you," I cooed.

"Were you really?"

"Umm hmm," I whispered softly.

"What were you thinking about?"

"A lot of stuff," I answered with the innocence of a young girl experiencing love for the first time. I sat on the couch in the living room and cradled the phone between my ear and shoulder. "I was just sitting here listening to one of Jill Scott's CDs and thinking about how much fun we had the other night."

"That was nice," he said with a laugh. "That was real nice!"

"So you liked that little sexy number I had on?"

"Couldn't you tell!" he exclaimed. "You caught me by surprise with that move."

"Well you caught me by surprise, too."

"Did I really?" he asked.

"Andre you're such a wonderful and thoughtful man," I confessed, feeling inspired to open up and allow my feelings to flow without hesitation or fear. "You always seem to call when I need to hear kind words. You're a great person and I want you to know how much I appreciate you and how grateful I am to have you in my life."

"Thanks La," he responded. "So are you looking forward to the concert?"

"Can't you tell?" I asked. "I've been playing Jill Scott's music all day long."

"Yeah I can hear her singing in the background."

"You must've been reading my mind?"

"Why you say that?"

"Because I had overheard a lady in the office that same day telling someone she had gotten tickets to the concert and how they had sold out so quickly. I was thinking how I would have to try to catch her the next time she came to Chicago; then I get to my car and find a ticket on my windshield. That's amazing."

"No," he corrected me. "You're amazing."

I blushed like a school girl and lounged across the couch and cradled the phone next to my ear holding on to Andre's every word.

"I'm just glad no one took that envelope off your car," he said.

"So am I!"

"Yeah that was a gutsy move."

"Well you know what they say," I teased in a frisky tone. "No guts no glory."

"And I'm trying to get all the glory I can, Ms. La," he flirted.

"I bet you are, but before we start getting carried away on the phone, I need to go through my closet and find something glorious to wear."

Andre responded reassuringly. "I'm sure you'll look lovely in whatever you decide to put on . . . with your fine ass self!"

I giggled. "You think?"

"Yeah I think."

"So what time should I be ready?" I asked.

"The show starts at eight. I'll pick you up around seven."

"I'll be ready."

"Cool."

"Andre. . ."

"Yeah La?"

"I love you."

"I love you, too, La"

I hung up the phone and floated around my condo with the freedom of a butterfly being released from its cocoon, ready to live life like I'm golden. I cranked up the volume of the stereo and listened to Jill sing as I embraced my body and rocked myself in a cradle of joy.

Andre will be here in two hours so I need to go through some stuff in my closet and see what I can wear tonight. I need time to try on a few outfits to see what still fits and hugs my body the right way.

I took a quick shower and applied my makeup. The phone rang while I was in the process of pulling a pair of sexy, black, leather pants out from the back of the closet. I looked at the clock and figured it was Andre calling to say he would be on his way soon. I didn't check the caller ID.

"Hey baby," I said, answering the phone on the second ring.

"La-La," it was Mama speaking in a rattled voice through labored breaths. "I need you . . . to take me to the emergency room."

20
MAMA

    The intensive care unit is always so noisy and busy. Once again I can hear loud machines beeping all around me. It's hard getting any rest when doctors and nurses are constantly coming in disturbing me. They were in here all night sticking me with this and checking me for that. Hmm . . . and I don't know where they got this one nurse from who was in here earlier this morning, trying to find a vein to put the I-V in my arm. I thought I was gonna have to do it myself. I get more rest at home.

    Friday was one of my best days; I felt better than I had in a long time. I was able to move around the house with ease and my body wasn't aching as much. The weather was nice so I had even gone outside on the porch and got some fresh air. It felt good getting out of the house. Lord knows I get tired of sitting up in the house everyday watching the same television shows all the time.

    Julian came over Friday evening and brought me some catfish to eat. It had too much salt on it and I think that was what set me off because I got sick during the middle of the night. I tossed and turned all night, unable to rest. I closed my eyes and slept for a couple of hours, but when I woke up my wrists and ankles were all puffed up. I done gone through this stuff long enough to know fluid was building up in my body again. Lord I'm tired of living like this. Being a senior citizen has its advantages, but getting old sure is an inconvenience.

Getting old and being sick is also an inconvenience to my kids, especially Julian and Lauren. She was so upset last night. I didn't know about her big date and never . . .

"How you feeling, Ms Collins?" asked a light-skinned nurse with a funny accent.

"Better."

She walked around the small space, checking the numbers on the beeping machines, writing information down on my chart.

"Your blood pressure is much better," she added. "It was a very high last night."

"Can I have some water?"

"I need to check with the doctor," she mumbled quickly.

"What you say?" I asked. I can't understand a word she said.

"I must check with the doctor on call. First we need to get some of the fluid out of your body and off your lungs," she mumbled as she left the room.

She must be one of them Filipinos because I couldn't understand a damn thing she said. Foreigners are taking over these hospitals. Lord Jesus we almost need to know how to speak another language just to go to the hospital now days.

A few minutes later another nurse entered the room, pushing a rolling stand. She was a dark-skinned, heavy set, black woman with blonde hair.

"Ms. Collins it's time for your breathing treatments."

"Okay," I answered, nodding my head. I didn't mind talking to her because we spoke the same language. Blondie leaned over the bed and placed the oxygen mask over my face with the strap going over the back of my head.

"Take some deep breaths and I'll be back in a little while to check on you."

I held the mask close to my face with my left hand and nodded to the nurse. Oxygen traveled through my nostrils and into my lungs. Suffering from asthma and emphysema over the years has ruined my lungs.

I've been in this hospital so much over the last few years that I'm expecting them to name a section of the building after me. Maybe they can call it the Hope Ann Collins Rehabilitation Unit or something fancy like that. Lord knows I've earned it.

Nurse Blondie returned to the room after about twenty minutes and removed the oxygen mask from my face. My eyes had started to water from the constant pressure.

"Ms. Collins do you want me to turn the television on?"

"Please do," I answered quickly. "I'm tired of sitting in here listening to these machines go beep beep beep."

"I know," she said with a smile. "We want you to get better and these machines help us monitor your progress."

I returned the smile. "Nurse I'm thirsty. Can I have some water?"

"The doctors don't want you to have too much water because of all the fluid in your body. But how about I bring you a cup of ice to suck on to wet your whistle," she said with an understanding grin. "Will that help to quench your thirst a little bit?"

I nodded. "A little bit."

I was hoping to find a church broadcast on television, but all I found was college basketball games. I don't know a lot about college basketball, so I kept flipping channels until I got to the local news.

The lead story on the evening news was the discovery of a body found in the Little Calumet River. I listened as a reporter on the scene described the pitiful details and the events leading up to the finding.

'According to authorities, the body found in the Little Calumet River is believed to be that of Dwayne Patterson. Patterson also known as Smiley was the ten-year-old boy suspected of killing Chiquita Richards earlier this month when he fired three bullets from a nine millimeter handgun into a crowd at the Cleophus Hubbard Elementary School on Chicago's south side. Witnesses on the scene said Patterson was shooting at an older boy who he had had an altercation with earlier in the day. Ironically, funeral services for little Chiquita Richards were held at Stamps Funeral Home this past Friday.'

"Lord Jesus," I mumbled to myself and continued to listen to the reporter as Nurse Blondie returned to the room with a cup of ice.

'A spokesperson for the Chicago Police Department said they believe ten-year-old Dwayne Patterson had been in hiding since killing Chiquita Richards nine days ago, and was most likely afraid for his life; and that he was probably murdered by members of the gang he was associated with. The police spokesperson went on to say higher ranking members probably killed young "Smiley" Patterson to avoid the risk of him being apprehended by authorities and perhaps giving names of higher ranking gang members.'

"Lord Jesus," I said, shaking my head. "Kids are killing kids. That boy Smiley was just a baby. Parents shouldn't have to bury their babies."

'I'm standing on a bridge at Ashland Avenue not far from I-57. There are a lot of camera crews out here, but the Illinois State Police will not allow us to get too close. However, if you take a good look at the location where Patterson's body was found, you'll see it is a very polluted area. The water is very dirty, and has a creamy, milky green color. The Little Calumet is a river of many sewer pipes which run into the water from almost everywhere. It is believed to be one of the worst rivers in the state in regards to pollution. Patterson's body was found floating face down. He had been shot twice in the back of the head, execution style. Authorities said an autopsy will be needed to determine how long Smiley Patterson's body had been floating in the river.'

Nurse Blondie and I watched and listened in shock as the reporter on the scene provided more gruesome details of the young child's death.

'Once again, just to recap on what has transpired within the last two hours. Authorities have found the body of ten-year-old Dwayne "Smiley" Patterson floating in the Little Calumet River with two gunshots wounds to the back of the head. This is Kimberly Vanderkam reporting from the brutal murder scene overlooking the Little Calumet River near I-57 and 130th Street.'

Seeing something like this makes me worry about my own children. I pray for their safety everyday of my life. I don't know what I would do if I had to bury Julian, Kendall or Lauren. That is my greatest fear.

Under The Same Roof

    I worry about Julian and the legal problems he's having. He didn't want me to know about it, but I forced La-La to tell me what was going on with him. She told me about the FBI breaking into his office and taking files and stuff. I asked Julian about it one time when he came over to the house, but he avoided the subject. I didn't press him on it. I figured he would tell me in due time. I could tell something was wrong because he hadn't been acting himself lately.

    When I think about it, it seemed like he had a lot on his mind the day he took me to the doctor and left to go meet with his friend Steve. Julian has always had a gentle spirit and it's not like him to snap at me; that's not his character. Also, I can tell he's lost weight. He's not eating because he's worrying about that case. Julian won't tell me anything because he doesn't want me to worry, so I try to get La-La to fill me in on the latest developments.

    La-La has always been quick to tell on everybody else, but she wants to keep her problems to herself. I worry about her also. Even as a child, she was always a very serious minded individual. She's such a dedicated and hardworking person that I pray she doesn't let life slip away. I hope the goals she has for down the road don't get in the way of her being happy now.

    She spends so much time preparing for the future that she doesn't take the time out to enjoy the present. La-La needs to realize that insurance company is gonna make it with or without her. And if she drops dead tomorrow morning, they'll have someone else in her office to replace her by noon. I understand La-La's desire to be successful and make a lot of money, but she needs to take some time and enjoy life. I've been to a lot of funerals in my day, but Lord knows I ain't never seen a Brinks truck follow a hearse to the cemetery.

    I think La-La is serious about the young man she's dating now, but I'm not gonna get my hopes up yet because La-La is a hard woman to please and expects everybody to be perfect. She's stubborn and set in her ways. Any man dealing with her is gonna need a lot of patience.

    I don't know what's going on with Kendall. And to be honest, I'm not sure I wanna know either. I just know it's something shady; I can see it in his eyes and in his mannerism when he's around me. He's uncomfortable around me.

Kendall was a mischievous child, he was always into something. I remember finding one of them magazines with pictures of naked women in it under Kendall's bed when the boys were about ten and twelve years of age. When I asked Kendall about it, he said it was Julian's magazine and that Julian had gotten the book for them from a store up in Roseland. Both of them were too young to buy that kind of magazine, so I got my belt and threatened to beat the truth out of them. Julian remained loyal and took the punishment to protect his younger brother even though Kendall had lied on him.

Years later, I found out the magazine was really Kendall's and that he had stolen it. He has ways that reminds me of his father.

On another occasion, Kendall got into a fight in the neighborhood and tried to hit the boy in the head with a brick. Fortunately, a policeman, who lived in the area, saw Kendall and the other kid fighting, and broke it up before either child got seriously hurt. The officer brought Kendall home and tried his best to explain to me what happened. However, instead of me taking a belt to Kendall's behind, I lashed out at the policeman, who was trying to do the right thing. I started ranting and raving and cussing and fussing about what my child would and would not do, and that my thirteen-year-old son must have had a damn good reason for wanting to hit someone in the head with a brick.

Lord Jesus, what was I thinking?

The officer stood on the porch with his gun strapped in his holster and his night stick by his side, and looked at me in disbelief. I remember his words vividly and what he told me before walking back to his squad car. He shook his head and said, *"Ma'am that boy of yours will break your heart one day."*

On that cloudy day, I saw the officer's gun in the holster, the nightstick at his side, the badge on his chest, and the disapproving frown on his face, but I failed to recognize the prophesy in his words because I didn't want to.

Sometimes a mother can see the handwriting on the wall and still not read the message.

21

JULIAN

Panic set in the moment I saw the hospital's name on my caller ID. Being afraid to answer the phone is a horrible state of mind to be in. I let the phone in my office ring twice before I finally decided to pick up the receiver. Somehow I knew it wouldn't be good news on the other end of the line.

"May I speak with Mr. Julian Collins please?" a female voice asked.

"Speaking," I answered nervously.

"I'm calling from Roseland Hospital to let you know your mother has taken a turn for the worse and that you should get here as soon as possible."

"I'll be right there."

I left the office immediately and drove like a bat out of hell to the hospital hoping Mama wouldn't be dead when I got there. Fortunately, it was the middle of the day, so I didn't have to contend with rush hour traffic on the Dan Ryan. My foot was pressing the accelerator with no regard for the police. I darted in and out of traffic better than a stunt driver in a chase scene from an action movie, and nearly got sandwiched between two, eighteen wheelers. Traffic, trucks and troopers were the least of my concerns. I risked my life hoping to find Mama still alive. By the time I got to the hospital, I was a nervous wreck and probably needed medical attention as well.

Seeing Mama in this condition scares me. She's unconscious and the excess fluid in her body makes her face look bloated. Mama is hooked up to a ventilator with a tube inserted into her throat. It makes me uncomfortable just looking at her with all these machines attached to her body.

I take a seat in a chair next to the bed and try to keep myself from crying. Mama hasn't opened her eyes yet and doesn't even know I'm in the room. My mother is very sick!

Once again, Mama had gotten sick during the middle of the night. It's strange how it happens because yesterday Mama was bragging about how much better she felt, and that she was excited about her doctor transferring her back to a regular room. Then, all of a sudden, she suffered another severe asthma attack and had to be rushed to ICU again. Mama was feeling great one moment and near death the next. This was an emotionally draining experience. Caring for an elderly parent was no joke.

Still, it shouldn't be so difficult for us to work together in looking after Mama, since she raised us all alone. Mama didn't have a choice; she had to be both mother and father. I can only imagine the times Mama lost sleep and had to take off work to rush Kendall, Lauren or me to a hospital or doctor's office. Trips to the emergency room are never convenient.

It reminds me of the time when I was in third grade and got sick. I was already coughing and battling a cold, but insisted on going to school because I wanted to take gym class. Unfortunately, for me, the gym teacher thought he was an army drill sergeant running a boot camp instead of a physical education instructor teaching eight-year-olds. He had us running laps around the gym until I passed out on the floor with my tongue hanging out. I was wheezing hard enough to have the principal and teachers thinking I had just participated in a 25K marathon.

I wasn't the only child in the house suffering from medical emergencies because Kendall and La-La also had their share. Kendall, the risk taker, was always doing something dangerous that threatened him with bodily harm. For example, he went through his daredevil phase and thought he was the black Evil Knievel.

One time in particular, we were outside in the alley with three other boys in the neighborhood doing stunts on our bikes. Doing wheelies and riding with no hands was boring, so we decided to set up two ramps made of wood and anchored them with bricks. We all took turns lining up and taking jumps on our bikes like members of the five speed acrobatic team. All of us had been successful in making our jumps from one ramp to the next, but that wasn't enough for Kendall; he had to make the challenge more dangerous and adventurous.

For some bizarre reason, Kendall suggested we spread the ramps farther apart and put our bikes on the ground to give us something to jump over. Forever bold and daring, Kendall wanted to go first and told us to get out of his way. He called himself Kendall Knievel and started pedaling from half way down the alley. Kendall hit the ramp at a speed of about thirty miles per hour and launched into the air with his legs dangling from his brand new, blue Huffy bicycle. In mid-flight, the front tire of his new Huffy tipped the handlebars of one of the other bikes, causing him to summersault through the air faster than an out of control daredevil. I thought my little brother had killed himself or at least broken his neck. By the time Kendall finished tumbling on the concrete, he had a busted chin and a broken arm. None of the rest of us attempted the jump after that. We didn't have all of the protective gear like helmets and knee pads back then.

La-La's antics weren't as death defying as Kendall's, but that didn't stop Mama from having to race her to the emergency room for one thing or another. La-La's inquisitive nature had her always getting into something. Like the time she decided to swallow a few too many pills. My baby sister was trying to overdose on a bottle of Bayer aspirins. I guess that bottle didn't have a child proof cap. Mama didn't have to worry about her raiding the medicine cabinet anymore after the emergency room doctors had to pump her stomach.

It really makes me wonder why it's so hard for three children, who were all raised under the same roof, to work together and take care of one parent, when one parent raised and nurtured three children all alone. There's something about that equation that just doesn't seem to add up.

I don't know what it is, but it seems like every time I'm finally able to push a woman to the back of mind, they reemerge into the center of my consciousness. It's like they wait for me to get over them, then they pop up again wanting to rekindle romance. Annette was supposed to be out of my system ever since I wined and dined her at an expensive seafood restaurant, but now she was reeling me back in with her captivating sex appeal. With one unexpected call, I was on the phone line holding onto her every word, nibbling on her bootylicious bait like a horny fish out of water. I'm hooked.

Annette's phone call earlier today had definitely taken me by surprise. In her sassy and sexy way, she talked about how she was in the mood for some weekend fun and excitement. Annette explained how she had just completed a project for her boss and was finally able to relax and let her hair down. She also stated how she was finally in the frame of mind to go in a new direction physically and mentally. She mentioned how she was in the process of moving to a new apartment and was attempting to start a clean slate.

Annette always talked a good game, so I was anxious to see if she would keep her game plan for the future. However, first things first, I want to make sure we kept our plan for tonight. Considering all the stress I've been under in dealing with my legal problems and Mama, I was game for just about anything. Besides it's the weekend.

The long week at work and running back and forth to the hospital every day has me exhausted. I came home from the office and took a nap so I would be fresh for my date with Annette later on. I called the hospital a couple of times and talked to the nurse on duty to get a report on Mama's condition. Each time, they told me she was resting comfortably. I was hoping nothing would change.

Originally, our plan was to go to a jazz or blues club to listen to some music, but instead, we decided to hang out in Millennium Park and enjoy the nighttime air. To my delight, Annette's mood was frisky and affectionate. We held hands and spent most of the evening laughing and joking as we walked around Chicago's latest tourist attraction. Some city taxpayers and critics have complained about the half a billion dollar price tag of downtown's newest playground, but my goal was to use the aesthetic atmosphere as a late night aphrodisiac. I hadn't read my horoscope for the day, but I was hoping the moon and stars were aligned in my favor.

After leaving Millennium Park, Annette and I stopped in Bennigans to get a drink and rest our legs from all the walking we had done. With it being a Friday night, the restaurant was crowded, but fortunately we didn't have to wait too long to be seated. I don't think we were hungry, but neither of us wanted the night to end. We ordered a couple of drinks and munched on a basket of chicken wings. A strong glass of gin and 7-Up had me feeling courageous, and Annette was perky and ripe, sipping seductively on strawberry daiquiris.

Annette stared at me from across the table and I stared back. The gin was making me fearless.

I reached under the table and grabbed Annette's right leg. I pulled off her stylish sandal and allowed it to fall on the floor. A surprised yet satisfying look covered her face. I held Annette's small foot in my lap and began rubbing her ankle and shapely calf. Her eyes smiled as she sucked on the fruity daiquiri with succulent lips. She wiggled her toes and allowed them to massage my throbbing penis as I fantasized about being the straw in her mouth. My eyes were on the verge of rolling into the back of my head when the waitress returned to give me the check. I had to stop this before I ruined my pants. I paid the waiter and left a big tip.

Annette and I cuddled and hugged each other playfully as we walked down Michigan Avenue en route to my car in the Grant Park Garage. The garage was nearly empty. We kissed each other for the first time. Our lips parted and allowed our tongues to taste the alcoholic fuel of our heated energy. It was if both of us were long overdue and in need of some sexual healing. Romance was trying to make its presence felt on the evening, but lust was dominating the night. The clacking footsteps of a customer entering the garage put the brakes on our semi-public display of passion.

The weekend activity and the nighttime construction work on the Dan Ryan made traffic a mess on the expressway. I put in the Isley Brothers Beautiful Ballads CD and let Ronald Isley set the mood in the car. While Mr. Biggs crooned the lyrics to "Don't Say Goodnight" in a honey rich voice, I gently caressed the inside of Annette's thighs with fingers anxious to discover unknown territory.

"You're bad, Julian," purred Annette.

"Does that mean you want me to stop massaging your thighs?" I asked.

"No."

I smiled with inebriated confidence. My intoxicated spirit made me willing to say or do just about anything to keep Annette under my influence. My words were bold, my actions were bolder. She had not seen this side of my personality; it had been a long time since I had seen it myself.

"You can let the seat back Annette if you want to relax more."

She reclined the seat and continued to hum along with the Isley Brothers. Ronald Isley was crooning on every track, and Annette was going along with the program. I rolled the windows all the way up and opened the roof to let the moon in.

"You know what I want you to do, Annette?"

"What?" she asked, still humming along with the Isleys.

"Put your feet up on the dashboard," I ordered confidently as the gin continued to give me courage. I wasn't drunk, but the liquor had me feeling bold enough to be daring with Annette.

Without hesitation, Annette put her feet on the dashboard and opened her legs wide enough to allow my fingers to delve into her sexual swamp. She was hot down there, and even the air flowing through my opened roof was unable to cool her off.

"What you doin', Julian?"

"Shhh," I whispered. "I'm just taking you back to my house to get your car."

"Mmm," she sighed. "It seems like you're trying to take me somewhere else."

"Only if you let me," I whispered.

Annette opened her legs wider and guided my sticky fingers on a Voyage to her private Atlantis. Her pleasure island was wet and inviting, and I was ready to get lost like Gilligan.

Ronald Isley was still crooning; my fingers were still stroking; and Annette was still moaning, and the driver blowing his horn and flashing his bright lights in my rearview mirror was annoying me. Folks do some crazy driving on Friday nights; in a hurry to get to their destinations. I know the feeling because I was in a hurry to get Annette back to my house.

I drove up the exit ramp at expressway at 99th and Halsted, with the crazy driving individual in the silver Jeep Cherokee still on my tail. I removed my hand from Annette's pleasure zone and raised it through the opened roof, and signaled for the anxious driver to go around me.

"If you in that big of a damn hurry, you should jump over me!" I hollered.

"What's wrong?" Annette sighed, keeping her feet in place on my dashboard.

"That fool in the car behind me keeps riding my tail."

The traffic light at the corner of 99th and Halsted turned red and stopped my progression, allowing the driver in the silver Jeep to pull up to me on the passenger side. He rolled down his window and began shouting at me.

"Pull over goddammit!"

"Who the fuck are you!" I yelled back, pointing at him with sticky fingers.

"Get outta that car bitch!"

"Oh shit!" Annette exclaimed, taking her feet down from the dashboard and adjusted her reclined seat to an upright position.

"Oh shit what?" I yelled.

"That's my man, Ted!"

"Your what?"

"Do something, Julian!" she screamed in fear.

The light turned green and I hit the gas. Instead of going straight on 99th, I darted out in front of some vehicles and made a daring left turn on Halsted that almost caused my car to hit the curb and have an accident. Fortunately for us, Annette's boyfriend had pulled up on the passenger side because he got trapped by the flow of cars traveling westbound and couldn't make the turn with me. Looking back through the rear window, Annette claimed to see his car go into a service station to turn around. Like me he was trying to merge into the traffic moving southbound, but by the time he did, I was off the beaten path and was zipping down side streets faster than Speed Racer.

I turned off the Isley Brothers CD and stopped Ronald's crooning. The "Caravan of Love" is over.

22

KENDALL

Ever since Smiley's body was found floating in the river face down with two slugs in the back of his head, things have gotten hot. Cops were coming with the heat and were sweeping the area day and night. They've been harassing a lot of the younger guys in the neighborhood and making it tougher to do business. Some of my crew members had been taken in for questioning and were beaten by cops trying to coerce a confession, but so far the police still hadn't come up with any concrete information to charge anyone for Smiley's murder.

Once we found out where Smiley was hiding, it was just a matter of time. I knew Ray was gonna have him killed because he was mad at himself for not doing it sooner. I'm just surprised Ray didn't make sure the body was burned or buried instead of just dumping it in the river. Ray is getting very reckless.

The media has been all over this story. The accidental killing of Chiquita Richards was a local tragedy, but the murder of Smiley raised the bar and put things on another level. The Sun-Times and Tribune had put a mug shot of Smiley on the front page of their newspapers and had done in depth research about his upbringing. Cable news programs were doing reports on the case, making Smiley the poster child for youth violence in the inner-city. This is all fucked up.

And I have a strange feeling that things are only going to get worse.

A caravan of luxury vehicles traveled downstate, through the hick country and cornfields of central Illinois; commanding rural roads in Cadillac limousines with the driving force of a presidential motorcade. However, instead of choosing the state capitol in Springfield, where the governor resides as our destination, we'll be stopping thirty miles north in the town of Lincoln. It's where one of our most notorious leaders has been governing our policies from behind bars.

I've never seen Ronald Green before; wouldn't know him even if he had walked up and spit in my face. All I know about him is his rep and the stories I've been told from others in the game. According to them, he's an inner-city legend with a reputation deadlier than the grim reaper. Just the threat of his violent tendencies stretched way beyond the bars of his prison cell. I'd heard upper echelon members of the higher-ups talk about what Ronald Green would do about this or about that when he hits the streets. Sometimes a person's rep is all we need to know. Even though I hadn't met Ronald Green, in my mind, he was already a mythical monster or ghetto boogeyman.

Before entering the Logan Correctional Center back in 1980, at age twenty, Ronald Green had the nickname "Get Money" Green because he would do damn near anything to get money; including robbing, stealing and killing to take from others things he wanted for himself. From what I heard, his victims were of all ages, backgrounds and ethnic groups; he wasn't prejudice when it came to crime; Ronald Green was an equal opportunity offender. The only thing he cared about was getting someone's money for himself. Being convicted of murder, armed robbery and theft is exactly what had landed him in prison. The nickname "Get Money" is no longer used today, but it still applies because Ronald Green is still getting other people's money.

Ray and I sit in the fourth car of the four limousine convoy as we wait for Ronald Green to emerge from the facility that has physically detained him for the last two and a half decades. Top ranking members of the higher-ups are represented in the first two cars. Following the higher-ups down here was Ray's idea not mine.

Ray considered the gesture a way of us showing proper respect to Ronald Green and the higher-ups. In my opinion, we show respect every time we pay them tribute by giving them a large percentage of our profits.

I would've rather stayed at home and waited for the big party planned to celebrate Ronald Green's release. Considering the fact that he's already receiving the royal treatment, the homecoming party will probably be more extravagant than a presidential inauguration. And if I didn't know better, I probably would've thought that Ronald Green was some kind of political prisoner because the higher-ups were treating him like Nelson Mandella.

B-Rob and Charlie-O, two ranking officers of the higher-ups step out of the first black limo and greet their newly freed partner. Finally, I'm able to see the face of the street legend. I focus to see if the man before me matches the mental picture I've had in my mind over the years. It's my first time laying eyes on him, but I can only imagine him having the same sinister scowl on his face when he entered Logan Correctional Center several months shy of his twenty-first birthday.

No one else from the other limos parked in the procession get out and greet Ronald Green. It wouldn't make much sense because he's been in prison too long to know most of us anyway. For him, this is just a ceremony; a way of allowing him to leave prison with an entourage and respect. It's another enhancement to his rep. Guys still inside the joint can say Ronald Green left the scene with the status of a grand marshal in a parade of limos. From the back of the limo I'm sharing with Ray, I try to size him up from a distance.

Ronald Green appears to be close to six feet tall, with a stocky build that's probably a result of him lifting weights to kill time instead of somebody else. He's slightly hunched over with a short, thick neck. A chocolate complexion full of bumps resembling almonds show nothing sweet about his character. His clean shaven head is accented by a menacing goatee. Cold steely eyes greet the outside world with the glare of an animal whose been trapped in a cage for too many years. There's nothing pretty about Ronald Green. He's a gruesome guy to look at.

Because of Ronald Green's dignitary status within the higher-ups, he still manages to get a piece of the profits from the action on the streets. From behind prison bars, Green lived better than a lot of people in the outside world. He played a major role in making business decisions, settling disputes, dividing turf, and when necessary, even sanctioning murders. Now as a free man about to leave the medium-security penitentiary in downstate Illinois, I can only imagine what changes are about to happen once he gets home in Chicago.

Ronald Green's release from prison yesterday set off a wave of parties and fanfare. Earlier today, the higher-ups celebrated in Palmer Park with a barbecue for the neighborhood. We're a few blocks from where we do a lot of business and about a half a mile from the police station. As a matter of fact, a few officers even came through to munch on some rib tips and hot links. It was a blast. Men, women and kids participated in softball, sack races, bid whist games and other outdoor activities suited for a day of fun under the sun.

At the picnic, I was formally introduced to Ronald Green. The higher-ups described me as a good earner. He shook my hand, but remained distant. I guess years in prison had made him guarded and uncomfortable around people he didn't know or trust.

Once the sun went down on the festivities in the park, a few members of the higher-ups and some crew captains drove out to B-Rob's new recording studio in Calumet City. We had spent most of the day singing, dancing, stepping, and doing the latest version of the electric slide. Now guys were trying to make music and dance to their own tunes.

I don't know what it is, but it seems as though everywhere I turn I see entertainers pretending to be thugs and thugs pretending to be entertainers. The two appear to go hand in hand like guns and money. Up and coming rap artists are almost ready to die or do jail time in order to have street credibility and platinum status with a hit record. On the flip side, real life gangsters are willing to turn the tables and order a hit on anyone keeping them from taking advantage of an opportunity to become a money making music mogul.

Upright and clean-cut, prep school poets fantasize of being the next Tupac, whereas down and dirty degenerates dream about becoming another Suge Knight. Myles Montgomery and Benny Robinson are just two of the latest entries into the music industry hoping to get rich by shooting up the charts with a bullet.

For the longest, B-Rob has been bragging about this new, young rapper by the name of Myles, and tonight it seems like I'll finally be able to hear him for myself. I'm anxious to find out what all the hype is about.

By day, Myles Montgomery is a seventeen-year-old senior at Gwendolyn Brooks College Prep on the city's far south side. He's a straight A student, a member of the National Honor Society, speaks Spanish fluently, and since he got a twenty-seven on his ACT exam, he will probably receive a scholarship to a prestigious university. His school attire consists of neatly creased khakis and starched collared shirts.

By night, the prep school scholar transforms his well grounded demeanor into that of a lightning rod lyricist by the name Wild Myles. Preppy school clothes are exchanged for a Kevin Garnett basketball jersey and baseball cap. Myles is trying his best to be something other than a middle-class school boy. He has already completed a demo and is willing to sell his CD on street corners while he hopes to land a record deal.

Most drug dealers use their profits from heroin and crack to buy lavish homes, fancy cars and expensive jewelry, but Benny "B-Rob" Robinson emptied his fat pockets into a south suburban recording studio. B-Rob's studio is very impressive. He bragged about spending over $125,000 on top flight, state-of-the-art music equipment which included a three-inch reel to reel recorder, a forty channel mixing board, computerized drum machines and sophisticated digital equalizers. B-Rob is very committed to being a music tycoon and has spent more than enough money to prove it.

At age thirty-seven, B-Rob is unlike many players in this game; he didn't grow up taking short cuts in life. He always kept a job. As a kid, he had a paper route, and later worked as a stock boy in a paint store as a teenager. One of his relatives had even helped him get a job at one of the banks on the south side.

In some ways, B-Rob reminded me of myself because he's extremely smart. He didn't need to hire sound engineers and technicians to come in and work the controls in the recording studio because he's a gadget junkie and had studied computers and electronics at DeVry. B-Rob probably could've done almost anything professionally, and could've perhaps been a computer programmer or electrical engineer. However, the lure of fast money in the early nineties had short circuited any career opportunities he may have envisioned in corporate America.

It's understandable to see why B-Rob would attempt to enter in the music industry as a behind the scenes executive. There are a million kids on the streets of Chicago trying to be the city's next R. Kelly or Kanye West. The music industry is also another way for drug dealers to hide money and come across as legit businessmen. B-Rob considers the young, charismatic Wild Myles as his version of Bow Wow.

Watching B-Rob tonight, I can see he is frustrated by the negative energy flowing through the studio. Too much partying is being done and not enough music is being made. Dope is getting smoked and snorted, and alcohol is being poured nonstop. To make matters worse, folks are clowning and acting careless around very expensive equipment.

A handful of freeloading women are drunk and shaking their asses as if they're auditioning for a skin flick or G-Unit video. Also in attendance are members of a local rap group by the name of Strait Jackin. B-Rob is working with them and trying to sign them to his record label. In the meantime, Ronald Green is spraying a bottle of champagne in the air as he receives a free get out of jail blowjob by a woman too drunk to remember his name or hers.

"Yo Myles," B-Rob shouted angrily over the commotion. "I need you to get in the booth and start rhyming, dawg. We're wasting time and money up in here."

"Yo B. I'm not really feeling this," he said, trying to respond in a tone that supported his cool stage name. "It's too crazy up in here tonight."

"Yeah, but I need you to get the fuck in there and flow anyway." B-Rob warned.

Myles is right. His nickname may be wild, but his personality is much too tame for this environment. He probably doesn't have a clue to how rowdy some of the individuals in this room can be. This atmosphere is too crazy to be creative.

After Wild Myles enters the booth and puts the headphones over his Minnesota Timberwolves baseball cap, the funky beat from the drum machine causes his head to bob up and down; his wiry frame begins to rock back and forth. Finally it appears as though he's ready to get his groove on. Wild Myles is flowing off the top of his head with out pen or paper in his small hands, and B-Rob is grooving at the mixing board with the enthusiastic high of Dr. Dre recording "The Chronic" or some other funky shit.

I'm sitting here with my mouth wide open because this prep kid by the name of Wild Myles is coming with the heat. Damn. I wouldn't be surprised if B-Rob has found a goldmine with this young cat.

"Flow dawg!" I yelled after swallowing another gulp of expensive champagne.

The combination of reefer and alcohol has me grooving and rocking with my eyes closed. As Wild Myles continues to spit lyrics, one of the drunken members of Strait Jackin trips and falls on Ronald Green. The rapper's stumbling ways causes Ronald Green to spill champagne on his silk slacks and the woman welcoming him home.

"Oops my bad," the young rapper said, nonchalantly. His mind is occupied by the music and his body occupied by too much cheap liquor and weed.

"My bad?" Ronald Green snapped, pushing the woman's head away from his lap.

"Yeah, my bad," said the rapper with outstretched arms. "What's the problem? I said my bad, what else am I 'posed to say?"

Almost before the young member of the rap crew is able to finish his sentence, Ronald Green is beating him across the face with the half-empty bottle of champagne.

"Yo chill Ronny chill!" B-Rob hollers as he pulls Ronald Green off the bloody and champagne drenched rapper.

"It's cool, B-Rob," Ronald Green chides. "I just want his punk ass to know what Cristal tastes like."

"It was a mistake!" the beaten rapper hollered, wiping blood and champagne from his mouth with his right hand. "It didn't take all that!"

"Say what?" Ronald Green asked with his eyes full of attitude.

"Let him be, Ron," B-Rob urged. "This is supposed to be 'bout us having a good time and enjoying you being home."

"Yeah I'm wit' that," Ronald Green nodded. "But I don't like the attitude of some of these young niggas. They need to learn how to respect their elders."

"Man, fuck this shit," mumbled the beaten youngster. "I'm outta here."

"Yo, dude!" barked Ronald Green. "You got beef wit' me? I'm old enough to be your muthafuckin' daddy nigga. You 'posed to respect me."

"But you ain't my daddy!" yelled the young rapper, not knowing when to keep his mouth shut.

Silence filled the room. The booming sounds of B-Rob's expensive recording equipment had been reduced to its lowest decibels. Wild Myles' ferocious voice was now tame and back to its original prep school state of innocence. This drama was blowing everybody's high, especially mine.

Ronald Green has only been out the joint for two days and has already violated his parole over a dozen times. Here he is a free man, celebrating by guzzling Cristal and getting a blowjob, and he's beating a guy over the head with a champagne bottle. Damn. I'd hate to be around him when he's really pissed off.

Now I can testify to the myths I've heard about Ronald Green; he really is a ghetto boogeyman. Even though he's dressed in the silk suit and alligator shoes the higher-ups gave him as homecoming gifts, he'll never be able to conceal the sharp, jagged edges of his persona. Twenty plus years behind bars hasn't rehabilitated him one bit. He's still tailor-made for a life of crime.

"You right Shorty," Ronald Green whispered slowly as he pulled a gun from the waistband of his trousers. "I ain't yo' daddy at all, so maybe you don't feel the need to show me the respect I deserve. I understand you just a young nigga tryin' to come up and be heard. I admire your boldness. I wanna ask you a few questions, then I'll let you raise up on outta here and that will be the end of it."

"I'm sorry," the kid apologizes. "I didn't mean . . ."

Finally, the kid has fear in his eyes as the room remains silent, wondering what questions Ronald Green will ask.

"How old are you, partner?"

"Twenty."

"So you think you a man, huh?"

". . . Yeah" he answered hesitantly.

"Don't you know I was in the joint longer than you been alive?"

He shook his head. "Nah I didn't know that."

"I didn't think so," Ronald Green reprimanded the kid with the gun still in his hand resting by his side. "Do you get a lot of pussy?"

"Huh?"

"You a man and all," Ronald Green laughed. "So I wanna know if you get a lot of pussy, or are you a virgin bitch?"

"I gets mine," he bragged. "I ain't no bitch."

"Oh yeah!" Ronald Green grinned. "You gets yours, huh?"

"Fo sho," he boasted. "And Ima keep gettin' mine."

Ronald Green responded by firing two shots between the boastful kid's legs.

"No you won't," Ronald Green grumbled with an intimidating stare as the barrel of the gun smoked in his hands. "And by the way young nigga, I hope you already got some kids 'cuz if you don't, you never will."

Disbelief invaded the room as the bragging kid with the big mouth fell to the floor. Blood gushed from his premature manhood, soaking the fabric of his oversized, baggy jeans.

Ronald Green tucked the gun into the waistband of his slacks and roared for everyone to hear.

"Anybody else in here wanna interrupt my welcome home party?"

The king of the jungle is back.

23

LAUREN

It feels good being on vacation this week even though I'm not going anywhere. Mama is still in intensive care, so I wouldn't feel comfortable leaving town. To be honest though, I wish I could get away for a few days to clear my head and recharge my spirit. Ever since Mama called me the night of the concert, telling me she needed to go to the hospital, my mind has been racing with a lot of thoughts and questions regarding my future. My mind is on Mama, Andre and my job.

Right now, I'm just grateful for being able to sleep late and have some time away from the insurance company. Having some days off will allow me to catch up on some things. I need to pay bills, do laundry, clean my condo, and run the errands I don't have the time to take care of when I'm working twelve hour days. Also, I'm very excited about spending some quality time with Andre.

Lately, Andre and I have been spending a lot of time in movie theatres, but since spring is here and the weather is nice, I persuaded him to use his creative mind to think of something different for us to do. I know I could've suggested some ideas and gave my preference, but since he's the man I stroked his ego and deferred to him. It was easy. I rubbed his head a few times and whispered encouraging words in his ear to motivate him to take charge in planning our afternoon of fun.

Andre is very punctual, so I was dressed and ready to go when he rang my doorbell promptly at eleven o'clock. I buzzed the door so he could come up. As I waited, I checked my lipstick in the living room mirror. I liked what I saw. This new Cinnamon Frost looked good on my lips and matched my complexion perfectly.

I also liked what I saw when I opened the door to greet my man. Damn Andre looked good. His starched blue jean shorts and white T-shirt were rugged and sexy at the same time, and enhanced his athletic build. Well toned muscles defined his arms and legs. He smiled at me and stood in the doorway with both hands behind his back.

"Come in," I said, smiling back, with luscious lips ready to kiss.

He walked towards me and pulled a dozen red roses from behind his back with his right hand.

"You brought goodies for me?" I cooed, kissing him gently on the lips.

"Yep," he smiled, licking his lips like L.L. Cool J. "Goodies for you."

"Thank you."

"You like them?"

"Of course," I said, holding them close to my nose to inhale the scent.

"I'm glad you like them."

"I love them, Andre; they're beautiful."

"No, La, they're roses," he grinned. "You're beautiful."

"Thank you," I smiled. "Well I need to get a vase, so I can put them on my dining room table," I grinned as I headed for the kitchen to run some water in the vase.

"Well don't forget these," Andre grinned, pulling another dozen of red roses from behind his back with his left hand.

"Two dozen," I asked with surprise.

"Yep."

"You're always so thoughtful."

"I try my best."

"Keep this up and you're going to have me thinking I'm special."

"You'll be thinking right."
"You're a sweetheart."
"Am I your sweetheart?"
"You better be," I responded seductively.

Andre follows me into the kitchen. I could feel his eyes examining my rear with the intensity of a human X-ray machine. He's looking right through my tan Capri pants and pink polo shirt; his mental probing is stripping away my Victoria's Secret panties and bra. I'm fully clothed, but Andre's eyes are penetrating my naked flesh. I run some water for the vase and clip the stem on the roses.

Andre approaches me from behind and presses his body against mine. I close my eyes and moan softly. The vase nearly falls from my grasp when his hands grips me by the waist and moves upward slowly until they reach the fullness of my breast. He pinches my nipples gently through the fabric of my bra.

The soldier in Andre's jeans is erect and standing at attention, ready to pledge its allegiance to me. His freaky flag is flying full staff and eager for me to blow it in the wind. He nibbles tenderly on my earlobes and neck.

"Not now, Dre," I moaned.

"Come on," he begged. "Lemme get a piece of nookie before we go."

"Later on," I whispered, removing his hands from my breast. "You know if we get started, we'll be here all day and will never leave."

A postponement of sex quickly changed Andre's mood. All of a sudden, the kissing and nibbling on my earlobe ceased. He backed up, allowing space to finally come between our bodies. I turned around to see that the smile he entered my condo with was no longer on his face. He backed away and returned to the living room, leaving me alone at the kitchen sink. If I hadn't known better, I would've thought he had just blown an electrical fuse. All the spark and voltage of his passion were gone. Andre had completely turned off and disconnected himself from me. He could've at least stayed in the kitchen and talked to me.

I shook my head in amazement as I heard him walking around in my living room. It's amazing how quickly a big, strong man can exhibit childlike behavior when he doesn't get his way, ready to take his balls to another room. I can't believe he's actually moping like a spoiled brat. It's like watching a kid get mad because he can't have any cookies. I didn't say I wouldn't give him any; I just said not right now! Instead of crying for cookies, he's pouting for pussy.

Ugh! I could strangle him!

Suddenly, the footsteps get louder as I hear Andre returning to the kitchen. Now my mood has changed. My arms are folded across my breast, and my eyes stare at the ground. I'm so angry right now. I can see and hear his feet moving in my direction. There aren't any marks on my kitchen floor because I just mopped and waxed it, but there's still a line drawn on the ceramic tile defining my territory.

He keeps coming closer.

Now he's invading my space.

Andre better not cross that line. My thoughts are daring him to cross that line.

"I'm sorry, La," he says, reaching for my wrist to unfold my arms. "I'm sorry."

I want to be tough and resist, but I can't. I accept his apology and wrap my arms around the same neck I was ready to strangle just a few moments ago. We hold each other tightly in a warm embrace. Still, I wonder if he's apologizing because he knows he has hurt my feelings, or if he's just trying to make up so he can get his hands in my cookie jar later on. Maybe I should strangle him anyway.

After driving around the block a couple of times, Andre finally finds a parking spot on a meter near Museum Park. Museum Park is a charming stretch of land, just southeast of downtown, off Lake Michigan, where the Adler Planetarium & Astronomy Museum, the Field Museum, and the Shedd Aquarium sit side by side housing a wealth of educational information about the constellation of stars above, the world's cultures and environments, and animals living beneath the sea.

The trunk of Andre's Nissan Maxima is stocked with enough items to make our private picnic last until the sun sets. First, he pulls out a large, burgundy blanket for us to lounge in the midday grass. A large green cooler is filled with ice to keep the juice, pop cans and water bottles cold. The small, yellow cooler will keep the apples, oranges and grapes fresh. Wheat bread, lunch meat, condiments, and plastic utensils are neatly placed in a wicker basket for us to feast on sandwiches. He's also included other snacks for us to munch on during the course of the day. A portable Sony stereo system and a CD holder full of music will allow us to keep our romantic party going well into the evening hours. He even brought a Scrabble board. Andre has really put a lot of effort and energy into making our afternoon along the lake memorable. I'm impressed.

I sit between Andre's long legs and lean back, resting my head on his chest. Once again, he's nibbling on my ear and kissing me on the neck. I'm glad I didn't strangle him after all.

"A penny for your thoughts," Andre whispered as he nibbled on my ear.

"I'm just enjoying the day," I responded. "It feels good being out here today."

He grinned. "I'm just glad the weather cooperated."

"It's perfect," I agreed. It's not too hot or too cool, and the breeze off the lake feels wonderful. I could just sit here forever."

"Yeah this is nice."

This has to be one of the most tranquil places on earth, or at least in the city of Chicago. Sitting here gives us a perfect view of the skyline and the corporate landmarks occupying the Loop. The John Hancock building, the Sears Tower, Prudential, and the big red CNA building are all within my focus. And even though the Ferris Wheel at Navy Pier is about two miles away, I still feel like I can touch it and go for a ride. I feel like I can go anywhere in the world right now. Calm, refreshing moments like this bring out the dreamer in me.

A homeless man pushing a shopping cart full of belongings brings me back to reality. The temperature is in the seventies, but he's wearing a winter coat. Downtown Chicago is the epitome of people who have and those who have not. A lot has changed over the years, but in many ways it's still the same.

High rise condominiums and lofts are reaching for the sky with upwardly mobile citizens calling the area home. I would love to live down here if I could afford it because I would be walking distance from the Magnificent Mile, popular entertainment venues and elite restaurants. Meanwhile, lower Wacker Drive remains the outdoor shelter for homeless people living under the footprints of the privileged. A homeless shelter is just a few yards away from half a million dollar condos.

The homeless man and his cart have moved on and the dreamer in me returns.

"So where are we headed, Andre?"

"You mean when we leave here?" he teased.

"No silly," I snapped, pinching him on the thigh with my fingernails. I was hoping my questions about the future wouldn't cause him to retreat. He didn't. Instead, he held me tighter.

"I'm just messin' with ya," he laughed, pulling me closer to him.

"Do you see me as a part of your future?"

"Yes."

"What do you think the future holds for us?"

"I don't know where we're headed, La-La. Only God knows that," he replied in a theological tone. "Let's just keep going and see where we end up."

I kept asking questions. "Where would we live?"

"In a big house in the city," he replied quickly.

"Where in the city would we live?"

"I don't know, La," he laughed uncomfortably. "I hadn't really thought about it."

"Would we take vacations every year?" I asked.

"Of course," he answered, lifting my braids and kissing me on the back of my neck; probably willing to say almost anything to make me shut up and stop asking questions. "I'll take you on a trip to the islands."

"Oh really," I cooed. "Which islands?"

"First I'll take you over to Stony Island; then we can go to Treasure Island; and then perhaps we can visit Blue Island," he laughed loudly.

I turned to look at him with a playful look of disapproval. Stony Island is a street on the south side, Treasure Island is a store on the north side, and Blue Island is a southwest suburb.

"I don't think so."

"Give me some time to think about it and I'll let you know."

"You need to do some thinking then."

I stopped interrogating Andre and tried to keep the rest of the afternoon light. However his lack of ambition troubled me. I'm a very goal oriented individual and want to make plans for the future. I need to know where I'm going in life, so I can map out my path. He's content on just living for the moment, going step by step with no specific course of action.

I guess it's impossible for him to know where he's taking me, if he doesn't even know where he's taking himself yet.

Andre's a lovely man, but he's a man without direction or purpose. Lord how did I end up with a bus driver who doesn't know where he's going? Sometimes I wonder if I should get off this bus and take another route.

24

JULIAN

The sound of the telephone startled me; it interrupted my sleep and awakened me from the strange dream I was having. The coming of dawn was set to usher in a new day and my alarm clock was thirty minutes early in fulfilling its daily obligation. Who could be calling me this early in the morning? I wiped the sleep from my eyes and turned on a lamp next to the bed so I could read the caller ID.

It was Roseland Community Hospital.

My heart began beating at an accelerated pace. I prayed for the best before picking up the receiver just before the fourth ring.

"Hello," I answered, in an anxious and fearful tone.

"Good morning, Julian."

"Hi Mama," I replied, as my heart rate decreased to a calmer pace.

"Are you okay?"

"I'm fine, Ma," I answered. "I was asleep and the phone scared me a little."

"I'm sorry, Julian" she laughed. "I just wanted to call you and let you know I'm out of intensive care and in a regular room now. They wheeled me in here about two hours ago."

"So you must be feeling better, huh?"

"I feel better than I did a few days ago. I'm not coughing up as much phlegm and the swelling is gone from my ankles and hands."

"Well that's good."

"I just wonder why they had to move me from ICU in the middle of the night. Maybe they had another sick person to come in who needed the ICU bed more than me."

"Maybe the people at the hospital knew you wanted to be near a phone so you could call and wake me up," I replied sarcastically.

"Ha ha ha," Mama giggled. "Maybe that was the reason why they did it. When my doctor comes in I'll be sure to tell him you said thanks."

"Well since you're feeling better and spreading good cheer all around the hospital, then why don't you tell Vanessa I said hello if you see her."

"I ain't in that," Mama countered.

"What?"

"You heard me," she snapped. "I ain't in that."

"Ma, you were in it before."

"Well I retired and ain't in it no more," she repeated. "If you wanna say hello to Vanessa, then you should call her yourself."

"So Ma, you mean to tell me your matchmaking career is over already?"

Mama didn't respond right away and silence dominated the early morning phone lines. Right then I realized I had played into her trap.

"I asked you about Vanessa a few months ago and you got all huffy and said 'I got other things on my mind right now' so I said I wasn't gonna ask you about her again."

"Ah come on, Ma," I pleaded with a laugh. "Why you have to go and get all historical on me and stuff?"

"Get what?" she asked.

"Historical, Ma," I laughed. "You know, Ma, you could have been a high school teacher because you always remembering history and bringing up stuff that happened a long time ago."

"Well, Julian, you gotta know where you came from in order to know where you goin'," she wisely suggested.

"Okay, Ma," I replied, not too anxious to engage in this type of philosophical dialogue so early in the morning.

"Okay nothing, you the one who brought up Vanessa," she quipped. "Not me."

"Yeah yeah yeah," I countered, not having much to say after Mama's clever response. "Well, Ma, I need to get off this phone so I can start getting ready for work."

"Oh so now you're in a hurry to get ready for work, huh?" she teased.

"You're a card, Ma."

"You're a card, too."

Mama would've done an excellent job of cross-examining witnesses in the courtroom.

The rhetoric at my court hearing was much calmer today. Gary Banks, the lawyer representing the State's Attorney's Office was still stalling in his attempt to produce an affidavit and Judge Nathan hadn't dismissed himself from the case yet. My attorney, Charles White and I were working diligently to step up our efforts to have a special grand jury take over the case. If nothing else, we at least want Judge Nathan to quash the search warrant he authorized so that I can have my computer and files returned. I have to attend another hearing next month. I'll be glad when all this is over. It's starting to take up too much of my time.

All of this legal confusion has greatly affected my professional and personal life. I'm busy trying to catch up on cases to satisfy my clients, and other than a teasing night with Annette, and a high speed chase from her stalking ex-boyfriend, my social activities have been non-existent. To add to my worries, I'm still concerned about Mama's deteriorating health.

I left the courthouse at 26th and California around three-thirty and made my way back to the Loop. The nice weather created congestion on the streets. Balmy temperatures encouraged people to bask in the afternoon sun which welcomed the first days of spring. I drove down Roosevelt Road and enjoyed the scenery. Kids were out on bikes and folks were cruising with their sunroofs open and tops down. Today would be a lovely day to have a convertible. I turned left on Canal Street and headed north to the Union Station parking garage.

Pedestrian traffic rushed towards me as I elbowed my way through crowds of downtown workers with the desire of a running back trying to reach the first down marker. They're in a hurry to catch Metra trains to exit the Loop as I made my way to the office for the first time today. It's four-fifteen. Ladies strutted with jackets under their arms while guys wore neckties that flapped in the wind. I walked swiftly across the bridge and heard my belly rumble in hunger. I haven't eaten all day and my stomach is growling louder than an angry dog. I stopped in a Subway on Jackson and got a sandwich, a bag of Ruffles and a large Coke to take with me to the office.

I entered my office and took a look around to make sure everything was the way I had left it. Ever since the FBI raided my office, I've felt nervous each time I entered my workplace. Now I know how a person feels after their home has been burglarized: completely violated.

I took off my jacket and got settled in at my desk. My mouth watered as I anticipated devouring my foot-long Subway melt. I dialed my voicemail and put in my password. Twelve new messages awaited me. The first message began playing as I took a bite into the sandwich consisting of ham, turkey and bacon with extra mayonnaise. Damn this is good. I licked my lips and wiped my mouth with a napkin. One of my clients left a message canceling his upcoming meeting with me. I deleted the message and took another bite. The second message was from a client advising me the date of his real estate closing had been postponed until next week. I grabbed a handful of potato chips and kicked off my loafers before moving on to the next message.

The third message was from a client requesting help with his taxes. Tax preparations for procrastinators will keep me busy for the next several days since April 15th is right around the corner, and of course, a lot of people have waited until the last minute. I sipped on my drink through a straw and listened to message number four as the cold liquid flowed to the back of my throat. This time the voice was that of an elderly lady inquiring about a living will and advanced directives.

Because of the recent legal war that had taken place involving Terri Schiavo, the importance of living wills and advanced directives were getting much more attention from people who normally wouldn't have given it a second thought. Schiavo was the Florida woman, who was severely brain-damaged and had relied on a feeding tube for fifteen years. Michael Schiavo, Terri's husband, had been engaged in a bitter court battle with her parents because he made the decision to have Terri's feeding tube removed.

The parents wanted to have the feeding tube reinserted, but Michael Schiavo insisted his wife never wanted to live in a vegetated state. Even though Mr. Schiavo had moved on and was now involved with another woman and has children, he was still Terri's husband and maintained power as her legal guardian. What a shame; a family dispute played out in the media, with politicians using the personal tragedy to advance their own agendas. The family battle had even continued after her death.

Seeing the family tragedy play out every night on cable news programs made me consider drawing up a living will for Mama. Lord knows I wouldn't want to battle Kendall and Lauren about how to address our mother's health and wishes. My siblings and I don't always see eye to eye, so the last thing I need is to be at odds with them regarding what's best for Mama. Dealing with Mama being sick is already stressful enough.

Besides, Mama has already said she doesn't want to be hooked up to any machines and wants to go in peace. Loved ones and caretakers often have difficult decisions to make. A lot of my friends are facing similar challenges in caring for aging parents. I guess that's the road we must travel and the cross we must bear. I wrote the elderly lady's phone number down so I can call her later on.

I filled my mouth with more Ruffles and washed them down with a large gulp of Coke. The sandwich and chips definitely hit the spot. I propped my feet up on my desk and leaned back in my chair, watching my toes wiggle through dark blue socks. The next message started. I put my pop down and removed my feet from the desk. I listened closely to make out the voice that sounded somewhat familiar.

"Hi Julian," said the female caller, speaking in a raspy tone. "This is Vanessa Stinson from Roseland Hospital. It's been a while since you and I spoke. I had a chance to check on your mom today.

She's in good spirits and was very talkative as usual. Your mother is something else. Take care, Julian."

Yeah she's something else alright.

25

KENDALL

Lately, I've been spending more nights in the city, so that I could keep a closer watch on things in the hood. Since Mama was still in the hospital, I've been able to stay at the house and use it as another location to switch up my whereabouts.

The day after Smiley was killed, I moved out of the spot I had on the block and hooked up with this little chick named Tammy. Tammy is a sexy, tattooed, hood-rat, in her early twenties, living in an apartment around the corner with her young children. Getting in with Tammy was simple because she was easily seduced by the money and the chance to live hood rich. All I had to do was say I was gonna do this and that and in no time I was in as the new man of the house. She lived in a run-down, two-flat building which rested between an abandoned building and a vacant lot. No one would ever expect to find me living here.

Tammy was trying to do right, but she was struggling. The crumbs she made working a part time job at McDonald's was hardly enough to feed herself and two sons, but the mice in her apartment were eating happy meals all day long. One night, I turned on the light in the kitchen, and saw two mice chilling in the middle of the floor. They squeaked and moved around as if they were about to step in the name of love at a family reunion. I stomped my foot and watched them run in different directions. The critters were moving so fast

I thought my vision was blurred. They raced across the floor like track stars on steroids trying out for the Olympics. Eating crumbs off the kitchen floor was one thing, but if I didn't get rid of them little bastards soon, they would've been up in the crib drinking Hennessy and watching the movie *Willard* on the new plasma television I was about to bring in.

Fortunately for me, one of my boys worked for a pest control company and came through and exterminated the place for a couple of bags of weed. I don't know how long I'll be staying here, but I plan on being comfortable while I'm around. I like to be comfortable wherever I am, whenever I'm there.

I took a bouquet of flowers and a get well balloon to Mama at the hospital. A petite nurse, wearing wire framed glasses, was leaning over the bed checking Mama's blood pressure when I entered the room. She had on blue hospital pants and a floral print top. Her shiny, black hair was pulled back into a bun with a large clip holding it in place. Seeing her leaning over the bed made me fantasize about waxing that ass doggystyle; she was in the perfect position to get blazed from behind. I could sit her little ass on my lap and spin her around like a top.

"Your blood pressure is much better today, Ms. Collins," she said, removing the black wrap from Mama's arm.

"Thanks, Vanessa," Mama replied.

"I got a feeling you may be able to go home soon."

"And I'm ret to go too," Mama said with a laugh. "I'm tired of this food."

The nurse laughed. "Oh you want some real food, huh?"

"Yes indeed."

"I heard that," the nurse agreed.

"Maybe you'll let me take you out to dinner," I said, interrupting their girl talk. The nurse turned around to face me, giving me a clear view of her appearance. The glasses and the conservative hairstyle reminded me of a brainy school teacher.

"Ms. Collins, you have a visitor bringing you gifts," she said, taking the flowers from my hand and putting them on a counter next to the bed. "These are beautiful."

"Umm hmm," Mama mumbled, showing a lack of enthusiasm.

"You sure are getting a lot of love and attention today," she added.

"Umm hmm," Mama repeated, looking at me out of the corner of her eye. "Vanessa this is my son, Kendall."

"Hello Kendall."

"Nice to meet you, Vanessa," I said, extending my hand to shake hers.

"Nice meeting you, also, Kendall," she said, gripping my hand with her long, slender fingers. "So this is your other son?" she asked, turning her attention to Mama.

"Umm hmm," Mama mumbled.

"Who's the oldest, you or Julian?" she asked.

"Julian is," I smiled. I see she has already met the golden child.

Nurse Vanessa cleaned off the tray next to Mama's bed and threw away paper cups and wrappers. She adjusted the height of Mama's bed and made her way towards the exit.

"Ms. Collins I need to go check on some other patients down the hall. I'll try to get back in here to say goodnight before I get off work."

I turned around and watched her leave. She looks like a librarian, but I bet she's probably the biggest freak in the world. Yeah, I could pin that small frame up against the wall real good.

"Okay, I'll see you, Vanessa," Mama replied, in a tone that seemed very familiar. She acted like she was more excited about having Vanessa in the room than me.

I started to lean over the bed to kiss Mama on the forehead, but her icy attitude froze me out, so I kept my distance and sat down in the chair next to the window. Hopefully, the rays from the afternoon sun will take some of the frost out of the room. Sometimes I feel like Mama forgot she gave birth to me also. Maybe she wants to forget. That's why I don't come around more.

"So what blew you this way?" Mama asked, sarcastically.

"I just wanted to see you," I answered sheepishly. "That's all."

"Umm hmm," she chided. "You sure took your time about it. It's almost time for me to go home now."

I should've just sent the flowers with a card and called it a day. I don't need this bullshit. How can she love one son so much and hate the other. According to her, the sun rises and sets with Julian, but I guess I'm just some fuckin' storm cloud ready to blow in and destroy some shit. Sometimes I feel like she holds me responsible for what Daddy did to her. It's like she looks at me and sees him.

I'm his namesake and bear a strong resemblance to the pictures I've seen, but I never really knew him. I was too young when he died to have formed any kind of relationship with the man. Mama is always talking that I'm just like my daddy bullshit. What the fuck does that mean? And how is it I'm the only one of the children who happens to be just like him? They make it seem like I'm the one who got all of the fucked up traits and nobody else. Julian and La-La are God's little angels all dressed in white, but I'm the son of Lucifer dressed in black with a red tail dangling from my ass. I admit, Mama didn't raise me to be a drug dealer, but she didn't raise me to be a pussy either. She encouraged me to be tough. It was as if she knew I had it in me.

I remember getting into a fight at school when I was in the fourth grade with a boy named Chris Phillips. Chris was a punk kid who enjoyed playing the dozens, and talking about kids' parents. He called Mama all kind of names and then talked about my father, cracking jokes and laughing about me not having a daddy. That punk didn't even care about my father being dead; he just wanted to get a laugh. It was on after that. At first, we fought during recess and then agreed to meet again after school on the playground at three-fifteen.

The older boys on the playground surrounded us and instigated the matter by saying shit like the baddest one hit my hand and pushing us into each other to force contact. Deep down, I was a little scared because Chris was bigger than me, but I was still willing to fight because he had talked about my daddy. Here I was defending the honor of a man I hardly knew, who had been killed while fucking around with a stank ass, home-wrecking ho behind my mother's back.

Chris threw wild looping punches and fought like a little bitch. Somehow he was able to swing and kick at the same time. Chris hit me in the mouth and kicked me in the shins, but I was determined to go toe to toe with his punk ass. We fought all the way to my house.

As usual, La-La ran inside and told Mama. Mama came out on the porch and broke up the fight. She told Chris to shake my hand and make up, but he wouldn't do it. Mama asked Chris about his parents, and he laughed at her and said it was none of her damn business. His bad attitude had Mama fuming. She ordered me to kick his ass, and said she wouldn't let me inside the house until I won the fight. Mama went back inside, locked the screen door, and looked on with her arms folded across her breast and a scowl on her face.

Chris laughed at me and said he was going to cause me to have to live in a foster home, because after he kicked my ass Mama would never let me back in the house again. I got mad and got even by kicking him twice in the nuts. He wasn't laughing after that. A swift boot to the balls always ended a fight in a hurry, and this time was no exception. While Chris was bent over with his hands clutching his jewels, I pounded him in the face until I saw blood flowing from his nose and lip. I won the fight.

Mama watched everything unfold and unlocked the screen door to welcome me in the house. I strutted inside with the pride of a champion, chest stuck out, ready to receive my crown. I watched an episode of *The Three Stooges* and laughed while basking in my glory. Mama rewarded me with a ham and cheese sandwich and a tall glass of red Kool-Aid. Nobody fucked with me after that. I earned major props in the hood that day. Everyone knew Kendall Collins could fight and would never back down.

Army & Lou's has long been one of the finest places to eat in the city. Located on the south side, a block east of King Drive at 75th Street, the restaurant specialized in soul food; the kind of food Mama used to cook for us when we were little. I was tired of eating bacon double cheeseburgers and pizzas, so I knew a couple of smothered pork chops, with a side order of greens, sweet potatoes and two pieces of corn bread would be a welcome treat to my stomach right now.

Instead of dining in, I got my dinner to go. Within minutes, I was back in my truck headed west towards the Dan Ryan Expressway. I increased the volume of my stereo and inhaled the aroma of the soul food causing my stomach to scream louder than James Brown. I was feeling good and couldn't wait to get home and get my grub on.

I pulled down the visor and tried to decide which CD I wanted to listen to on the drive home. All of a sudden, a brown Ford sedan pulled in front of me and cut me off; a case full of CDs fell in my lap and on the floor. Before I could gather myself, they were screaming and cussing at me with guns in my face.

"Get the fuck outta the car with your hands up!" shouted a big, dark-skinned guy, wearing an orange Illini T-shirt with a blue and orange Illini baseball cap.

"Keep your fuckin' hands where we can see 'em!" yelled a short and stocky, light-skinned guy wearing a Nike cap turned backwards. "Lean up against the truck."

My heart was beating hard enough to rip a hole through my chest. Once I gathered my composure, I realized they were rogue cops. I was pissed at myself for not being more alert and getting caught off guard.

"This a fancy ass vehicle you pushin'," said the dark-skinned guy in the Illini cap.

"Real fancy," added the light-skinned guy.

"You got any goodies for us in the truck?" the dark-skinned guy asked as he ran his hands through my pockets, pulling out close to a thousand dollars in cash. "If you got this much money in your pocket, I know you got some other goodies in the truck for us to grab," he warned while striking me in the kidneys with his night-stick. "I wish we had the canine unit with us so we could sniff that muthafucka out real good."

"Oooh," I groaned as the dark-skinned cop used excessive force and slammed my head onto the hood of my truck.

"What's this all about?" I asked.

"Don't worry about it muthafucka!" hollered the dark-skinned cop, shoving my head back down on the truck. "It's 'bout whatever the fuck we want it to be 'bout."

The hot engine made the surface of the hood warm; the heat burned the side of my face. A million thoughts ran through my mind as the other cop searched the inside of my truck looking to find or plant evidence. I was glad I didn't have any drugs with me.

The nine-millimeter gun under the seat was registered in my name. Damn! Where was an innocent bystander with a video camera when I needed them? Five-O is jacking me in broad daylight in the middle of 75th Street.

Black cops are just as scandalous as the white cops; they're gangbangers with a badge. I'm confused because I don't know these guys and I'm not sure why they pulled me over. Neither of them ever acknowledged me by name so I'm thinking this was just a random jack. They just saw me driving a shiny black Escalade and figured I was rolling with a lot of loot in my pocket. They figured right. Crooked ass cops.

As the right side of my head remained pressed to the truck, I saw an elderly lady walk by. Immediately, I heard Mama's voice speaking inside my head saying *I pray to God you don't break my heart.*

"Should we take this muthafucka in for questioning?" asked the dark-skinned cop as the light-skinned cop continued to search my glove compartment and under the seats of my vehicle.

"What the fuck man," the light-skinned replied. "It's almost time for our shift to end. I don't feel like dealing with all this shit now. I'm ready to go home, eat a hot meal and lay up on some ass."

"Well if we go and get sumpin' to eat, our Escalade driving big shot has agreed to treat," said the dark-skinned cop, holding the wad of hundred dollar bills he took from my pocket.

"Man, fuck that," laughed the light-skinned cop. "I got my food right here, I ain't gotta go get nuttin' to eat. Ima eat me some pork chops, some candy yams, some greens and some corn bread. Man this shit looks good."

"I got an idea," the dark-skinned cop said, finally releasing my head from the warm surface of the truck.

"What?"

"If you share what you got, I'll share what I got."

"Of course," agreed the light-skinned cop. "We thick as thieves. Besides them Benjamins you got over there will last a lot longer than this dinner I got 'cause I'm hungry as all get out."

"Well buddy since you cooperated with us, me and my partner gonna let you slide this time. Now be careful 'cause we gon' be lookin' for you again," the dark-skinned cop promised with a sarcastic smirk on his face. "Oh yeah, and thanks for the dinner and the donation."

26

LAUREN

Shock and disappointment covered Andre's dark, brown eyes with a moist daze as he fought to hold back tears. There's no need to explore the window of his soul for evidence; the pain is written all over his face. He sighed and took deep breaths, trying to decrease the impact of the heartbreak. It's too late. His mouth is wide open with confusion and dejection has him gasping for air. Andre never saw it coming. I never wanted to hurt him. It just happened. Things have changed. Besides, I'm not sure if we have long term compatibility, so it's best to end it now before investing too much emotionally.

"What are you saying, La?" Andre asked.

"I think we need to take a break," I urged, biting my lower lip nervously as we sat in my car near Pirie Park.

I turned off the radio to avoid distractions from the on air personalities chattering about nonsense. People were in the park getting exercise, but after a while it seemed as though no one else in the world existed. Andre and I were left alone with all of our memorable months and timeless thoughts. The warm climate steered a breeze of silence and awkwardness through the car. Dark clouds began moving in to make its presence known, letting us know a storm of life would soon be raging.

I saw a little girl with cornrows like mine spinning on the carousel near the swings. The scene made me ponder my predicament and mindset. I was praying God would stop the merry-go-round of life long enough so I could get off for a little while and regroup. The world was turning too fast and the constant motion had me dizzy. I've been feeling overwhelmed ever since Mama called me to take her to the hospital the night of the Jill Scott concert. I felt guilty about being selfish because I was angry at Mama after I had to miss the concert and stay with her in the emergency room. How could I be so self-centered? What was I thinking? That's my mother. I had to ask God to forgive me for my selfish attitude.

Stress is altering my way of thinking. It seemed as though I'm being pulled in too many different directions. How can I be productive at work, be a caregiver for Mama, be a good lover and companion to Andre, and still have time for me? I don't think my current state of mind is conducive to me being in a relationship. The world is closing in on me and if I turn in the wrong direction I'll probably step on my own shadow. I'm suffocating and need room to breathe. Being by myself allows me to know exactly which moves I want to make next.

"What did I do?" Andre inquired in bewilderment.

"You didn't do anything, Andre," I assured.

"Well why, La?" he asked. "I thought everything between us was cool."

"It's not you, Andre, it's me," I replied, shaking my head as I felt the tears welling up in my eyes. "Andre, you're a wonderful guy with an enormous heart. I just need time to gather myself and regroup. My life is in chaos and I have too many things coming at me from different directions at the same time. Right now, I just have too much going on and need to take control of my life."

"What about me?" Andre sighed, rubbing his hand across his face. "I love you, Lauren. I need you."

"Andre, I love you, I care about you, but right now I need myself," I pleaded, trying to get him to understand my emotions. He's too focused on his own heartache to fully understand my pain.

"Whoa," he sighed, shaking his head. "You caught me by surprise with this."

"It's not something I envisioned myself saying," I confessed as I caressed his sweaty palms. "Things have been happening so fast for me lately. It's getting crazy and nerve-racking at the insurance company; Mama's condition is worsening; and right now I'm just trying to figure out my next move, Andre. I'm trying to decide if I want to move back home with Mama or have her move in with me. I got all these decisions I need to make, and I'm afraid. I'm scared to death. And right now I need to be able to make decisions without impacting the life of someone else."

"That's what I'm here for, La," Andre begged. "I want you to lean on me so I can help you get through it. You shouldn't have to deal with all this stuff alone. La-La relationships are all about being there to help each other go through tough times. If I can't be with you when times are tough, then what's the point?"

"Andre," I pleaded. "Please . . . just let me have some room to breath."

"But La . . ."

"Andre," I interrupted him. "Please just give me a little room to breathe."

Finally he consented. "I will."

The drive back to Andre's house seemed like the longest ride of my life. Our hearts pounded to communicate with each other, but our tongues remained mute. My lack of concentration on the road caused me to hit two huge potholes before reaching the street Andre lives on. I just broke up with my man and now I'm about to tear up my car. Life seems to be full of unexpected holes for us to fall in.

I parked my car in front of Andre's house, but didn't turn off the engine. We embraced, kissed each other gently on the lips, and said our goodbyes.

Falling in love is tremendous; falling out of love is traumatic.

My eyes watched Andre walk up the porch to his front door with his head down and his broad shoulders slouched. He never looked back in my direction. Tears rolled down my cheek as I saw him unlock the door and enter his home.

Thoughts flooded my mind with the force of a tsunami. I wonder if I'll ever step through those doors to be with him again. I wonder if I'll ever lounge with him again on the leather sofa in the living room and watch television. I wonder if I'll ever enjoy another bottle of wine while listening to a Will Downing CD with him again. I wonder if I'll ever have another breakfast served by him in bed. I wonder if I'll ever pray with him in the middle of the night again. I even wonder if I'll ever wear the black, silk shirt he gave me to sleep in when I spent the night there. Deep down, I wonder if this is just a brief intermission or the end of our love story. But most of all, I wonder if I've made the biggest mistake of my life by making my move too soon. Lord I hope I don't regret what I just did.

 I sped away from the scene of the crime, hoping I wouldn't have to pay the price for stealing and breaking Andre's heart somewhere down the road. He didn't deserve it. I just don't think I can give a relationship my all right now; my emotions have taken a detour. Maybe I shouldn't approach life from an all or nothing perspective, but I've always been this way. I need to give my best in everything I do. That's me, Lauren Janine Collins, the perfectionist. To give less than one hundred percent would be cheating. I don't want to cheat life or love. It wouldn't be fair to Andre or me.

 I left work early so I could pick Mama up from the hospital since the doctor is going to release her today. This time Mama had been in the hospital for twenty-eight days; that's a long time to be away from home. However, before going to the hospital, I needed to stop by the house and tidy things up and get the place suitable for Mama's homecoming. Also, I needed to pick up some clothes and a portable oxygen tank for Mama to have for her return home.

 I park my car in front of the house and admire the bungalow style house I grew up in with new appreciation. The neighborhood is relatively stable, but time always brings about a change. Many of the neighbors who had hosted and attended block club meetings back in the day are no longer around to watch over each other's house the way they used to in the past. A lot of the people on the block who were here when I was a child have either died or are now near death. Many of those suffering from failing health now reside in assisted living facilities. The thought of Mama in a nursing home scared me and sent chills down my spine.

 Next door to Mama's house was where the Gilberts used to live. They were an older couple who were both fair-skinned enough to pass for white. Their kids were already grown so they treated us like an extension to their family. The matriarch, Maureen Gilbert, was a very sweet lady who baked cookies for kids in the neighborhood and gave out lots of candy on Halloween. We called her the candy lady. Everyone liked going to the Gilbert house for trick or treat because she always filled our bags with miniature Snickers, Now & Laters, Tootsie Rolls and Jolly Rancher wine candy.

The patriarch, Melvin Gilbert, was a lanky gentleman with white hair who loved to play ball with Julian and Kendall. They used to play running bases in the front of the house or softball in the alley. Mr. Gilbert was too old to swing the bat or run, but he enjoyed being able to pitch and catch while my brothers ran around until Mama called for them to come inside. Also, the Gilberts allowed us to stay at their home and eat dinner if Mama was working late.

Across the street from us lived the Newman family. They were as different from the Gilberts as night and day, in complexion and attitude. Mr. Newman was a short, bald-headed, evil man who seemed to hate all the kids in the neighborhood. He used to get mad and threaten to sick his dog on the boys who let their baseball roll in his yard or on his grass. It's hard to imagine Mrs. Newman being worse than Mr. Newman, but she was.

Mrs. Newman was a dark-skinned, fat woman, with bulging eyes which looked like they were about to jump out of her nappy head when she got angry. Her eyes were so wide that it always looked like she had been surprised by a ghost. She had big lips and a permanent frown. Kids on the block referred to her as the mean lady. We didn't bother to stop at the Newman house on Halloween because we were afraid the mean lady would put a razor blade in our apples.

Both families are gone from the block and I don't know the new residents taking their place. One thing I do know, the people now living in the Newman house need to cut the grass and do some yard work, or at least hire some Mexicans to do it. The weeds and dandelions are the eyesore of the block. This is the street I grew up on, but I'm nothing more than a stranger on the block now.

I entered the house and was startled by the sound of men talking in the kitchen, and the smell of smoke coming from the same direction. Fear almost caused me to turn around and leave, but foolishness made me stay in the house. The chatter didn't stop, so they must not have heard me come in. Wall to wall carpet allowed me to step lightly without making a lot of noise. The closer I got to the kitchen, the voices became more recognizable, and the smell of smoke got stronger.

"Kendall, what's going on in here?" I asked, shocked by the sight of him and Ray counting money with guns and drugs covering the kitchen table.

"You better be careful rolling up in here like that," Kendall warned, his bottom lip and right eye swollen; a large gash on his forehead was just above his blackened right eye. "You'll fuck around and get blasted coming up in here unannounced."

I was too shocked to respond to his statement.

"You not gonna speak to me, La-La?" Ray asked, with a cigarette dangling between his fingers and a lustful grin spread across his rugged face, gazing at me from head to toe.

I replied unenthusiastically. "Hi Ray."

I always had an idea what my brother was involved in, but now it was staring me in the face, in our mother's kitchen of all places. To say it was too close to home would be an understatement. Here I am on my way to pick up Mama from the hospital, and my older brother is in the kitchen, with his renegade henchman, packaging drugs and counting blood money in a cash machine at the same table Mama eats breakfast and drinks orange juice every morning. I can't believe my eyes. I've never seen so much money at one time.

"Kendall, you and Ray need to get your shit and get out of here!" I ordered, trying to be stern, but hoping the confrontation with my older brother doesn't get out of hand, and hoping he doesn't laugh at my uncharacteristic use of profanity. "Mama is being released from the hospital today and I want this place cleaned up before I go to pick her up."

"Oooh weee," grinned Ray. "You a feisty lil' number, La-La wit' your sexy skirt and high heels on. Shit Kendall, I need to drop dem hood-rats I been fuckin' 'round wit' and get me a professional woman like baby sister. Yo La-La you got any friends you can hook a nigga like me up wit'?"

"Please," I mumbled under my breath, not in the mood to deal with Ray and his drunken nonsense, wondering how I can get this place in order before going to get Mama.

"You got a man, La-La?" Ray asked.

"Ice that shit, Ray!" Kendall snapped.

"Kendall, Julian would have a fit if he knew you were doing this is in Mama's house. You shouldn't bring your illegal activities into our mother's home."

"Fuck Julian!" Kendall barked with a menacing scowl that was unfamiliar to me. "You act like Julian gon' roll up in this muthafucka and kick my ass or some shit!"

"Yo Kendall," Ray teased. "If big brother, Julian 'bout to roll through and save the day, then maybe I need to go and get more artillery."

"Goddammit, Ray!" Kendall shouted, slamming his hand down on the table, causing one of the guns to fall to the floor. "Stay the fuck outta this!"

My heart skipped a beat as the cold steel hit the floor. Fear had my chest pounding fast enough to go into cardiac arrest. Oh Jesus! I'm scared of guns. Pearly white teeth frantically gnawed my bottom lip as I thanked God for not allowing the gun to fire shots accidentally in the house.

Kendall is angry and on the edge.

"Yo, dawg," Ray retreated with his arms in the air. "I ain't even tryna get caught in the middle of no family shit. Things seemed kinda tense so I was just tryna lighten the mood a bit. But I see the two of you need to resolve some shit, so I'm gonna raise the fuck up and break camp so y'all can have some space."

"Thank you," Kendall said, reaching down to pick the gun up from the floor.

Ray gathered his things and his portion of the money. He walked by me with the reek of alcohol and cigarette smoke on his bad breath. Ray disgusts me. He always has and always will. I didn't like him when he asked me out when I was in high school and I still don't like him to this day.

Ray was always vulgar and loud, too much cheap liquor flowed through his bloodstream. I can't stand nasty, trifling ass men who disrespect everyone they come in contact with and that pretty much sums Ray up in a nutshell. In my opinion, Ray has always been a bad influence on Kendall and had introduced him to the wrong crowd.

When they were young boys, Ray and Kendall would throw stray cats off roofs and out of two story windows just to see if the flying feline would land on its feet. They said they were just trying to find out if the cat really had nine lives. For them, it was entertainment. They were downright inhumane. Ray was a bad influence when they were kids and he still is.

I watched Ray walk through the living room to leave the house, and immediately followed him to the door so I could lock it and keep him from getting back in. Ugh! Goodbye and good riddance! As much as Ray drinks and smokes he should keep a truck of breath mints parked close by. I need to spray the house with a bottle of Febreze to remove some of the stench he left behind.

I returned to the kitchen to find Kendall still sitting at the table with a gun, money and drugs at his reach. Instead of joining him at the table, I stood at the doorway next to the refrigerator to keep a safe distance between me and his element. Sitting at the table with him would've put me too close to the danger, too close to the dirt. I've never seen my older brother like this. Usually, he's calm, cool and collected, never rattled or out of control.

Ebony in tone with skin smoother than a chocolate swirl, Kendall was always a lady's man whose penetrating eyes could hypnotize the souls and break down the wills of women young and old. I stared at the bruises and scars taking up space on his normally unblemished, cocoa colored face and tried to understand how it had gotten that way. His gaze told a violent story today. Now he appeared raw and vicious, much more dangerous than the big brother who used to threaten male admirers walking me home from school when I was a teenager.

Kendall stared back at me. His eyes were cold and conniving.

I don't like what I see.

27

JULIAN

Anticipation has me pacing back and forth on the hardwood floors of my home anxiously awaiting my first date with Vanessa. My mind has been wavering back and forth on where to go and what to do. I want to do something different that will allow us to hang out and have some fun while being able to talk and get to know each other at the same time. It seems like I'm always under pressure to plan the first date by suggesting something exciting, enjoyable and fresh while keeping the mood light and relaxed.

In a way, its ridiculous how much I contemplate over an initial outing with a woman; spending large sums of energy and money trying to make a good impression. It's totally in character for me to go on a date looking sharp as a tack, carrying a bouquet of flowers with tickets to a first run play and reservations at a fancy restaurant. The idea of dinner and a movie will be too typical and uneventful, but I don't want to go overboard either. I had already made the mistake of spending too much money on Annette with nothing to show for it. Now, I'm ready to turn my attention to Vanessa.

So far, the telephone conversations between Vanessa and I have been both humorous and easy going. We shared a laugh about Mama's not so subtle ways of playing cupid in trying to hook us up. As a matter of fact, Vanessa expressed deep admiration for the way I cared for Mama. She said being a nurse had allowed her to witness children who had turned their backs on their aging parents. Vanessa told me about a lady who was in a room down the hall from Mama, who had been in the hospital three weeks and was crying because none of her five children had been there to visit her.

Vanessa understands what I'm dealing with in seeing my mother age. In my opinion, the old adage about women being attracted to a man who maintained a good relationship with his mother was a bunch of crap. Many of the selfish women I had encountered viewed a man's mother as competition and a threat. I had even been labeled a Mama's boy by a woman unable to understand the love I have for my mother. All of this made me appreciate Vanessa even more. I really hope Vanessa and I can hit it off and have good chemistry since she and Mama already like each other.

Vanessa lives on the southeast side of Chicago, not far from the lakefront in a neighborhood known as South Shore; an isolated area known for its large, multi-unit apartment buildings with spacious rooms. South Shore is also home to the city's largest number of section eight residents, which sometimes welcomed a group of unsavory characters who don't always give a damn about how they may negatively affect the property values of the area they dwell in because they're living cheap.

Some of the residents might not have known the value of the area, but real estate developers knew. Shrewd white folks with deep pockets and oil rich Arabs were grabbing as many abandoned buildings as they could because they knew they would be able to rehab them and charge an arm and a leg or a tenant's first born son in rent.

I heard the sound of the train moving northwest down the Metra tracks on Exchange Avenue as I looked for a parking space close to Vanessa's apartment. So far, I'd been around the block three times without having any luck. Being prompt was important to me, so I called Vanessa from the car and explained my challenges in finding a place to park. She understood and agreed to come down and meet me outside. I double parked next to a white Volvo in front of Vanessa's building and eagerly awaited her arrival.

Vanessa's understated appearance as a nurse in hospital scrubs and wire framed glasses failed to give her natural beauty its proper justice. I was expecting to see the same conservative looking lady whose warmth and care had won over the heart of my mother in Roseland Hospital, but that wasn't the woman I saw walking through the iron-gated courtyard with the pleasant smile. I waited for Vanessa to walk to the car, but she stopped at the edge of the curb. After a momentary brain cramp, I realized she wanted me to get out and open the door. Oops. I guess I was just captivated by how amazing she looked. I quickly got out and met her curbside, opening the passenger door to help her get in the car.

Gone are the wire-rimmed glasses that I've been accustomed to seeing Vanessa wear at the hospital. Contact lenses instead of spectacles allow me to get a clear view of the soft brown eyes that had looked after my mom in recent weeks. Coiffed hair is fluffed and flowing, freed from its style restrictive bun. Low riding, hip-hugging jeans reveal the petite, curvaceous figure previously concealed by floral printed medical garb. Four-inch patent leather pumps gave her added height and made my temperature and nature rise at the same time.

I sure hope Vanessa has a stethoscope in her purse because I think I'm about to have a heart attack, and will need some outpatient rehabilitation treatment real soon. She can revive my spirit anytime. Looking that fine can bring a brother like me back to life in a hurry. Damn girl.

During an earlier conversation, I recalled Vanessa mentioning she enjoyed playing arcade and video games, so I decided to drive down to Dave & Buster's for an evening of lighthearted fun. The affluent Gold Coast area is always congested and finding parking is always difficult. I drove slower than usual, hoping to find a spot on the street near a meter.

Parking garages in the city are outrageously priced, and I don't want to take a chance of parking illegally and getting a ticket or having my car towed. I explained to Vanessa my dislike for paying for parking, and to my surprise, she agreed, and supported me in my efforts of being patient and driving around the block, as I hoped to find a driver pulling out of a spot not far from Dave & Buster's.

"There's a guy coming out across the street, Julian," Vanessa said, pointing in the direction of a man driving a convertible Nissan

350ZX. "If you can make a U-turn you can get the spot when he pulls out."

I wheeled my Infiniti coupe around in the middle of Clark Street and snatched the space before an Asian man in a Honda Accord could beat me to the spot. This is excellent because we're right down the street from Dave & Buster's.

"Thanks Vanessa."

"You're welcome," she grinned, with eyes sparkling with the brightness of a child heading to an amusement park for the first time.

I went around to the passenger side of the car and opened the door for Vanessa. I looked at my watch and realized it was after six o'clock so the meter didn't have to be fed. This is perfect. I helped Vanessa out of the car and smiled.

"You must be good luck," I said, praising her for helping me find a good spot as we walked down Clark Street.

"You're welcome," she replied. "I hate paying for parking also."

"If you keep on coming through in the clutch like that," I grinned. "I'll have to give you some coupons."

Vanessa stopped in her tracks. "No you didn't."

I turned and looked at her with the expression of an innocent child. Her lips creased into a surprised smile. I doubled over into a laugh. I was feeling good about myself and being with Vanessa.

Once inside, I went to the cashier and got power cards for Vanessa and me. We made our way around the multi-level facility playing games with the enthusiasm of children on Christmas morning. Vanessa's very competitive, and took pride in beating me in skeeball. However, I saved my manhood by winning the racing video games and hitting the most points in the basketball Super Shots game.

It was good natured fun and I enjoyed having Vanessa walking beside me as we moved through the arcade. She had my full attention and was definitely being admired by many of the other guys in the arcade as well. I was able to walk around with my head up with added pep in my step.

After playing a wide selection of arcade games, Vanessa and I went to the dining area and got a bite to eat. Both of us were hungry.

Vanessa studied the menu for a meal without meat while I looked for something healthy since I was already aware of Vanessa's attention to maintaining a proper diet. I ordered catfish even though I had a taste for a bacon cheeseburger.

Vanessa and I engaged in conversation as we waited for our food to arrive. My mood was carefree, however she appeared careful. The experience I'd gained as a serial dater caused me to closely study her mannerisms and body language. Her posture was guarded and not as relaxed as when we were playing the arcade games. Vanessa sat in an upright position with her arms folded across her small breast. A yellow traffic light flashed in my mind, advising me to slow down and proceed cautiously down Romance Road.

"So Julian, do you date a lot?" she asked with her arms still folded across her breast and seriousness in her eyes.

"Not really," I answered.

"Why not?" she asked, in a raspy yet thought-provoking tone.

"Well lately I've been spending so much time worrying about Mama and dealing with legal stuff that I really haven't had the time to do a lot of dating," I said, using Mama and work as an excuse for not being more successful with women. "What about you, Vanessa, do you do a lot of dating?"

She shook her head. "No."

"You're an attractive lady," I said, studying her childlike features. "I'm sure guys are eager to take you out."

"Yeah until I'm able to read through their bullshit," she declared.

Just then the waiter arrived with our meals; his perfect timing allowed me to regroup and digest Vanessa's statement. Her words were stern and direct. I could tell she meant every word she said. She may have been gentle while dealing with patients, but her hospital garb had been replaced by a protective armor covering her heart. Her use of profanity caught me by surprise.

She continued after the waiter left. "I'm just tired of guys playing games."

"Sounds like you have some battle scars?" I asked, before sipping on a large glass of Coke through a straw.

"I've had enough," she admitted. "That's for sure."

"Is it hard for guys to get close to you?" I inquired.

Vanessa nodded. "Yes it is, for many reasons."

"You care to explain?" I asked, trying to get to the core of what made this lovely lady with the tough exterior tick; somehow yearning to pull the hurt out of her heart.

Vanessa chewed and swallowed her salad and sipped water threw a long straw before gathering herself to answer my question.

"I guess I don't let guys get too close to me because I'm afraid of being hurt," she replied. "Five years ago my fiancée was killed two weeks before we were supposed to get married. And unfortunately, the guys I've met since his death have been jerks who don't know how to treat a lady. If it doesn't seem right to me early on, then I don't let them waste my time."

"I'm sorry, Vanessa," I said, apologetically. "I didn't know your fiancée had been killed."

I felt bad because I wanted things to remain light, but now the evening had turned serious all of a sudden.

"It's okay," she shrugged. "You had no way of knowing."

"I'm sorry."

"No problem," she assured. "Talking about it is how I got through it."

"I'm sure it had to be tough."

"Life can be tough sometimes, but we have to keep on living and move on."

"True," I agreed. "However, sometimes moving on is easier said than done."

"Yeah, you're right about that."

"What happened?" I inquired. "That's if you don't mind me asking."

"He was murdered," she professed, taking another sip of water before continuing her story. "William, my fiancée went to pick up his sister who was working in a lounge as a barmaid. For some reason, her boss wanted to meet with her after the lounge closed. William was tired because he had worked all day and was anxious to take his sister home so he could go home and get some sleep."

Vanessa paused and took a sip of water as I waited patiently for her to continue.

"Instead of William waiting in the lounge until the meeting was over, he decided to go and wait in his car. A couple of guys who were in the club also had been watching him with intentions of robbing him. When William went to the car, they followed him and put a gun to his head and forced him into the trunk. The two men rode around for about an hour getting high before taking William to a nearby alley. They made him get out of the car and shot him twice in the head, once through the temple and once through the brain."

I shook my head in disbelief and in frustration about how blacks continue to kill each other. The value of another black life isn't worth a damn.

"Did they catch the guys who killed your fiancée?"

"Umm hmm," she nodded. "The police caught them the next day. They were convicted and received life in prison without parole. In court, they described it as a robbery gone wrong. They said they weren't planning on killing William, but he kept making eye contact, so they decided to kill him and be done with it."

Vanessa's recollection of William being murdered in cold blood was chilling and left me speechless. My mind traveled back to my childhood and revisited the day I learned my father was dead. I can still hear the sound of Mama wailing and screaming in a high pitched tone.

I stared at Vanessa, but remained silent.

Just then it hit me. Now I understood her connection with Mama. They shared a common bond. Mama had lost her husband to violence and Vanessa had lost her fiancée in the same way. And in some ways, both were still trying to put the pieces of their broken hearts back together again.

Mama had spent many days and nights in the hospital, and Vanessa hadn't hidden her pleasure for visiting and checking on my mother during her time there. They seemed to have more than your typical nurse/patient relationship. I wonder if the two of them had ever shared their pain with each other. Or were they just able to look into each other's eyes and know?

28

KENDALL

It took several days for the bruises on my face to heal from the abuse I received from the hands of Officer Unfriendly and his dinner snatching sidekick. I'm getting tired of this game now; they're too many players involved, and it's becoming more and more difficult to tell the good guys from the bad guys. Easy money can make even the straightest arrows shoot crooked.

Rogue cops are robbing dealers and selling more narcotics on the streets than a Mexican drug cartel. They're being paid off by the higher-ups, but they're still stealing our stash and cash. These thug cops are getting over like fat cats running away with all the cheese. They even stole my food. Rat bastards. In the meantime, I'm looking over my shoulder, changing locations on the fly, trying to sleep with one black eye open.

Ever since those undercover cops jacked me with excessive force on 75th Street, I've been changing vehicles and being low key. I stopped driving my Escalade and started cruising around town in either my black, convertible Ford Mustang or white BMW. The Escalade rolling on twenty-four-inch spinning rims attracted too much attention.

Because of my hookup on the west side, getting luxury vehicles at a reduced price used to be as easy as taking a test drive around the block. Unfortunately, the feds and the Chicago Police were putting brakes on that ride as well. Two auto dealership owners had been arrested recently and charged with federal racketeering. It had been a cool set up for us because we were able to pay cash for top flight vehicles without the dealerships disclosing the transactions. Guys like me were able to show up at the dealership with a duffel bag full of loot and pay for Benzes, Jaguars and Cadillacs in neat stacks of hundreds. It was sweet. I had come a long way from the days when I used to say *that's my car* when drivers zoomed past me in flashy cars. Now kids were pointing at me when I drove by.

The guys running the illegal car dealerships looked like some bin Laden terrorist type muthafuckas, but I didn't give a shit because they were helping me roll in style. It was a win-win situation for all parties involved.

I ordered some flowers and had them delivered to Mama for Mother's Day. I've been moving around and changing my cell phones so much that Mama probably doesn't know how to reach me, and I'm not sure if she would if she could anyway. Julian and Lauren usually take her out to some overcrowded restaurant for dinner on Mother's Day, but they didn't tell me about it. I can't really blame them because most times I didn't go when I was invited in the past anyway. I guess I was too busy handling business and doing my own thing.

I miss my family now.

La-La is probably still pissed about catching me at Mama's house with drugs, money and guns all over the kitchen table. That was fucked up. That was a real stupid move on my part. It seems like La-La is always the one catching me doing some shit I shouldn't have been doing.

One time La-La caught me and Ray in the garage getting high. I was about eighteen or nineteen at the time and had been smoking weed for several years. Normally, I wouldn't get high anywhere near the house, but on this particular day, Ray and I decided to go in the garage and light up a joint. We thought the coast was clear because Mama and La-La were gone to the beauty shop and Julian was away in college. We were getting fucked up. My eyes were red and squinty, and Ray was coughing more than a patient suffering from lung cancer. We were passing the joint back and forth to each other. Puff puff pass. Puff puff pass.

Ray was about to take another hit when all of a sudden the garage door began to go up. Here comes no driving ass La-La speeding down the alley using the electric garage opener to raise the door. I damn near pissed in my pants, meanwhile high ass Ray is running his mouth as usual, saying "Man, this here some . . . potent ass weed," in the middle of almost choking half to death. I had to bribe La-La to keep her from telling. She drove back to the beauty shop to pick up Mama, and Ray and I went back in the house flying high as a kite. We had the munchies and raided the refrigerator. I'm glad Mama wasn't the one in the car when the garage door went up because she would've been mad enough to tear the roof off.

Since I couldn't celebrate Mother's Day with Mama and my siblings, I decided to take Tammy out to dinner. I told her I wanted to take her out to a nice place, and encouraged her to get her older sister to watch her sons. Tammy has been real cool about allowing me to stay at her apartment when I want to hang out in the city. And as long as I give her a few dollars, she doesn't hassle me about transacting business there either. Taking her out on the town and spending a little loot also helped me to manage the guilt I sometimes felt for exposing her young boys to my lifestyle. I must admit, I was getting attached to the little guys. They like me and call me Uncle Kendall.

I enjoy watching Tammy's sons interact with each other because they reminded me of Julian and me as small boys. DeAndre and Dontrell are playing with each other one moment and fighting the next. They're just boys being boys. I trip out because Tammy hollers at them the same way Mama used to holler at us. In a lot of ways, having me around has provided DeAndre and Dontrell with a calming influence instead of having to listen to their mother screaming all the time.

Being around them allows me to see the importance of little boys having a father figure in the home. The murder of my father robbed Julian, Lauren and I of experiences that a child can only share with a man. I never thought I would say it, but seeing DeAndre and Dontrell makes me want to settle down and have a family of my own with all of us living under the same roof. However, I want to be living right and out of this game when I decide to start a family.

Women have always been easy for me. I can get all the pussy I want. However, I always strap on a raincoat to protect myself from diseases and chicks saying they're pregnant with my baby. I don't wanna be like Ray and have kids and baby mama drama all over the city. He has seven kids by four different women. Fuck that shit.

Chicks like Tammy are easy prey for guys like me. They haven't been exposed to a lot of things. They're struggling to make it, and a brother with a few smooth lines and some extra cash in his pocket comes along promising to rescue them and make life a little easier. Before long, she's pregnant with another child and the guy who was supposed to save the day is now dead, in jail, or trying to rescue another piece of ass. That's why Ray has kids popping up everywhere.

Recently Ray had hooked up with this young woman by the name of Monique. Monique was a twenty-five-year-old country girl from Jackson, MS with three children: two girls and one boy. She had moved here to be closer to the father of her children, who had come to Chicago a year earlier. Unfortunately, the man she moved here to be with was now living with his mother on house arrest, while Monique was in the heart of the hood all alone. To hell with trying to make her ends meet, she just wanted them to look at each other. It wasn't long before Ray set his sights on Monique and sized up the situation. She needed help.

Monique got financial help, and Ray helped himself sexually. Her apartment was another place for him to eat, sleep, shit and get his rocks off. Monique's a well-built woman with thick thighs and a big Mississippi booty, raised on collard greens, black-eyed peas, sweet potatoes, fried chicken and corn bread. Ray was feasting and getting fat on his country loving until he found out Monique was pregnant. After that, he was out of there faster than a nigga being paroled from the joint. Monique gave birth to twins. Now she has *five children* without a father. She would've been better off staying in Mississippi.

Tammy was excited about going somewhere other than Red Lobster or Fridays to eat so I decided to take her to an upscale restaurant on Michigan Avenue. It was fun seeing her get dressed up with the look of anticipation on her face. It doesn't take much to impress a woman who isn't used to having a lot.

The eighty degree temperatures allowed Tammy to wear something sexy and revealing, yet, still tasteful and cute. Her floral printed, spaghetti strap, summer dress exposed smooth, golden skin which featured a Tweety bird tattoo near her left shoulder blade. Shapely, stocking free legs strutted with me down the Magnificent Mile in a pair of pink, ankle strap heels, which showcased a colorful flower tattoo on the side of her right calf. These young ladies love covering their bodies with tats. Tammy already has five tattoos and a stud in her chin. And she's also talking about piercing her navel. She's such a freak.

Tammy and I dined at a restaurant on Michigan Avenue called Bandera. One day I had overheard La-La bragging about some guy taking her there to impress her, so I decided to check it out for myself. Of course, it was jam packed with folks celebrating Mother's Day, and it took us a while to be seated even though I had reservations. Money definitely talks. And the fifty dollar bill I gave the host to persuade him to get me a table by the window talked loud enough for everyone in the restaurant to hear.

The view from the window allowed Tammy and I to eat dinner while watching people walking and shopping along the Magnificent Mile on a spring evening with a summer feel to it. Tammy was soaking it all in. I laughed on the inside as I watched the twinkle in her eyes experience a whole new world.

After dinner, Tammy and I took a walk down the Magnificent Mile. Next door to the restaurant was Andriana Furs, an upscale furrier chain, with several stores around the city. They were closed for the day, but that didn't stop Tammy peaking through the window and daydreaming. Openly, she fantasized about having a white, mink jacket like the one she saw a popular rapper wear in a video on MTV Jams. I lied and told her I would buy her one like it later in the year if she continued to treat me right. Tammy was putty in my hands. Her delicate fingers cuffed my strong bicep as we enjoyed the breeze and continued our walk. I felt like I was on a date. This wasn't my nature. I normally don't date women, I just fuck women.

"What you wanna do now?" I asked.

"Whatever you wanna do," Tammy answered, still basking under a sun on the verge of setting for the day. "I'm just enjoying the moment, Kendall. This is the best Mother's Day I've had since I had my sons. This is incredible. This whole day has been off da chain!"

This was fun, so I decided to milk it to the max.

"I got an idea," I said.

"What?"

"Do you wanna go to the top of the world?"

"What you trippin' on, Kendall?"

"You'll see."

"Where you takin' me, Kendall?"

"You'll see."

Tammy and I rode the elevator to the John Hancock observatory to get another view of the world we live in. As we entered the observatory, I stood back, and let Tammy walk ahead of me in awe. It was her moment to wish on a star. We're still in Chicago, but she's a long way from the wild hundreds of the south side.

"I always wanted to do this but never had a chance," Tammy gasped.

"They say on a clear day, four different states can be seen from here," I lectured with the confidence of a geography professor.

"For real!" she exclaimed with the enthusiasm of a child seeing her first star.

"That's what they say," I replied, sliding up behind her with my hands on her hips, pressing my body against hers. The sun was going down, but my dick was about to rise up. I wanted Tammy to feel my presence.

"Wait 'til I tell KeKe and Tanisha about this!" she yelled.

I played it off and kept my composure on the outside, but on the inside my stomach was rumbling with laughter. Tammy's excitement is hilarious. I can't wait to see how excited she is later on.

"You like the view, huh?" I asked.

"Yeah," she responded gleefully. "It makes me feel like I'm on top of the world. Looking out over the city and the lake like this makes me believe everything will be alright. Just being able to stand here makes me feel like all my dreams will come true. Damn, Kendall, this is incredible!"

A sinister grin crossed my face. "Stick with me, Tammy, and I'll take you places beyond your wildest dreams," I bragged with the demeanor of a pimp promising to take one of his bitches to the player's ball. "I might not be able to give you the world, Tammy, but at least I can show you a piece of it."

Tammy turned her body to me and wrapped her arms around my neck. She hugged me tightly and kissed me on the cheek. I pulled her close and squeezed her body. I'm able to feel her warm body relaxing in my arms. She's having a tender moment. I can feel her heart beating. I can also still feel my stomach rumbling with laughter. That line worked better than I thought it would.

"I can't even believe this," Tammy declared, resting her small hands on my broad shoulders. Instead of looking at me, her eyes focused on the pavement beneath us. "This has been a wonderful day, Kendall. Thank you very much. Thank you for everything."

"You're welcome."

"You gonna let me show you how much I appreciated my special day?" she asked, now gazing into my eyes with a devilish smile on her face.

"Hell yeah," I smirked, trying to control the laughter raging inside my belly. I knew she would be impressed, but this was way too easy. It was Mother's Day on the calendar, but it might as well have been Christmas morning for Tammy. She was like a little girl getting her favorite toy from Santa Claus. And it will be like the 4th of July for me later on tonight because Tammy's body is hotter than a firecracker. I plan on lighting her little stem so I can feel her explode.

"Happy Mother's Day, Tammy."

29

LAUREN

Even though my flight out of Midway Airport was delayed by an hour, I still arrived at LaGuardia Airport in New York City by two o'clock in the afternoon. It's a business trip instead of a vacation, but New York's frantic pace and excitement is still a thrill compared to the bogged down existence I've been living back home. Although, I'll be in meetings and workshops on Wednesday, Thursday and Friday, I'll use the weekend to explore New York and enjoy some of the city's most popular venues. Dining at one of the four star restaurants and seeing a Broadway play are definitely on the agenda. Lately, life has been taking a bite out of me, so I'm definitely planning on taking a bite out of the Big Apple.

I slid into the back of the taxi and instructed the cabdriver to take me to the Park Central with conviction and power in my voice. While the dark skinned cabdriver with the strong island accent chauffeured me through the city that never naps, I hid the stars in my eyes behind brand new designer sunglasses. My goal is to give the cabdriver the impression I do this all the time instead of appearing like a naïve woman blinded by bright lights of the big city. I want him to know his job is to take me directly to Manhattan and not take the scenic route through the Bronx to increase his fare.

He needs to know Lauren Janine Collins is the new star in town. I fantasize about seeing my name on a marquee as I ride in the back of a black limousine disguised as a white taxicab. Get ready folks. I'm here. LJC is in the NYC.

However, before doing an encore and taking my final bow, I need to pay the cabdriver. Wow. I'm glad the insurance company provided a per diem for meals and transportation to and from the airport; the taxi ride from LaGuardia to the hotel in Manhattan cost close to fifty dollars. Gee whiz. New York is expensive.

Located in Midtown Manhattan on Seventh Avenue at 56th Street, across from Carnegie Hall, the Park Central is by no means the Waldorf Astoria, but it will serve the purpose while I'm here. The Park Central is probably a three star hotel at best, but the surrounding area makes it perfect for me. The hotel's convenient location is walking distance to Times Square, the Rockefeller Center and the Theatre District. And best of all, the stores on Fifth Avenue are just a couple of blocks away, and they're already calling my name.

Even though it's only three o'clock on a Tuesday, the area was already bustling with activity. I registered at the front desk and got the key to my room. I know this is the city that never sleeps, but I'm ready for an afternoon nap. As soon as I got up to the room, I kicked off my shoes, threw down my duffel bag, and stretched out across the bed to relax for a little while. Before drifting off into a deep sleep, I decided to call home and check on Mama. I want to let her know I had a safe trip.

"Hello," Mama answered on the third ring with heavy wheezing.

"Mama," I replied. "Are you okay?"

"Yeah . . ." she hesitated because of labored breathing. "I'll be okay."

"Are you sure?" I asked, troubled by the phlegm rattling in her voice.

"Yeah," she panted. "I'll be okay. Julian is going to stop by here when he leaves the office and bring me some medicine. And if that don't do the trick, then I'll have him take me to the hospital to get checked out."

"Oh Mama," I sighed.

"Don't worry 'bout me baby," she coughed. "You just enjoy your trip, and check on me when you get home."

I parted my lips to respond, but nothing came out of my mouth.

"Did you hear what I said, La-La?"

"Yes."

"Don't worry 'bout me," she repeated, clearing her throat. "I'll be okay."

"Okay Mama."

"Bye baby."

"Goodbye Mama."

I closed my flip phone and sprawled across the bed with my eyes staring at the ceiling. If it's not one thing, it's ninety-nine. It just never stops. The caring and worrying side of my personality makes me wish I were in Chicago looking after Mama, but the selfish part of my personality makes me wish I had never called home. Every time I call I wonder if trouble is going to greet me from the other end of the phone. I feel guilty when I'm not around to take care of Mama, but I get paranoid every time I see her name and phone number on my caller ID.

All of a sudden, a subway of sadness was speeding down the tracks of my mind. In less than a New York minute, one phone call had sent my emotions tumbling all the way from a Broadway marquee where the stars shine to ground zero where the towers fell. From within, I felt myself hollering like the George Jetson cartoon character; Jane stop this crazy thing!

Instead of wallowing in misery, I showered and put on some fresh clothes and a pair of comfortable sandals. The walls of the tiny room were beginning to close in on me. I'm in New York City. I need to see the town. I can cry at home anytime.

Designer shades cover my eyes again, but this time hides more tears than stars, as I walk along the congested streets of Manhattan. My anxiety stricken stomach is beginning to rumble. Nervousness about Mama is making me crave food. Diners are present on every block in Manhattan, but instead of dining in, I prefer to eat and keep moving. I buy a hot dog with all the trimmings from one of the many street vendors on Seventh Avenue. I take a bite out of the hot dog and lick the mustard from my lips, continuing my walk along Seventh Avenue towards the theatre district. The hot dog is nothing to brag about; I've had better hot dogs from the Maxwell Street Deli back home.

I kept walking until I got to the New Amsterdam Theatre on 42nd Street and saw the marquee for *The Lion King*. Andre had promised to take me to see it in Chicago, but now I had the opportunity to treat myself to seeing it on Broadway. I seized the moment and purchased a ticket to see the musical I've been anxious to experience for a long time.

The conference workshops and seminars on regulatory changes taking place in the insurance industry are not very exciting, however, it did allow me the opportunity to make contacts and meet vice-presidents and directors from the home office. Of course, most of them are uptight, bean counting executives who care more about profits than people. Also, on the negative side of the equation; there are never more than a handful of people of color in attendance at these conferences. My mental calculator immediately tallies black heads the moment I sit in on one of these forums. And the chances of seeing women of color are even slimmer.

Rising quickly up the corporate ladder has put me in somewhat of an awkward position because I always have to prove myself and have three strikes that go with me into every boardroom I enter. I'm young, I'm black, and I'm a female. Just one of those characteristics standing alone can cause a high achiever like me to get cut off at the knees. And I have to deal with having all three.

After seeing so many stuffy, white men in the room, a sense of pride flowed through my bloodstream when Jerry Farmer approached the podium to address the attendees. Since Mr. Farmer is an executive vice-president, I'd read his name on company correspondence, but had never met or seen him. It's good to see an African-American in position of authority.

Jerry Farmer is a very handsome man. He appears to be in his mid-fifties. A full head of salt and pepper strands provide seasoning for his wavy hair, and adds a spice of maturity and wisdom. Distinguishing good looks are accented by rich, caramel colored skin and dimples. Some men are handsome, some are cute. Jerry Farmer is undeniably *fine!!!*

Mr. Farmer's stimulating antidotes and witty analogies planted a feeling of hope amongst the upper level employees in attendance. He irrigated our spirits with passion and purpose and cultivated our psyche with the seeds to success. It's hard to believe, but he made me feel good about being an employee with the insurance company. I felt like I had just finished hearing a motivational speech by Les Brown. He was proving to be more than just a pretty face.

After his presentation concluded, I made an aggressive move to get close to Mr. Farmer to introduce myself. I've learned over the years from the self-help books and tapes to seize an opportunity and make my point quickly without beating around the bush and wasting time.

I'm greeted by a firm handshake. His demeanor is gracious and pleasant. It's like he's able to make everyone in the conference room feel important and essential to the insurance company's success. I'm a bit nervous, but Mr. Farmer possesses a smile that is both heartwarming and disarming. I stop biting my lower lip and relax.

My credentials and position with the insurance company roll off my lips effortlessly, and then I ask Mr. Farmer if he's able to recommend someone to mentor me in gaining a boardroom education to corporate America. With a fatherly smile, he promises to do the best he can and gives me one of his business cards and asks for one of mine. We shake hands again and say goodbye. I returned to my room feeling good about meeting a new contact and potential mentor.

I was shocked and flattered when Mr. Farmer called and asked if I were interested in attending Sunday morning service at his church. Since my arrival in New York a few days ago, I've done just about everything else to familiarize myself with the city and discover its rich culture. Tuesday night I saw *The Lion King*; Wednesday night I dined at a restaurant named Shelley's and spent way too much money on a steak; Thursday night I walked around Times Square and did some sightseeing. Friday night I dined and listened to some blues at B.B. King's club on 42nd Street; and this afternoon, I actually found the courage to get on the subway and ride down to Ground Zero. I even did some shopping and bought a couple pairs of shoes at Century 21. My first trip to New York has been a memorable blessing. It seemed only fitting to end my trip my going to the house of the Lord.

Mr. Farmer said he wanted me to attend the eight o'clock service, so that meant I had to get up early, much earlier than I'm accustomed to getting up on a Sunday morning; a task made even more difficult by the fact New York is on eastern time, and my body clock is still ticking on central time as if I were in Chicago. Mr. Farmer agreed to pick me up at seven o'clock. Somehow, I managed to be ready when he called to let me know he was waiting downstairs.

I had no idea how we were going to get to the church since Mr. Farmer mentioned that it's located in Brooklyn. The only thing I know about Brooklyn is that the late Notorious B.I.G., the greatest rapper of all time, called it home. Mr. Farmer is a native New Yorker, so I expected to find him waiting in his car in front of the Park Central, instead I saw him smiling from the backseat of a black, Cadillac limousine. Wow! It turned out Mr. Farmer also owned a limousine service.

I climbed into the backseat and allowed the luxurious leather interior to wrap its fabric around me. The overcast skies of early morning made it impossible for me to wear my designer shades to hide my excitement. I tried to act nonchalant and give Mr. Farmer the impression I do this kind of stuff all the time, but I couldn't. Perhaps I fooled the cabdriver who drove me from airport to Manhattan, but no way could I fool the man who was having me chauffeured from Manhattan to Brooklyn.

By the time the limousine chauffeuring New York's newest star reached the Saint Paul Community Baptist Church in Brooklyn, the first service was about to end. The elders of the church greeted Mr. Farmer with hugs and handshakes. He introduced me as his new protégé and explained I was in town for a conference with the insurance company. Everyone at Saint Paul made me feel right at home. The elder allowed us to wait in a small office until members attending the first service exited and folks attending the second service were ushered in. After the crowd lined up to attend the second service filed into the sanctuary, one of the elders led us to a pew near the front of the church.

The pastor of the church, the Rev. Dr. Johnny Ray Youngblood preached a powerful sermon about the faith and flaws of folks in the Bible. His words were candid and direct. Dr. Youngblood said straight talk made for straight understanding. Being in church service with Mr. Farmer was an unexpected blessing. This is something I'd missed by growing up without my father. I wanted the moment to last forever.

After the service concluded, Mr. Farmer and I returned to the limousine double parked outside.

"Are you hungry, Lauren?" Mr. Farmer asked.

"A little bit." I answered, shyly.

"Would you like to go to Sylvia's?"

"That's in Harlem right?"

"Sounds like you've done your research on New York," he said with the tone of a proud father. "Milton lets take our special guest to Sylvia's."

Storm clouds are dominating the Sunday morning sky, but I won't let the threat of rain dim my star or ruin my parade. What a trip this has been! I can't wait to call Mama when I get back to my hotel room.

As the limousine cruises through the streets of New York, Mr. Farmer fills my mind with knowledge about the challenges I'll have in succeeding in corporate America as a young, African-American woman. I listen closely and absorb his words like a sponge on a damp street. He's soaking my brain with the type of wisdom a woman can only receive from an older man. This is the kind of moment I wish I could've experienced with my father. Simple things like going to church together and having father to daughter talks. I'd missed a lot by growing up without a father. It would've been nice to have gotten an older man's perspective on life when I reached adulthood.

"Milton, looks like we got here early enough to beat the after church crowd," Mr. Farmer said as our limousine parked out in front of Sylvia's Restaurant in Harlem.

"I think so," Milton agreed.

I was so engrossed in Mr. Farmer's inspiring insight that I don't know what route we took to get here or how long it took for us to get to Lenox Avenue in Harlem. This has been a whirlwind experience to say the least.

While Milton went to park the limo, Mr. Farmer and I waited inside to be seated. An attractive, young hostess seated us immediately at a table near the front of the restaurant. Later, Milton came in and joined us. Shortly after, a friendly middle-aged waitress came to the table to take our orders.

Food is a secondary objective right now. I'm too excited to do a lot of eating. I order hash browns and sausages just to get something in my stomach. Soon after our meals arrive, a voluptuous female singer serenades the patrons with some soul stirring gospel tunes.

Oh I can't wait to tell Mama. This is excellent.

The vivacious singer struts and sings through the restaurant with the vitality of someone who has just been baptized in a pool of love. Her bubbly personality is contagious and spreads joy all around the Sunday morning brunch. She comes over to our table and puts the microphone in my face just as I'm trying to swallow a mouthful of hash browns.

"Good morning," she sang in a melodic tone.

I swallow quickly. "Good morning."

"What's your name?"

"Lauren Collins," I replied.

"And where are you from?" she asked in a rich soprano voice.

"Chicago," I answered proudly.

"Chicago's in the house," she crooned in a jazzy tone. "God bless you my sister. We're glad to have you here for our Sunday morning brunch."

The sassy singer taps Mr. Farmer on the shoulder affectionately and then moves on to other tables. People are here from all over the world, but she's making everyone feel at home. Before I can take another sip from my glass of orange juice, an older woman approaches the table. Mr. Farmer's lips part into a proud smile. It's Sylvia Woods, the owner of the restaurant bearing her name. She says hello and thanks me for visiting her restaurant. I didn't order any dessert, but being greeted by Sylvia Woods is icing on the cake.

By the time we finish brunch, raindrops are pounding Harlem's pavement hard. We rush to the limousine to keep from getting soaked. I settle into the backseat and take a deep breath. My eyes stare through the tinted windows once more.

"Did you enjoy breakfast?" Mr. Farmer asked.

"Yes indeed," I said, shaking my head in amazement. "This has been a wonderful morning, Mr. Farmer."

"Please, Lauren," he said with a disarming smile. "If we're going to continue our day, you're going to have to stop calling me Mr. Farmer. Please call me, Jerry."

"Okay, Jerry."

"So Lauren, you've been to church in Brooklyn, ate breakfast in Harlem," he smiled with the pride of a father showing his daughter a good time. "What do you want to do now?"

"To be honest, Mr. Farmer. . ."

"Hey!" he interrupted me before I could finish my sentence.

"I'm sorry," I apologized. "I mean Jerry."

"That's better."

"To be honest, I'm a little exhausted from having such a busy week. I'm ready to go back to my room and take a nap. I'm not used to getting up this early on a Sunday. Remember it's just ten-thirty in Chicago."

"I know," he agreed. "I also know black folks like to eat and go to sleep."

"Ha, ha, ha," I laughed. "This is true."

The sudden touch of Jerry's hand moving under my dress startles me and causes me to jump and fold my hands across my lap.

"What's wrong, Lauren?" he asked. "Aren't you having a good time?"

"Ah. . .yes I am," I responded nervously.

"So what's the problem, Lauren?" he asked in a controlling, manipulative tone.

"I just wasn't expecting this," I replied with my teeth digging into my lower lip.

"So what were you expecting?"

"I thought you were going to be a mentor or a father figure," I replied naively.

"Let me make myself clear, Lauren," he declared in a nonchalant tone. "First of all, I already have two daughters around your age who I've been trying to mentor for over thirty years. I worked hard, put them through college, and tried to get them on the right track professionally, and they still don't listen to me. I'm done teaching. Second: You asked me to show you how to navigate the structure of corporate America, and I'm trying to show you the quickest way for a woman like you to move up the corporate ladder."

Once again the stars in my eyes have been replaced by tears.

Mr. Farmer continued. "So if you want me to help you, then you'll going to have to help me in the process."

"But Mr. Farmer . . ."

"No buts," he replied coldly. "You're either in or you're out."

"What do you mean?"

"I mean we can go back to your hotel room and enjoy the rest of the day, or I can have Milton drop you off at the next light."

"Huh?" I swallowed as if I had one of his shiny shoes stuck in my throat.

"What's it going to be Lauren?"

"You're going to leave me in the rain?" I asked in disbelief.

"That depends on you."

"Why are you doing this to me?" I questioned, feeling disappointed and confused. "Please don't . . ."

"I don't have time for this," he said rolling his eyes and staring out of the backseat passenger window. "Milton, pull over to the curb and let Ms. Collins out."

"Yes sir," Milton answered.

My mouth is wide open with shock, but Mr. Farmer seems unfazed about kicking me to the curb in the rain. He isn't interested in being a mentor or father figure; he's only interested in getting between my legs.

"Please, Mr. Farmer," I begged as the limousine chauffeuring a fallen star pulls over to the curb on an unfamiliar street. "Don't do this to me."

"Goodbye Ms. Collins."

A downpour of rain drowns me in a state of abandonment. I can't believe this is happening to me. I don't even know where I am. Tears and raindrops are blurring my vision; I can't tell one from the other; the water cascading my face has become one. I pray to God for help as the limousine cruises away. Suddenly, I see the brake lights come on and the limo pulls over to a curb and stops. God is answering my prayer. Mr. Farmer has had a change of heart.

Mr. Farmer rolls down the window as I approach the limo's back door. I'm expecting him to unlock the door and let me back in. He doesn't.

"Here Ms. Collins," he taunts, handing me a black umbrella. "I don't want you to catch a cold. Have a safe trip back to the hotel."

"Please don't leave me," I begged.

"Good luck hailing a cab."

I thought the Lord was supposed to hear my faintest cry and answer by and by. Maybe God had His hearing aid turned down and couldn't hear my prayers.

30

MAMA

It's been a long time since I've been to a Sunday morning worship service and it feels good to be back in the house of the Lord. I was so excited about attending church this morning that I couldn't sleep last night. Anticipation had me tossing and turning 'til well past midnight; I was just too wound up. I was as restless as a child expecting a visit from Santa Claus on Christmas Eve, except this time, I was waiting on the Lord. Just plain giddy for God.

My Sunday, go to church clothes, had been hanging on the bedroom closet door ever since yesterday afternoon. Now that summer is here, I can wear all white: a white suit, a white hat, with a matching white purse and shoes. I even had my white, fold-up fan inside my purse just in case it got too hot inside the church.

The Lord says come as you are, but I always try to look my best; full of life instead of sick and shut-in. I know the Lord got healing power, but I still brought my portable oxygen tank to church with me. Believing in the Lord don't mean I gotta be a damn fool. I don't wanna suffer an asthma attack and pass out on the pew, and have the people in the congregation thinking I'm just happy and filled with the Holy Ghost in the process of turning blue.

A member of the Calumet Avenue Baptist Church greeted us at the door with a warm smile and a bulletin detailing the order of service. I had persuaded Julian and La-La to bring me to this church because I've been watching their broadcast on television for the last few years and wanted to come in person. God's been calling my name for a while, but the devil been trying to keep me from hearing a word from on high. Being in the house of the Lord is where I need to be. I might not have many more chances.

Calumet Avenue is one of the fastest growing churches in the city, and much bigger than what I'm used to. It isn't a mega church yet, but it's headed in that direction. One reason I came here is because I enjoy listening to the sermons by Calumet Avenue's dynamic, young pastor. I'd made a habit of tuning in every Sunday morning to see the Rev. Dr. Michael Newsome preach, sing, dance and shout his way around the pulpit with fire shooting through his bones. Hallelujah!

Rev. Newsome didn't look to be no older than Julian, but he seemed committed in his work for the Lord. He was called Dr. Newsome because he had actually gone to school to become a preacher. I know the Lord can work a miracle in anybody's life and can convert a sinner into a saint, but there are a lot of preachers out here who don't even know the word. Doctors and lawyers gotta go to college to learn their profession, but almost anybody can say they're a preacher. All they gotta do is turn their collar around and say they been called. Some of these preachers are up in the pulpit trying to lead people and don't even read the Bible. They just whoop and holler and pass the collection plate.

Calumet Avenue's congregation is a combination of young and old. A lot of families are coming in together. I'm glad Julian and La-La got me here early because the church is getting very crowded.

The service began with the praise team singing a melody of songs. Right away I could feel the spirit moving within my soul. It wasn't long before I was bobbing my head and stomping my feet. Watching at home on television is one thing, but being in the midst is worshipping on a higher level. I'm glad to be in the number. Julian laughed when he saw me tapping my cane to the beat.

When I was active at New Calvary, all we had was an organ, a piano and a tambourine, but Calumet Avenue got an organ, a piano, drums, guitars and a saxophone. They have more instruments than the clubs I used to sing in, and they know how to play 'em too. I love the sound of good music.

La-La tapped me on the hand and pointed to the Celestial Choir as they marched down the aisles wearing white robes, trimmed in royal blue, with royal blue sashes around the shoulder, showing the initials CABC. Watching them fill up the choir stand is a sight to behold. God is an awesome God.

One deacon read the scripture and another led the congregation in prayer. After that, the Celestial Choir rose to sing an A and B selection, and that's when the tears started to flow from my eyes.

"Let's have some church!" I shouted. "Let's have some church this morning!"

Hearing them sing "Safe in His Arms" caused me to drop my cane and rock myself in rhythm. It's my favorite song by the Thompson Community Singers. I always wanted to sing with the Tommies, but never got the chance. My lips matched the light-skinned soloist word for word as she belted out verse after verse.

La-La reached down and picked my cane up off the floor. She held onto the cane and whispered for me to put the oxygen tube back in my nose. I was too excited to realize I was breathing without it. My poor baby is afraid I'm gonna start wheezing and cause the ushers to come over here and cool me off with one of them fans advertising a funeral home with a picture of Martin Luther King on the front.

La-La and Julian just don't know; if I were thirty years younger and had the strength to hit those notes like I used to, I would go up in that choir and take that microphone from that young woman. I would tear this church up.

I put the tube back into my nostrils, but the next singer didn't give me a chance to catch my breath either. The short, dark-skinned gentleman didn't look to weigh over a hundred pounds, but he definitely had the lungs to breathe life into a song. My legs trembled as I listened to him sing the lyrics to the song "Faith" with conviction.

"Faith; I'm a living witness of what faith in God can do; faith to reach the unreachable; faith to beat the unbeatable; faith to remove the unmovable; faith that stands the invincible; faith that can conquer anything!"

Lord Jesus, that young man gonna make me take my hat off and throw it around the church if he don't end that song soon. My God!

What a voice! The best singers in the world come from the black church.

"Y'all glad I talked y'all into bringing me here?" I whispered to La-La and Julian as the male soloist finished the song and returned to his seat in the choir loft.

"Yes I am," Julian nodded.

La-La didn't respond to my question. She's been very distant lately. Her eyes are dazing into space without any particular focus. My baby girl's soul appears to be in a far away place, and her spirit seems to be somewhere even farther than any mother can reach. I want to connect with my only daughter, but I can't. Only God can reach into the depths of a person's soul.

Even though Lauren's mind is in some far away place, I'm still blessed to have her and Julian sitting next to me in church this morning. However, not knowing where Kendall is makes the service somewhat incomplete. I've been a nervous wreck worrying about him. That's why I had to come to church. I need to pray and settle my mind.

It's time for me to kneel at the altar and turn Kendall over to Jesus. I need to put all of them in the hands of Jesus. Lord knows I can't handle it anymore. I'm concerned about La-La and the troubles she's having on her job. I worry about Julian and his legal problems, and the strong resentment he has towards his younger brother. Worrying about my children has taken years off my own life.

Sitting here makes me think about the parable of the lost son. Just like in the Bible: Julian is the older son who has been loyal and dedicated, looking after me, making sure I'm okay. Whereas, Kendall is the lost son, and I have no idea where he is. He's wasting his life with reckless living. Kendall needs to come to his senses and turn those streets loose. I'm worried. I can't help but to worry because he's my son. I hate his lifestyle, but I would welcome him back with open arms. Lord I just wanna hug my son one more time and tell him I love him. He needs to know I still love him.

After the altar call prayer, Rev. Newsome stepped to the pulpit and announced it was preaching time. Shouts of amen filled the sanctuary as the youthful, energetic preacher flipped through the pages of his tiny Bible and announced the passage in which he was taking his text.

"For those of you with your Bibles," he said speaking with a voice that commanded respect and attention, "I want us to look at Matthew chapter 18 starting with the 21st verse which reads: Then Peter came to Jesus and asked 'Lord, if my brother keeps on sinning against me, how many times do I have to forgive him? Seven times?'

'No, not seven times,' answered Jesus, 'but seventy times seven.'

Rev. Newsome stared at the congregation over the top of his glasses and announced his sermon for the morning.

"I want to take a few moments to preach on the subject: Trying to forgive when we can't forget."

"Come on wit' it preacher!" hollered a middle-aged woman sitting behind me.

"Take your time, pastor!" yelled a deacon on the first row.

"Come on up!" screamed a man in the back.

"One of my best friends, I won't name no names, has a thing for Mafia movies. He has all of them in his collection on DVD: The Godfather series, Goodfellas, Casino, A Bronx Tale, Donnie Brasco and others; I tell ya, he has them all on his DVD rack lined up next to each other by his big screen TV and surround sound system. Often gangsters on TV like Tony Soprano will utter the phrase 'fuggedaboutit' in a thick Italian accent. For them, sometimes, fuggedabouit is a way of saying: don't worry about it, it's over with, it's no big deal, or it's in the past. I want to ask you a question this morning. How come it's so difficult for us to say fuggedaboutit and leave things in the past? Sisters and brothers I want you to know that it's hard leaving some things in the past."

"I know that's right!" hollered the lady behind me.

"Can I get a witness?" asked Pastor Newsome with a broad smile.

"Amen!" answered the congregation.

"It's really hard when someone we love has hurt us and disappointed us in a way we never imagined. We hold onto that pain and allow it to contaminate our inner-spirit. We may say fuggedaboutit, but deep down we want the people who hurt us to get hurt themselves.

We want them to feel the same pain we have. Bottom line, sisters and brothers, we want revenge. We don't get mad, we get even. We want them to suffer, so they'll know how it feels. Some of us even want the Lord to settle the score for us. We only wanna give folks one chance to make a mistake, but we want the Lord to forgive us over and over again. They disappoint us one time and we're washing our hands of them forever. I'm glad the Lord doesn't treat people the way we do."

"Say it preacher!" hollered the lady behind me. She was loud and animated and kept hollering in my ear. If I'd been wearing a hearing aid, I would've had to turn the volume down. La-La looked at me and rolled her eyes.

I leaned over to La-La and whispered. "You gotta fuggedaboutit, La-La."

Both of us chuckled, but deep within I definitely needed to search my own heart for forgiveness. I done lived with a lot of anger and resentment over the years. Some things I'll never be able to forget about. I was mad at Kenny for cheating on me and being killed, leaving me with three kids to raise alone; I was mad at Barbara Dixon for pretending to be my friend and church sister, while having an affair with my husband behind my back. However, most of all, I was angry at God. In my opinion, God had let me down.

"Isn't it ironic it's Peter who wants to limit how many times a person is forgiven, even though he is the one who denies knowing Jesus. He denied his own friend. Can't you hear Peter saying 'man I don't know nuttin' bout that dude, Jesus' when Jesus was probably feeling his lowest. The Bible says Peter went out and wept bitterly. I bet Peter wanted to be forgiven then!"

I tried to concentrate on Rev. Newsome's sermon instead of looking back on the past. God must be speaking through Rev. Newsome because he's reading my mind. His sermon is driving down my street.

"Forgiveness frees us from our past, and allows us to embrace the present. Our unwillingness to forgive causes us to live life focusing on what has already happened, instead of what can be. I call it rearview window religion. We spend so much time looking back that we fail to see our blessings or the blessings on the way. It's hard to focus on the road ahead when we're busy staring at the road behind us in the rearview mirror. I know you're saying: Rev. Newsome you don't know what that person did to me. Maybe I don't, but the Bible says: If you forgive others the wrongs they have done to you, your Father in heaven will also forgive you. But if you do not forgive others, then your Father will not forgive the wrongs you have done."

I nod and say amen because Rev. Newsome's sermon is parked in front of my house, and now he's about to walk up on the porch and ring my doorbell. I can't help but answer the door and let him in because he's preaching the truth.

"We have accidents when we don't watch the road ahead; we hit potholes when we don't pay attention to the street we're driving on. The Lord knows where He's brought us from, now we have to allow God to order our steps for the present and the future. For the Bible says: Trust in the Lord with all thy heart and lean not onto thy own understanding, but in all thy ways acknowledge Him and He shall direct thy path."

The lady behind me stood up and hollered. "Yes Lord! Yes Lord!"

La-La looked over at me and rolled her eyes. "I already fuggodaboutit."

By now, most of the congregation are on their feet, shouting with outstretched arms. The lady behind me is dancing with the Holy Spirit and is hollering to the top of her lungs. People come to church all dressed up, ready to sing and shout, but we never really know what problems they're carrying inside, or what situations they've left at home, or what's going on in their life. It seems like the Lord is working in her; I know it because He's working in me also. Sometimes we have to just let stuff go.

I bet a lot of my sickness is due to the anger and pain I've carried in my body all these years. It's toxic. I'm suffering from congestive heart failure probably because of all the heartache I've felt over the years. Just like other people perhaps suffer from ulcers because they allow stuff to eat away at them for so long.

While people danced and shouted around me, I prayed for God to heal me. I wasn't asking for Him to heal my body; I wanted God to heal my spirit. The congregation is shouting with joy by the time

Rev. Newsome concludes his sermon on forgiveness and hope. Lord he's in my house and calling me by name. Hope.

"The doors of the church are open!" Pastor Newsome shouted.

My mind and heart are having a spiritual tug of war. Both sides are pulling me in different directions. I'm listening to voices on each shoulder telling me what I should and shouldn't do. God is making His case and the devil is doing an excellent job of cross-examining me.

The Lord is pardoning my sins and granting me forgiveness; the devil is laughing at me and saying I wouldn't be in this position if I hadn't been guilty of loving Kenny so much and trusting Barbara Dixon as my friend. God reminds me of how He had brought me this far and helped me get through it; meanwhile the devil reminds me that I had met both Kenny and Barbara in church, and that they were sleeping together while I was serving God. The devil is a cheap shot artist who hits below the belt.

A malicious mind is telling me I'm too old to join a new church; a healed heart is encouraging me to be born again. Lifeless legs are urging me to remain seated; a saved spirit is warning me I might not get another chance. I feel like the Bible character, Jacob: I'm wrestling with God. I can't keep fighting the Lord.

I grab my cane and stand up. With my cane, a portable oxygen tank strapped to my back, and a tube of fresh air flowing into my nostrils, I walk slowly down the aisle. Shouts of thank you Jesus and hallelujah fill the spacious sanctuary with joy. The loud cries of praise energize me. Tears stream from eyes while strength pours into my legs. God's feeding my feeble body with enough power to make it to the altar by myself. My spiritual cup is overflowing with happiness as years of hurt and anger spill out of me.

Julian and La-La remained seated with shocked expressions on their faces. They're surprised yet happy. Both of them have tears in their eyes. They looked as though they were waging their own internal battles. Neither of them trailed me to the altar; I didn't want them to follow my lead. Some journeys we have to make alone. By the time I made it to the front of the church, I was too excited to be tired. I gave my hand to Pastor Newsome, but gave my heart to God.

31

JULIAN

    Media crews representing Chicago's major television stations are on hand with cameras and microphones positioned to snag a scorching quote from the lips of the city's newest headline grabber. Charles Owens is taking pleasure in having cameramen and reporters clinging to his every word. He's right where he wants to be. He's the center of attention, basking in another chance to be on the ten o'clock news.

    As of late, the activist has been a regular on local television and radio programs speaking out against black on black crime and police brutality in the inner-city. The high profile tragedies of two children had catapulted the articulate and charismatic Owens into the Chicago limelight. He'd held a prayer vigil with the family of six-year-old Chiquita Richards after she was shot on a school playground and lingered in a coma for almost two days before dying. And a week later, he paid for and spoke at the funeral services for ten-year-old Dwayne "Smiley" Patterson.

    Owens was noble in reaching out to members of both families, saying everyone in the community suffers when our children die too soon. He even had a motto: It's time to silence the violence.

    Today Owens is blasting the police department for using excessive force against an innocent eighty-four-year-old man.

Two nights earlier, working off the tip of an informant, plainclothes officers from the narcotics unit had bolted through the residence of an elderly gentleman. The police handcuffed the weak and ailing man as he tried to protest. They shoved him to the ground and made him lay face down with his hands behind his back while ransacking his bungalow with dogs sniffing for drugs. Overzealous cops knocked down doors, ruined furniture, emptied closets and cabinets, and even ripped holes in bed mattresses and sofa pillows looking for drugs. Later, after nearly destroying all the contents in the home, the police realized they were at the wrong address and had caused havoc at the wrong house on the wrong person.

Cameras flashed as microphones recorded the nattily attired Charles Owens while he addressed the media in a taupe, single-breasted suit and brown crocodile shoes; accusing city government and law enforcement of incompetence and insensitivity. His caramel colored skin and curly black hair made him photogenic; his vast vocabulary and oratorical flair made words line up for the chance to flow from his mustached lips.

I listened on as Owens mesmerized the crowd with the abused, elderly gentleman standing by his side.

"Our community can no longer afford to tolerate the injustices delivered by the hypocritical arms of law enforcement. With one hand, they serve and protect us, but with the other hand, they unnerve and upset us. Their abusive actions must cease. The gentleman standing next to me didn't deserve the treatment he received. Mr. Lawrence Sanders is a good man, an honest man, a God fearing man; he didn't deserve to have his home shattered and his spirit battered by angry, abusive cops. It wasn't right for ornery officers to leave Mr. Sanders feeling rejected, dejected and disrespected. Ladies and gentlemen, Mr. Sanders is one of our own; he's one of our community's elder statesmen. He's a courageous crusader, not a corrupt criminal; he's an angelic liberator, not an angry lawbreaker; he's a conqueror, not a convict; he's a full-time father, not a first time felon!"

The words coming from the mouth of Charles Owens are passionate. He's galvanizing a community committed to wrapping its arms around an abused, elderly victim. A crowd of captivated supporters hold on to his every word inspiring a challenge to make a difference. Eyes became misty and frowns became smiles as Owens made the people living in the crime infested neighborhood believe that the promised land was right around the corner.

"It's time for the city of Chicago to issue a public apology to Mr. Sanders. It's time for the city to rebuild his house after destroying his home; it's time for the city to resurrect his spirit after burying his manhood. Ladies and gentleman, the city of Chicago must be held accountable. We can't allow police officers to continue vandalizing the homes of law abiding, tax paying citizens because they carry a badge of dishonor. And then they leave the premises with innocent lives left in shambles and say oops my bad we made a mistake."

"See . . . that's what I'm talkin' 'bout right there!" hollered a young man, wearing baggy jeans and a White Sox baseball cap cocked to the side. "The popo always rollin' up in the hood doin' that rank ass shit."

"Say that!" shouted a middle-aged woman. "It ain't right!"

Others in the revolutionary crowd roared with the hope of a civil rights movement, as Charles Owens spoke passionately with his arm placed around the shuddering shoulders of a gentleman old enough to be his father. The fragile and slouched over Sanders looked distraught and defeated. Meanwhile, a confident Owens stood on solid ground as he inspired residents of the community to rebuild the foundation of a man whose world had been uprooted beneath him.

"This is an eighty-four-year-old man standing next to me! Look at him ladies and gentlemen! Look at him! This is a beaten man; a violated man. He could be your father, your grandfather, your husband, your brother, or your uncle! He's one of our seniors, one of our ancestors! He's a member of our village! He's our family!"

I stood in the background and watched Charles Owens work the crowd. Cameras and microphones are turned off, but that didn't stop flirtatious female reporters from trying to get an exclusive interview with the magnetic bachelor blessed with good looks and the gift of gab. Like the rest of the awestruck citizens in attendance, I look on with civic pride. I'm proud because I know Charles better than most. To me, he's more than just a media savvy, public servant. He's a mentor. And he's also one of my clients.

My representation of Charles Owens is the reason the FBI and the Cook County States Attorney's Office raided my office. They didn't like the idea of him buying and rehabbing so many dilapidated buildings and accumulating so much wealth in real estate. His outspoken personality and continuous verbal attacks against the city and the police department fueled the fire of law enforcement to have him extinguished.

Charles and I met a couple of years ago when I worked on a committee sponsoring a scholarship banquet at one of the downtown hotels. He was very supportive in helping us raise scholarship money for African-American high school graduates attending black colleges and universities. He seemed to be a real cool guy, willing to give something back to the community. I also admired his style and presence; people were drawn to him, and he seemed comfortable interacting with all kinds of people from all walks of life.

With him being a developer and me working in real estate law, the two of us hit it off immediately. I could help him and he could help me. Being in his late-forties, and almost fifteen years older than me, I saw Charles as a big brother and somewhat of the father figure I had always yearned for. He's beyond his years and full of wisdom.

I guess having an older male to confide in is what I missed the most by not having my father around. Whereas, Kendall was able to find refuge in the gang he hung out with, I was always a loner and kept problems to myself. In the past, when I suffered heartache or disappointment, I internalized my emotions and used school or work as an outlet. I've always had a close relationship with Mama, but there are some things a young man just can't share with his mother. A young boy needs to hear a strong male voice. Sometimes a mother and a boy just are unable to relate well to each other.

My love for Mama has grown over the years; I guess maturity has allowed me to understand her better. As a child I didn't understand her mood, her rage, and the way she sometimes took her frustrations and loss of Daddy out on us. I wouldn't consider Mama an abusive parent, but her lack of patience often rattled my sensitive temperament enough to wish I had the number to DCFS. Sometimes it just didn't take much to set Mama off.

I can look back on those days and smile now, but I wasn't laughing then. I remember Mama flying off the handle on one occasion vividly. One time, we were riding down 95th Street, on our way home from shopping for new clothes for the upcoming school year. It was the month of July and the temperature was blazing. Mama's gray Buick Electra 225 felt like an oven on the inside and was hotter than charcoal at a backyard cookout. We were being roasted. There was no air-conditioner and the rolled down windows only provided humid, suffocating heat. Mama was hot, tired and irritable.

Up ahead was Fun Town, the largest amusement park on the south side. First La-La looked at Kendall, then, Kendall looked at me. As the oldest, I was supposed to ask Mama to stop so we could get on some rides, but I was scared. We were all scared.

As the 225 degree Buick approached Fun Town, the three of us sighed in unison "Oooooh", hoping Mama could find it in her heart to stop. She couldn't. As a matter of fact, Mama was rather heartless in her response.

My God-fearing, church loving, Mama unleashed a tirade full of four letter words that made me wonder when and where she found her religion. She quickly reminded us of how much money she had just spent on pants, blouses, shirts, skirts and shoes, and that dollar bills didn't grow on trees or come out of her ass.

Mama was steaming mad and her blood pressure was close to reaching its boiling point. I thought she was going to suffer a stroke. Sweat was rolling down her face faster than kids on a water slide. She was cussing and fussing, and huffing and puffing so loud that I thought the top of her head was going to explode. By the time Mama finished blowing her stack, I was pouting, Kendall was crying, and La-La was shaking more than a child with Tourette Syndrome.

Those were the times I wish we had a cool, calm and collected fatherly voice at home telling us everything would be okay. Back then, we were too young to understand the reason behind Mama's ranting and raving. It was just her of way of coping with being overwhelmed and stressed out.

After most of the crowd disappeared, Charles came over and greeted me with a firm handshake and gracious smile.

"How did I do?" he asked, in the way a politician seeks approval from his campaign adviser after giving a big speech.

"You hit a homerun."

"So I knocked it out the park, huh?"

"Better than that," I added. "You hit a grand slam."

Charles nodded and grinned boldly. "Julian, there's nothing like clearing the bases and bringing everybody home."

"Well you definitely cleared the bases."

Mr. Sanders, the media, and all of the neighborhood protesters have moved on. Only Charles' inner-circle of aides and security remain on the scene. I'm happy to be a member of his team.

"Are you hungry, Julian?" he asked.

"Sure," I replied.

"Excellent," he smiled. "Leave your car and ride with me."

Two guys, the size of NFL linemen, sit in the front seat of Charles' dark red, Lincoln Navigator while he and I ride in the back. As engaging as Charles is in front of the camera, he is extremely private and guarded. It's almost as if he has two personalities; one for the public and one for his inner-circle. In some ways, he reminds me of a shy entertainer who is at his best only on stage in front of an audience. Charles said he always travels with security because he wants to shield himself from people with bad intentions trying to get too close. Beware of jealous people he warned.

"See Julian," he stated, as we rode around the south side in his luxury SUV. "Some folks don't like me because I'm trying to do some things. They know I have the power to make a difference."

I nodded in agreement, but remained silent.

"Look at all the nonsense happening around this city," he lectured. "Man I grew up right over there," he said, pointing at a vacant area where buildings of the Robert Taylor projects used to line up next to each other.

I remain silent and keep listening.

"Some of us got out alive, but a lot of us didn't."

"I can believe that," I said, feeling the need to say something.

"And a lot of us who did get out are wasting away," he added.

"That's a shame."

The security team never said a mumbling word. Instead they kept their eyes on the road ahead, as the four of us navigated around the streets of Chicago, surveying the demographics of the inner-city on a warm summer day. From the back seat, Charles and I watched African-American men, young and old, congregate on corners near liquor stores, vacant lots and abandoned buildings. They had no place to go and didn't appear to know where they had come from either. It's a sad scene to view.

Charles keeps talking as he focuses through the tinted windows, using his eyes to shoot a cerebral photograph of the picture in front of him. It seems like some of the subjects are gazing back at us in the Navigator, almost as if they know they're being observed and are posing for Charles' mental snapshot.

Charles keeps talking and the gator keeps rolling.

"They tore down those projects and are now forcing black folks to move out into the suburbs while white folks reclaim the city. Remember, Julian, the city is where the money is, and is where it will always be," he affirmed, tapping me on the leg to make sure he had my attention.

"I know," I concurred.

"Julian, with your legal mind and my business acumen and credibility with folks on the street, you and I can do some things. Our problem is we get distracted and caught up in nonsense. Look at the news. Kids are killing kids. We got little girls getting shot at school and ten-year-old boys getting killed and thrown in the river. Julian, I plan on getting to the bottom of that nonsense and eradicating the situation as soon as possible!"

And the gator rolls on.

32

KENDALL

Birthday celebrations are meant to be special, so I decided to throw Ray a surprise party. Because he's such a suspicious individual, surprising him with a party was going to be extremely difficult. However, I was determined to pull it off. The two of us have been through a lot together. I love Ray even though his reckless attitude sometimes pisses me off. We don't always approach matters in the same way, but I know Ray will have my back in crunch time and I'll have his. He's crazy as hell, but he's been my partner in crime for a long time. We've been friends since grammar school. Ray's my brother.

I lured him in for the surprise by telling him I wanted just the two of us to hang out and kick it like we did back in the day. I told him we needed to get out and forget about business for a little while and have some fun. No women, no crews, no bullshit, just us. For some reason, I needed things to be like they were back when life was simple. Back then, we weren't so occupied with hustling, managing street teams, and looking over our shoulders. We were broke as hell and didn't have a damn thing, but we still had a good time because we knew how to create our own fun.

Now, Ray and I have more than we ever dreamed of. Greed sometimes makes me consider increasing our territory to make more profits, but deep down, I know it isn't worth it. Expanding our turf will bring us more money, but also more problems. I have enough stuff to worry about already.

Life is good. Both of us are already living in the fast lane, with fast money, fast women and fast cars, moving at a speed faster than a time machine. We're burning rubber on the game. Pockets still winning, rims still spinning.

And as long as we keep traveling in the express lane, no one will ever be able to pass us by. Nevertheless, we still have to keep looking in the rearview mirror to see whose trying to creep up on our tail. I don't know when it will happen, but at some point, we're gonna have to ease off the accelerator. Lately, I've been thinking it may be time for me to shift gears and slow down a little bit.

"Surprise!" screamed well wishers as they greeted Ray and me aboard the Odyssey for a midnight cruise on Lake Michigan.

"Ah hell nah!" Ray hollered with eyes wide as saucers.

"I got you didn't I," I bragged.

"You got me dawg!" he yelled in amazement. "You got me big time!"

"I know!" I laughed.

"All evening you been talkin' that just the two of us bullshit, and here you . . ."

I laughed and slapped hands with crewmembers and buddies from around the way, as Ray looked around to register the faces on board.

"Well I'll be damn!" Ray shouted.

"Ha ha ha," I laughed.

"Kendall, you my nigga for real!"

"I know, Ray. I know."

Ray hollered to get the attention of the well wishers on board and then turned to me. "Can you believe this nigga even went out and bought me a white linen outfit, so I could wear it here tonight, and here all you niggas up in here got white linen outfits on, too. He got me y'all. I got much love for you, K!"

"I love you, too, Ray," I said embracing him with a hug. "You my brother, man."

"No doubt."

Family and friends clad in the coolness of white linen, gathered around to shower Ray with hugs and kisses as we celebrated on the water. For two hours, we sailed the shores of Lake Michigan, wining and dining, styling and profiling, with me playing the big shot and picking up the tab. Why not, it was my partner's surprise birthday bash.

We danced and partied like ghetto superstars, with one of the world's greatest skylines providing the backdrop to our titanic festivities. The cool, late night summer breeze and endless bottles of champagne made the occasion even more sparkling and bubbly. And as usual, Ray enjoyed being the toast of the town.

In all seriousness though, I'm a little concerned about Ray because he's been toasting the town a bit too much lately. His actions have been wild and reckless. He's out of control sometimes; too much alcohol and drugs. In light of all the craziness going on in the game, I've been trying to tone down my act and operate under the radar, but Ray's getting bolder and more flamboyant. Sometimes, he acts like he's invincible and above the law. The police can spot him a mile away. I'm driving around town in a Ford Mustang GT, and he's high rolling through the hood in a hundred thousand dollar, convertible Jag.

I was trying to relax and remain festive, but I couldn't help but observe Ray's actions on the Odyssey. Several times on the cruise, I heard him bragging about how he was gonna run the city; the future king of the C-H-I. He strutted around the ship, drinking champagne out the bottle, doing his Al Pacino impersonation of Tony Montana in the movie *Scarface*; talking about the world was his and everything in it. At first it was funny, but after a while, I thought I was watching a rerun of Wesley Snipes in *New Jack City*. It was annoying. Ray's intoxicated, but some of his actions didn't even make drunk sense. I laughed and played it off, allowing him to enjoy his moment under the stars. What can I say? It's his party and he can brag if he wants to.

"I can't stand you, Kendall!" Tammy shouted, as I reached for my keys on the table near the front door.

"Yeah, yeah," I laughed. "You'll be awight."

"You said you was gonna stay here wit' me tonight!" she screamed.

I snickered. "I changed my mind."

"I got my sister to keep the boys tonight 'cuz you said you wanted to be wit' me."

"I was with you," I countered. "Now I gotta go."

"You know what Kendall," she pointed. "You full of shit!"

"If you say so," I teased.

"All you wanna do is come over here get yo' freak on and then leave."

"I thought that was our quality time, baby."

"Fuck you, Kendall!"

I heard the ashtray hit the door as I left Tammy's apartment. Lately I've been trying to take a break from her. Ever since I took her to that fancy restaurant on Mother's Day, she's been trying to be possessive and questioning my comings and goings. Now, she's complaining and sweating me about why I don't spend the night at her apartment as much as I used to, or if she and the kids can move in with me. A lot of it is my fault because I lured her into my web of seduction and deception.

I'd taken Tammy out to my house after the Mother's Day dinner so she could see how I really lived. It was her first time visiting my home; she was captivated. That didn't surprise me because I pulled out all the stops. First, I ran some bath water and let her bathe in the tub for about a half hour. Then I let her relax in the Jacuzzi with a glass of wine. She was feeling tipsy and was ready for just about anything. I gave Tammy a full body massage, rubbing her tender body down with some hot oils. She was putty in my hands after that. I had her cooing, purring and whispering my name all night long. She could've just called me Calgon because I had taken her little ass away.

I must admit, I like Tammy and enjoy having her little tattooed body rubbing me the right away in the middle of the night, but she's in love, and I'm not feeling that shit.

Tammy's been pissed ever since she found out about the party I threw for Ray on the Odyssey, and didn't invite her. Taking her to that party would've been worse than taking sand to the beach; it was a boat load of freaks on that cruise, and most of them were looking for a place to dock at the end of the night. And I was determined to put my anchor down.

The ladies on board that night gave me major props for being able to rent out the Odyssey for our own private party. They were eager to show me how much they enjoyed themselves, and I allowed them to do just that. Just like athletes and entertainers, drug dealers get plenty of groupie love. Gold digging skeezers are always looking to have a good time at somebody else's expense. They use us and we use them.

Ray and I took four of the women back to my house that night just so we could keep the party going. Those chicks were hot and wet way before they got in the Jacuzzi. Tammy's mad because she knows what went on that night.

To make matters worse, Tammy's two boys, DeAndre and Dontrell have grown too fond of me. I started off being Uncle Kendall, but lately, they've been asking me if I'm gonna be their daddy. I really care about those boys, but I don't want them getting too attached to me. It's probably because I'm afraid of getting too attached to them.

I dropped the top on my high-powered Mustang and sped off into the humid nighttime air, leaving Tammy to cool off at home alone. Ray and I had made plans earlier in the day to hook up at his house to shoot some pool and tally our profits for the week. When I spoke with him earlier, he said he had to visit a few currency exchanges and some casinos in Indiana to launder some money. Our plan was to meet at his place around eleven, but I was running behind schedule because of my drama with Tammy.

It's Friday night and the warm weather has people out and about. 79th Street is congested with weekend activity. Folks have been waiting for consistent warm weather and now we have it. People are pounding the pavement and hanging on corners. Taverns and liquor stores are making a lot of money tonight. I wonder how much cash we made this week?

In recent weeks, our sales have dropped due to increased police activity, but we're still raking in about $8,500 a day. That gives us over a quarter of a million dollars a month. That's chump change to a lot of guys in the game, but I can live with those numbers any day of the week.

As usual this time of year, rocky roads and bright orange construction signs are making driving difficult. It seems like detours and lane closings are dominating every major thoroughfare and expressway in the city. There's just no way to avoid it and no fast way to get anywhere. It's ridiculous. I hate it. I thought about calling Ray on my cell phone to tell him I was going to be a little late, but knowing Ray he may be late getting home as well.

Suddenly flashing lights appear in my rearview mirror. The loud siren is deafening. It's a blue and white police vehicle, and the officer behind the wheel seems to be in a big hurry to get to his emergency destination. The police cause almost as many accidents as they prevent. I pulled over and let the squad car pass. Within seconds, I saw two other squad cars and an ambulance rushing in the same direction. Typical Chicago in the summer time; the temperature is hot and folks are acting a damn fool. I got out of the way and let them by.

I tried to turn right onto the block Ray lives on, but police cars have denied entrance to the street. I wonder if they're the same vehicles that passed me a few minutes earlier. The sirens are mute, but the lights still flash. I park my car on the next block down and got out to see what was going on. People are all over the street and sidewalk.

"Hey man," I said, stopping a guy wearing a blue North Carolina basketball jersey with Jordan 23 on the back. "What happened down there?"

"Some guys in a truck just rolled up on this nigga in a white Jaguar and opened fire on his ass!" the guy testified enthusiastically. "Man, that nigga in the drop top Jag got straight smoked! They can put a fork in that nigga 'cuz his ass is done for real!"

I can feel the air leave my body as I gasp in disbelief; I realize he's talking about Ray. My knees buckle from the blow of the information. I try to compose myself as the young man rambles on with the delight of an eyewitness on the ten o'clock news.

"Damn, this shit is crazy!" he continued. "They say blood is all over the seats and dashboard. Cops done already pulled out the yellow tape; they tryna search the scene for evidence, hoping they can find some shells and shit. And ole boy is still in the ride. Dude that's some wild shit! The folks in the truck just pulled a straight up hit! It's time for the coroner to do an autopsy on that nigga."

I'm fighting to keep my emotions in check. I can't believe this!

The eyewitness keeps reporting. "Man, I don't know who that nigga's family is, but I think it's time for them to pull out the black clothes, order a bunch of flowers and have a funeral."

33

LAUREN

"Did you hear what happened?" I asked, as I watched the news on CLTV while talking to Julian on the telephone.

"What are you talking about?" Julian asked, sounding groggy and half asleep.

"Ray was killed last night!"

"Ray who?"

"Kendall's buddy," I replied. "Ray McNeal."

"Whoa!" Julian replied, now sounding more awake. "What happened?"

"I heard on the news that he got shot and killed in front of his house. Ray was sitting in his car and some guys pulled up next to him and shot him seven times."

"Damn!" Julian gasped. "Have you spoken with Kendall?"

"No," I answered. "And that's what I'm worried about."

"Have you talked to him or seen him lately?"

"Yes," I admitted begrudgingly. "Julian, we need to talk, but I don't want to discuss this on the phone."

"What's wrong, La-La?" Julian asked with concern.

"We need to talk!" I warned. "I need you to come over here now!"

"What's wrong?" Julian repeated.

"Julian I need you to come over here now!"

"Okay!" he hollered. "I'll be there in a half hour."

Butterflies flipped around inside my stomach as I paced the floor waiting for the repeat broadcast of the news on CLTV. CLTV is Chicago's version of CNN and provides around the clock news coverage. "Where's Kendall?" I whispered softly to myself. I looked at my watch again, wondering what was taking Julian so long to get over here. There shouldn't be a lot of traffic on the streets since it's a Saturday morning.

Unable to be still, I went to the bathroom and turned on the radio to hear the news on WBBM-AM. Instead of local news, they were broadcasting the president's weekly radio address. I mumbled some more thoughts to God. "Lord if Ray has been killed, is Kendall next?"

The doorbell rang before I had an opportunity to ask God another question. Julian announced himself through the intercom and waited for me to buzz him in. Tearful eyes and a warm embrace greet my oldest brother at the door. I bury my head on his shoulder and hold him as if I'm holding on to him and Kendall for the last time.

"Its okay, La-La," he assures.

We go to the living room and sit down by the window; I'm hoping the fresh breeze of a Saturday morning will cool my concerns and fears.

"So what's so important that you couldn't talk about it on the phone?"

"Kendall."

"What about, Kendall?" Julian asked. "When was the last time you saw him?"

I took a deep breath and recalled the scene at Mama's house.

"The last time I saw Kendall, he was with Ray at the house."

Julian interrupted me. "What house?"

"Mama's house," I sighed, biting my lower lip with anxiety.

"What?" Julian snapped. "What were they doing at the house?"

"It was the day Mama was getting out the hospital, and I went by the house to get some clothes and the portable oxygen tank for Mama to have on her way home. When I got there, they were in the kitchen counting money and packaging drugs."

"They what?" Julian yelled.

"Let me finish," I pleaded.

"That trifling..."

I continued. "When I walked in the kitchen, they had money, drugs and guns all over the table."

"Who else was in the house?" Julian asked, interrupting me again with a look of rage in his eyes.

"Just Kendall and Ray," I answered. "But the look in Kendall's eyes scared me that day, Julian. I'd never seen him like that before. He looked deranged."

"That's because he's trifling!" Julian shouted with an uncommon frown of anger present on his otherwise pleasant face. "Why didn't you tell me about this sooner?"

"I was scared!"

"Scared of what?" Julian barked, pounding his fist on the sofa with his words becoming meaner by the sentence. "Scared of whom? Are you afraid of Kendall?"

"No," I answered, but not really sure what my brother is capable of doing.

"Well what?" he chastened. "Why didn't you tell me?"

"Because I didn't want the situation to get out of control," I pleaded. "I was worried about the two you having a confrontation and making it even worse."

"So what else happened?"

"Ray left and then Kendall left. I cleaned up the house and then went to get Mama from the hospital. Julian, Kendall didn't look right that day. His face was all swollen with cuts and bruises; he had a gash on his forehead and his eye was black and puffy. He was edgy. Kendall looked as if he was capable of doing just about anything."

"How was Ray acting before he left?"

"He was the usual, Ray," I said, recalling the events of the day, not realizing that would be the last time I would see Ray alive. "He was drunk, chain smoking and trying to hit on me, talking a lot of nonsense."

"Typical Ray," Julian sniped.

"That's what scared me about Kendall that day."

"What's that?"

"He was edgy and mean spirited. Ray was talking a lot of crap about how I looked and wanting to meet a woman like me and Kendall went off. I was so scared because they had guns sitting on the kitchen table and I didn't know what was about to happen next. It was a very volatile environment. Anything could've happened."

"We can't have him taking his lifestyle into Mama's house."

I nodded. "I agree. When I went to pick Mama up from the hospital I was a nervous wreck. Just think if I had gone straight to the hospital to get Mama instead of stopping by there first."

"He is so trifling!"

"Wait, Julian," I interjected, pointing to the television. "They're talking about the murder now."

Hearing the story again made me shudder with chills. It was a horrific scene. Julian and I looked on in disbelief. The weekend news anchor said Ray had been shot seven times with most of the bullets striking him in the chest and head.

"That's why I wanted you to come over here instead of discussing this on the phone. Who knows who may be looking for Kendall right now? We don't know what he knows about Ray's murder, and if the same people who killed Ray may be after Kendall next. We don't know anything because he doesn't talk to us. Julian, I know you don't like Kendall and his lifestyle, but he's our brother. And if something happens to him, it will kill Mama."

"Yeah because she loves the ground he walks on," Julian chided, with a trace of jealousy flowing from his small lips.

"She loves you, too," I urged. "Mama loves you because she's knows she can depend on you to be there and be responsible. She loves Kendall because she worries about him more than she does us. He's unpredictable. I think his reckless ways remind her of Daddy. Julian, you're like the sun and Kendall is like a solar eclipse."

"Huh?" Julian asked with a quizzical smirk, not understanding my solar analogy.

"You hear how the meteorologists make a big deal every time we have a solar eclipse; they talk about when it's going to happen, when it last occurred, and where the best place to view it is. That's Kendall. He pops up every now and then, and gives her a few dollars and pays for some prescriptions and she's happy as a lark. She takes his money because she loves him even though she despises what he does. His lifestyle is letting her down, but he's still her child. She's prays for us, but she prays a little bit more for him because she fears he'll end up dead or in jail. Mama may try to act like she doesn't worry about Kendall, but she does."

"So how am I the sun?"

"You're the sun because she expects you to rise to the occasion every day. She knows you'll be there to brighten her day. It's like we make a big deal out of seeing a solar eclipse because they're rare, but we often take the sun for granted because it rises everyday."

"So I'm the sun, huh?"

"Yes you're the sun."

"And still I rise! And still I rise!" Julian grinned with his arms raised in the air with the strength of a Maya Angelou poem.

"You're silly."

"Mama loves you, too, La-La," Julian smiled. "Because you're observant and see things other folks can't."

"Sometimes I can and sometimes I can't," I said, reminiscing about my encounter with Jerry Farmer in New York and being abandoned in the rain up in Harlem. I didn't see that coming at all.

"As a matter of fact, with your braids like that, you kind of resemble Miss Cleo," Julian kidded me with a hearty laugh.

"I don't think so," I said, rolling my eyes. "You know I don't look anything like that phony psychic chick."

"Come on La-La," he teased. "Tell me my lucky numbers."

"Yeah I love you, too," I responded sarcastically.

"Call me now!" he yelled, mimicking the pseudo psychic's late night commercial.

"Whatever. She's not even Jamaican."

The spurt of laughter is a brief relief to our souls, but concern lingers in the air. I sit silently as Julian rubs his hands across his round face. I look at him and see the striking resemblance to Mama; they share the same caring eyes which agonize way more than they should. Now, instead of speaking angrily, he's thinking quietly. Julian is being stubborn and doesn't want to admit he's worried about Kendall also. He loves his younger brother, but he hates him also.

The ticking seconds announcing the start of *60 Minutes* signal the end to another weekend. Hearing the clock is a weekly reminder there are only a few short hours left in Sunday and that another work week is about to begin again. Seeing the distinguished and debonair Ed Bradley is the only thing I like about this show. Other than that, it's just an alarm clock counting down to doom minute by minute. Tick tick tick tick. . .

My mood was restless. Before long, sixty minutes had turned into four hours and I didn't know where the time had gone. I don't want to watch the ten o'clock news; I don't want to listen to music; and I'm tired of pressing my remote searching for something to see on cable. I have a million channels that seem to show the same movies over and over again; if it came on last night then it's coming on again tonight. I'm bored, I'm lonely and I'm worried, and I wish I had someone to talk to. I need a strong shoulder to lean on. I miss Andre. I want to call him, but my pride won't allow me to pick up the phone and dial his number even though he's still on my speed dial.

I turned the television off and went to run some bath water. As the tub filled with warm water, I lit some candles to help soften my mood and relax my mind. I dipped my fingers in the tub to test the temperature. Waving my hand back and forth increased the foam of bubbles. I need to jump in and meditate happy thoughts. The sudden sound of the telephone burst my bubble. I cut the faucet off and rushed to the phone.

"Hello."

"It's me, La-La," Kendall whispered. "I'm okay."

Hearing Kendall's voice was the best sound I'd heard all weekend. Just knowing my brother is still alive and is able to speak to me brought tears to my eyes. Usually, I'm inquisitive and would've asked him a lot of questions about his whereabouts and what actually happened with Ray. I didn't. Instead, I looked to the heavens and uttered softly.

"Thank God."

34

JULIAN

Flashy SUVs, fancy cars and fast motorcycles dominate the overcrowded roads near Slaughter Funeral Home on east 75th Street. As expensive Hummers, BMWs and Harleys remain immobile outside, hundreds of people file inside the chapel to pay their respects to Raymond Arthur McNeal Jr. Some of us are mourning his death; some of us are just witnessing the theatrics; and some of us are using the wake to catch up with old friends from the neighborhood and classmates from elementary and high school.

Being reacquainted with old friends and classmates is nice, but Kendall is the person I'm hoping to see. Mama's nearly worried to death and is depending on me to find him. He called Lauren a couple of times to let her know he's alright, but didn't reveal where he was calling from. I'm hoping he'll show up for the funeral, but my instincts are telling me he won't.

It's absolutely amazing how funerals can allow us to revisit faces from our past, giving us a chance to see and talk with people we haven't seen in years, and in some cases decades. The memorial service for Ray is providing me with such an opportunity.

"Julian Collins!" screamed a voice from years gone by.

I turn to acknowledge the voice coming across 75th Street. The sound of the voice is familiar, but the shape of the person isn't.

"It's me," she responded in a sultry tone. "Nikki Coleman."

"Damn," I mumbled to myself.

When we were in high school, Nikki was fine and refreshing with the figure of a Coca Cola bottle with the ability to quench any man's thirst for something wet. That was then. Now she has the shape of a big gulp, super-sized with enough pounds of extra meals to feed a small army. The years haven't been kind to Nikki.

"It's good to see you!" she yelled, wrapping her meaty arms around my neck and squeezing me tightly. "You haven't changed a bit. So whazzup?"

"Nothing much," I responded.

"I ain't seen you in years."

"Yeah it's probably been close to twenty years."

"I saw you as I was comin' 'cross the street and I said he kinda looks familiar then I got a real good look and seen it was you."

"Yeah it's me," I smiled.

"Damn it's good to see you again."

"It's been a long time," I added.

"So you married or got some kids yet?" she asked.

"I'm single, no kids."

"Whatcha waitin' on?"

"I guess I'm still waiting on the right person." I replied with a shy smile.

"Well don't be waitin' too long, sweetie," she teased.

"What about you?" I inquired. "Are you married with children?"

"Huh . . . been there, done that and got the T-shirt," she quipped sarcastically.

"Oh really?" I asked, hoping for her to elaborate.

"Yeah baby, I'm twice divorced and got six kids."

I tried to play it off, but Nikki's declaration raised my eyebrows and caused a look of astonishment to sweep across my face.

"Sounds like you got a lot more than just the T-Shirt to me," I joked.

"Okay!" she laughed loudly and countered with a witty reply. "I got a whole box of T-Shirts and a shit load of diapers."

"I bet."

"So where you be stayin' at?" she asked.

"I'm over in Beverly," I answered. "Where are you, now?"

"I'm back with my mama and nem over on 104th and Calumet."

"So you're back in the neighborhood."

"Uh huh," she confirmed. "I'm back in da hood."

"Well that's cool."

"I guess I'm gon get on in there so I can sign the register and view the body. It's a shame we don't see each other 'til sumpin tragic happens."

"I know."

"Well it's been good seein' you, Julian."

"It's good seeing you, too, Nikki."

"Oh yeah," she hesitated, as if she had one more thing she wanted to tell me or ask me about. "Where's Mr. Kendall?"

"He's around," I responded quickly, not wanting to answer questions concerning my brother's whereabouts.

"Well tell him Nikki Coleman said hey," she said with a wide grin as she turned to enter the funeral home.

"I will."

I watched Nikki walk away and shook my head in amazement. I had the biggest crush on her back in high school. I was in my junior year, and she was a freshman and had classes with Kendall. Nikki wouldn't give me the time of day. She said I was a square and wasn't her type. I was an upperclassmen being rejected by a freshman. That was a disappointment for me back then.

At fourteen, Nikki's hazel eyes still had the innocence of the girl next door, but by fifteen she was a round-the-way girl gazing at roughnecks. She was right, I definitely wasn't her type. Nikki liked thugs. It wasn't long before she had earned the nickname Skippy. Guys in the neighborhood called her Skippy because they said she had thighs as creamy as peanut butter and legs easy to spread. Watching Nikki skip into the funeral home made me glad she'd told me no. Being rejected by her had proven to be a blessing in disguise.

I entered the crowded funeral home and got in the long line to sign the register. There were so many people coming in and out that I didn't even realize I was standing behind one of my closest friends from grammar and high school. After confirming it was indeed my old buddy, I tapped him on the shoulder to get his attention.

"George Moore," I said. "What's up?"

"Julian Collins," he replied. "Long time no see."

"No kidding!"

"Man, it's good to see you!"

"It's good to see you, too," I replied. "It's been almost twenty years."

"Damn it seems like I'm running into everybody today."

"Tell me about it," I laughed.

"It's like a class reunion around here," he nodded.

"I know."

"You're looking good."

"So are you."

The years have been kind to George. He's clean shaven and still maintains his lean, athletic frame from the days he ran track and played football in high school.

"So what are you up to these days, Julian?"

"Working hard," I answered.

"Doin' what?" he asked.

"I'm an attorney and have my own law firm."

"Straight up?"

"Yes," I nodded proudly. "What about you?"

"I'm a state trooper," he boasted.

"Get out!" I laughed loudly. "You mean to tell me they gave you a badge and gun even though you were one of the main guys in the middle of all the fights when we were in high school."

"Yep," he grinned. "Do you remember Ronny and Michael Gibson?"

"I think so," I replied. "The names sound familiar."

"Ronny was in our class and his brother Michael was two years ahead of us."

"Oh yeah," my memory registered. "Didn't they play football with you?"

"That's them."

"They used to always want to fight people after basketball games."

"Yep," he confirmed. "They're in law enforcement also. Ronny is a state trooper and Michael is a Cook County Sheriff."

"That's amazing," I declared. "They caused more trouble than anyone in school."

"Isn't it incredible how things work out?"

"Sure is."

"It's good being able to see people from the hood again," George said, looking around at all the familiar faces in the funeral home. "It's just a shame we have to come together because somebody died."

"I know," I agreed. "Have you heard anything about why it happened?"

"I don't really know why it happened," he said with a quizzical expression on his face. "But I have my suspicions. I have some buddies with Chicago PD investigating some info for me."

"It'll be interesting to know what they find."

"Man, from what I been hearing," George stated solemnly. "They say that crime scene was nothing nice."

"That's scary," I replied with my thoughts suddenly turning to Kendall.

"Have you been inside the chapel yet?" George asked.

"Not yet," I answered. "After I sign the register, I'll go in and view the body."

"You can sign the register, but you can't view the body."

"Why not?"

"Closed casket, dude," George whispered. "They damn near blew his face off."

"Damn."

George signed the register and then handed me the pen so I could jot down my name and address.

Sad organ music and loud crying welcomed me into the overcrowded chapel. One of the funeral home employees gave me an obituary with a photograph of Ray on the front; it's the same picture that's on a stand near the copper colored casket. Not being able to view the body one last time makes the service a somewhat surreal experience. I open the obituary to study the words chronicling Ray's life.

Ray's story is incomplete. The obituary mentions his date of birth, the parents who preceded him in death, where he went to school, when he was baptized, the date of his death, and the name of the siblings he leaves behind. That's the sanitized version of his life story. The words fail to mention where and why he went to prison, the people he robbed and stole from, or the extended family members he used and abused.

The multi-page obituary shows pictures of Ray at various stages in his life. They show Ray as a child posing with family and friends during his school years and at his eighth grade graduation. There are also photos of him partying in nightclubs, smoking fat cigars, leaning up against fancy cars, and vacationing in Costa Rica. Unfortunately, the pictures can't show the faces of the folks he sold drugs to, the men he shot, the boys he beat up, the vulnerable women he took advantage of, and the fatherless kids he leaves behind.

I turned to the back of the obituary and saw Kendall's name listed as a pallbearer. He's posing with Ray on a couple of photos in the obituary, but his face isn't present amongst the mourners inside the chapel.

The high pitched wailing of a young woman with burgundy hair startles me. She's dressed seductively in a tight-fitting, mini-skirt and clear stilettos which make her look like a clothes shedding polecat eager to collect a wad of single dollar bills in a strip club. She has a small boy in her arms, and is screaming loud enough to wake up the dead, or at least everyone except Ray.

"Rayquan," she yelled, pointing at the casket. "That's yo' daddy in there! Why can't they open it, so my baby can see his daddy one last time? Why can't they open it?"

Friends of the woman came to console her as she tried to open the casket. The little boy looked confused and too young to understand his mother's anguish, or the significance of the moment. He'll understand later on in life.

The sound of the woman's voice still echoed through the chapel even after she had been carried outside.

"We wanna see Ray!" she screamed. "Oh God we wanna see Ray!"

The toddler was unable to see his daddy in death, and probably hadn't seen much of Ray while he was alive either. I scanned through the obituary again. Rayquan's name wasn't even listed.

To my surprise, after the service, I spotted Charles Owens conversing with a few men outside in front of the funeral home. I hadn't seen him inside, but the enormous crowd would've made it difficult to know who was or wasn't in attendance. There aren't any cameras present, but Charles is still the center of attention, with one of his burly security guards by his side. He didn't notice me, so I stayed back and observed from a distance. Dressed impeccably in a gray, sharkskin suit, Charles is holding court with his usual sartorial splendor.

In my opinion, some of the people seeking Charles' attention appear to be a bit unsavory, but he has expressed to me his willingness to rub shoulders with folks from all walks of life. He's comfortable in all settings and commands respect from everyone.

The repeated vibration of my cell phone disconnects my concentration on Charles. It's Vanessa. I answer the call and walk down the block to get away from the commotion so I can better hear our conversation. Her words bring a smile to my face. She's inviting me over for dinner. I quickly accept her offer. Our brief chat ends with a warm sensation running through my veins. I place the flip phone back in my pocket and walk back towards the front of the funeral home. I look to see if I can find Charles again, but he's no longer in sight.

Instead I see the young woman again in the tight dress and burgundy hair sobbing hysterically. Little Rayquan is also crying and clinging to her left arm. It's a lot of drama for such a young child to endure.

It's been nearly thirty years since I stood in the shoes little Rayquan is forced to wear today. Like him, I couldn't understand why Mama was crying so hard and had to be taken out of the church so many times during the service. I thought my father was playing sleep in his Sunday clothes. The magnitude of the moment didn't register until later. I later realized Daddy would never return home to play with his three children again. At least, I got a chance to see my father's face one last time. Rayquan didn't even get that. He's going to be another boy raised without a father.

When will the cycle end?

35

KENDALL

Las Vegas feels different to me this time around. The last time I was here, I was watching prize fights and setting up drug deals with Hector. This time I'm in the desert trying to find myself and determine my next move. I'm lost and looking for a way to recover from the madness taking place in the Windy City. It's blazing hot out here and the temperature is hovering over the century mark, but unfortunately, things are even hotter back home.

I've been on the move since Ray's murder. The day after Ray was killed I went to several banks and withdrew close to two hundred thousand dollars. It was from the business accounts I'd set up for my barbershops, carwashes and real estate holdings. I had about a quarter of a million dollars at home in a safe, but I was scared to go back to my house because I feared my life was in danger.

Even though I had blown lots of money over the years on cars, women, clothes, jewelry and fast living, I still had the sense to put some money aside. At an early age, Mama had instilled in us the importance of saving some of the money we made. She used to tell us to save money so that money could save us on a rainy day. I'm glad I listened because right now I'm in the middle of an extremely violent storm and bullets are raining all around me.

At first I got in my car and drove to St. Louis for a few days. I wasn't down there to see anybody or anything; I was just trying to sort things out and clear my head for a little while. The open road allowed me to solve the pieces to the puzzle occupying space in my mind.

Ray's murder was definitely no random hit. For days I've been wondering if things would've turned out differently if I had made it to his house on time. Instead of meeting up with him as we'd planned, I was busy messing around arguing with Tammy because she hadn't wanted me to leave. Arguing with Tammy may have saved my life. If I had been there on time, the shooters would've probably killed me, too.

Living on the run is fucked up. I haven't talked to any of my crewmembers because I don't know who to trust right now. Besides with Ray dead, the guys back home are running scared also. He was our enforcer. If they could get him, then they can get anybody.

La-La has been my only source of communication. I've been calling her at night from payphones to find out what's going on and to get an idea of how much attention Ray's murder was receiving in the news. She said the media had described it as a gangland style execution, and that no arrest had been made yet. No shit! I didn't need the people on the news to tell me that.

The police will never make an arrest on Ray's murder because nobody really gives a fuck. With Ray's violent past and long criminal record, the police are glad to see him dead. Now there's one less menace in society to worry about. As a matter of fact, I really wouldn't be surprised if the police knew the murder was set to take place before it happened.

The shooters blasted Ray right in front of his house; that means they were waiting for him. They knew which car he was driving and the approximate time he was gonna make it home. For all I know, Ray could've actually spoken to his killers that day. He was a sitting duck in a white Jaguar.

Since La-La had kept me aware of the funeral arrangements, I'd driven back to Chicago to attend the services. I didn't go anywhere near the funeral home, but I was able to sit in a stolen van and see a few things from down the street. Since the services were during the day, I was able to make out many of the faces in the crowd, including Julian's. I'm sure he and many of those in attendance were wondering why they didn't see me. Through high-powered binoculars, I saw them up close, but from a distance.

I saw one of the women Ray had fathered kids by hollering and crying in dramatic form. Also in my vision, were some of the crooked cops we paid off every month. There were old family members and childhood friends mourning and walking around in a dejected state. I also witnessed members of the higher-ups planning and scheming in a conniving way. They were wondering where I was too.

If the higher-ups made the hit, they probably aren't done yet. With Ray out of the picture, they know they've weakened me in the process. If they kill me also, then they can wipe out our entire crew and reclaim the blocks we sold drugs on. Instead of being satisfied with the slice they forced us to serve them, the higher-ups wanted to feast on the entire pie. It's time for them to have their cake and eat it too.

They probably figure our pockets are getting too fat, and that we're outgrowing our britches. People in the drug game are greedy; everybody wants to enjoy their share and someone else's also. And in this business, you can never underestimate the ambitions of another man.

After the funeral ended, I drove straight to Midway Airport and boarded a plane.

Now here I am, out in Las Vegas in the middle of the summer. It's Thursday night and I've been here since Saturday. The sun has gone down, but the desert heat is still suffocating. Usually, for me, Vegas sizzled with excitement, but my enthusiasm for the city has fizzled out this time around. I'm ready to go home. Unfortunately, I don't think it's safe for me to return to Chicago just yet.

Right now I'm agonizing over everything I've done. I don't know if I'm feeling this way because my soul is telling me I need to change, or if I'm afraid because my chickens are finally coming home to roost. Maybe it's time for me to reap what I've sown all these years. I've hurt and disappointed a lot of people in my pursuit of money, power and respect. And I captured all three with relative ease. And Mama said I was just like my daddy and would never mount to shit.

In a lot of ways, I've done a lot of my activities out of spite for my mother. It's hard growing up feeling like an underdog in my own home. They say parents should never have favorites, but that was never the case in the house I grew up in. Mama favored Julian because he was the first born after a lot of difficult pregnancies, and La-La was catered to because she was the baby girl. That left me as the middle child, usually caught in the center of a lot of bullshit.

Deep down, I wonder if Mama is even aware of how she treated us differently. As I see it, in her own way, she set me up to rebel. I can't even count the times she called me stupid ass nigger as a child. I wasn't stupid, I just wasn't motivated. Julian was the studious type and always had his head buried in a book, therefore my progress, or lack of, was always compared to his. That's probably one of the main reasons we're sibling rivals today.

While Julian and La-La were in the house eager to read books, I was the hyper outdoors type always looking for my next adventure. At the time, if there had been some medicine on the market to slow me down, Mama probably would've drugged the shit outta me and had me sitting in a corner dozing off and drooling like a heroin addict waiting for my next fix. Now that I think about it, I probably wouldn't have been blamed for so much shit that I didn't do if I had been in the corner taking a drug induced nap. And even if I were asleep, that wouldn't have stopped Mama from beating my ass if she thought I had done something wrong.

As a child, I remember one time I went to bed early thinking it would stop Mama from swinging the ironing cord, but it didn't work. I was in the third grade and Mama had gone to the school for parent-teacher night to pick up all of our report cards. I passed all my classes with some *Gs* for good, a couple of *Es* for excellent, and a few *Fs* for fair, but the teacher, a short, fat, white lady by the name of Mrs. Fitzgerald said my grades would've been higher if my behavior was better. She said I disrupted the class too much and was a distraction to the other kids trying to learn. Mrs. Fitzgerald gave me a *U* for conduct since my behavior was unsatisfactory.

When Mama returned home, I was in bed pretending to be asleep. As soon as she slammed the door and started stomping through the house, I knew I was in for a restless night. I knew I was the problem because Julian and La-La never got into any trouble at school. I had the covers over my head; my eyes were closed, but my ears were wide open. Fear had me shaking between the sheets.

Mama hollered and told me to get my black ass up, and that she knew damn well I wasn't sleep because I don't usually go to bed so early. She threw the comforter off the bed, and went on a rampage telling me how she wasn't gonna take no more shit off me. That ironing cord had my ass too sore to sleep the rest of the night.

Tonight roulette is beating my ass. I've lost a thousand dollars in less than an hour, and I'm down about twenty grand since I've been out here. The casinos are taking a bite out of my ass and so is life. My world has turned into one big gamble, and I'm beginning to lose. I'm crapping out in every direction.

I decided to leave the MGM Grand and took the tram over to the Luxor to see the sights and find out if my luck will change. Instead of hanging out around the video poker machines and blackjack tables, I got a glass of rum and Coke from the bar and made my way over to the RA Nightclub.

The RA is one of the most popular nightclubs in Vegas and the sound of hip-hop can be heard from several yards away. It's jumping up in there. I'm really not in the mood for partying, so instead of waiting in the long line to get into the RA, I take a seat on one of the nearby sofas and people watch while sipping on my watered down drink.

This isn't a tourist crowd on hand tonight. Most of the people lingering around the club tonight are Vegas residents. A lot of people think Las Vegas is all glamorous, but there are a lot of thugs and hood-rats living out here too. Being here tonight is like hanging out at a club back home. Most of the guys are dressed like they're going to a picnic and the women are showing their assets.

Hookers run rampant in Vegas. I've been here so many times now that I can spot a Vegas ho a mile away. They're the ones who have moved here from all over the world to start a new life and end up selling pussy to make ends meet. Usually, they're easy to spot because they hang around the casinos in groups. They look for johns around slot machines or are requested by men calling one of the many escort services seeking sexual satisfaction from a certain type of woman. Special services are advertised by taxi drivers, foreigners passing out flyers on the street, and damn near everyone else in Vegas. Whatever ethnicity, body type, hair color, or complexion a man wants can be at his hotel room within ten minutes. Their services are monitored and organized.

However, I've also met my share of road warriors during my many trips here. Road warriors are the ones who fly in to do their dirty work and then fly back home.

The first time I came out here to transact some business I met a woman roaming through the Excalibur looking to hook up with a gentleman for the night. This chick had hopped on a plane and had come here with one of her friends from New Jersey to make some money over the weekend. Once again, a big fight was taking place and she knew a lot of cash would be changing hands.

It's been so long ago that I can't remember the broad's name, but she approached me and started a conversation. I really wasn't feeling her on the physical tip. She had average looks and was kinda on the chunky side. Her casual attire was unassuming and kept her from drawing a lot of attention. A rugged demeanor was subtly masked in a deceitful kind of way. She spent a good forty-five minutes gassing my head up about how fine and sexy I was, and how she would love to wake up with me the next morning. That chick was a straight East Coast hustler, and was trying to get up to my room and deep into my pockets.

While she made her move on me inside the Excalibur, her girlfriend was busy trying to set up a game plan of her own down at Mirage. They kept each other abreast of their progress with periodic cell phone calls.

Trick ass chicks probably got tired of walking up and down the strip all day looking for customers and wanted to find somewhere to sleep for a few hours. I dismissed that traveling tramp and went up to the room by my damn self. Fuck that shit. Those are the kind of broads who'll talk their way into your room and have you waking up the next morning not knowing who or where you are and without a dime to your name.

Now I must say, I've hooked up with a few freaks during my visits in Vegas, but something about that chick from Newark, NJ freaked me out. Any woman willing to spend a weekend in Vegas without a place to sleep is a bigger hustler than I am. And she's probably more dangerous.

My head must be in a funk because I'm not in the mood to kick it with any of these chicks here tonight, even though I've seen a few I would love to hit under better circumstances. I need another drink; something much stiffer than the weak rum and Coke I just finished. Right now, I need to gather my thoughts. My body is in Vegas, but my mind is in Chicago. I know I can't keep living on the run like this.

Maybe later on I'll call La-La to find out what's happening back home and ask about Mama. I worry about Mama. She probably doesn't think I worry about her, but I do. Even if I told her, I'm not sure she would believe me or not. I was always the guilty child whether I did something or not.

Being blamed for things I didn't do happened all the time when I was a kid. I remember one day when we were little, Julian, La-La and I were running through the house playing while Mama was in bed taking a nap. Somehow La-La stumbled and knocked a white, porcelain statue of Jesus off the living room cocktail table and broke it. The sight of a shattered Jesus had the three of us praying instantly for forgiveness. I was hoping that if Jesus could be raised from the grave, then maybe we could at least glue Him back together before Mama got up. Unfortunately our prayers weren't answered.

Instead the noise resurrected Mama from a deep sleep. She was mad and unforgiving. If there had been some crosses in the backyard, she probably would have hung us. Mama came in with the ironing cord and lashed out at all of us, but the venom of her anger was directed primarily at me. That was usually the case. I've always been the bad guy, and will always be the bad guy because I'm just like my daddy and will never mount to shit.

I guess I've spent all these years proving her right.

36

LAUREN

    It took everything I had to keep my eyes open while driving to Dawn's salon for my early morning hair appointment. Last night I was up until almost one o'clock taking my braids down, and was up at five, so I could get here to the salon by seven to have my hair shampooed and styled. I'm tired of wearing cornrows and want a new style. To make matters worse, fresh strands of gray are beginning to sprout up like aged vegetables planted in a garden of anxiety. I'm too young to be under so much stress. It's time for a new look and a new attitude.

    I closed my eyes and relaxed as Dawn cleaned and massaged my itching scalp. The mixture of shampoo and warm water caused a tingling sensation to penetrate my open pores. It feels good. It's therapeutic. I could stay in this chair forever. I can feel the dirt and dandruff being removed from my head. It would be nice to be able to rinse my troubles down the drain as well. Chaos is clogging my mind. If I stay stretched out in this chair for too long, I'll be in a deep sleep and snoring.

    With bouts of insomnia already dominating my nights, the wicked lifestyle of Kendall is the last thing I need invading my consciousness. I pray Mama never learns the depth of danger her youngest son dwells in. I know it would break her heart because it has definitely broken mine.

Carrying around the burden of worrying about my brother's illegal activities is taxing my brain, and not being able to really discuss it with anyone is causing me even more stress. I don't like discussing it with Julian because the tension between the two of them is already thick enough to cut with a butcher's knife. Julian is acting like he doesn't care about what's going on with Kendall. He's using his other activities as an excuse; saying he's busy running a law firm, attending hearings for his legal problems, worrying about Mama's health, and trying to establish a new relationship with his friend, Vanessa.

Like me, Julian has a lot to digest on his emotional plate. And adding Kendall's spicy way of life to his mental smorgasbord would surely have him battling indigestion as well. Maybe there's no sense in both of us wrestling with heartburn and sleepless nights. Besides, I think Julian is content with not knowing where Kendall is as long as he doesn't have to deal with him.

Thanks to Dawn, I had a new look when I walked through the doors of the insurance company. Goodbye bold and braided. Hello short and sassy. I looked different on the outside, but the same tired attitude marched inside my head. I'm exhausted, and a lack of sleep has me feeling like a zombie with a fresh hairdo. It's nine-thirty and I'm wondering how I can make it through the remainder of the day without falling on my face. And I'll probably have to sleep standing up because I don't want to mess my hair up yet.

I logged on to my computer and stared at the screen with weary vision. If I keep trying to function on three and four hours of sleep, I'll have bags under my eyes large enough to carry all my problems in.

My sleeping patterns have gotten worse ever since I went to New York and got kicked to the curb by Jerry Farmer because I refused his sexual advances. He left me in the rain on the corner of 127th Street and Madison Avenue. Thank God I made it back to the hotel safely. I've never been so afraid in my life. Right now, I despise everything about this company and what it stands for. I no longer feel like I can trust anyone. Jerry Farmer humiliated me. I hate him and I hate the company more than ever now, but I've worked too hard to throw in the towel and go someplace else to start over. At the present time, I'm not excited about having to go somewhere else and proving myself all over again for less money.

The computer detailed the items on my agenda for the remainder of the day; now I have an idea of what the next nine or ten hours look like. Unnecessary meetings and problems needing to be addressed dominate the emails in my mailbox. I have a long day ahead.

In the past, I complained about Andre sending a bunch of emails to my job because they interfered with my work, but now I miss them. The messages I get now are informing me of what corporate fires I need to put out; sometimes I wish Andre was around to put my fire out. At this point, I just wish I had his comforting voice to talk me through all the crap I'm going through.

Andre used to forward cute, electronic greeting cards to say hello and brighten my day just when I needed to read or hear a kind word. I don't get those anymore. I miss the early morning phone calls encouraging me to be careful and to have a good day. From time to time, Andre used to show up at my office on his day off with food for me to eat because he knew I would be working hard and skipping lunch. It's all the little things. I miss him.

Andre and I still talk with each other occasionally, but our conversations are much different now; they're forced and not as free flowing as they once were. I guess we're not sure exactly what to say to each other anymore. Both of us were accustomed to speaking from the heart, but now our words are calculated and measured; we're afraid of saying the wrong thing at the wrong time. It's like walking on eggshells.

Andre had promised to stand by me through thick and thin, but I still pushed him away. Now a burning ball of confusion had our emotions running high and bouncing off a wall of pain. Andre had extended his weary arms to grab hold of old times, but he was trying to catch on to something that may be long gone. He had been reaching out to me, but I never reached back because I wasn't sure if I was able to respond in the way he wants me to. I'm probably beyond his grasp right now. I thought ending our relationship would've helped me concentrate better on the other challenges dominating my life. I was wrong. I sleep even less now. I'm so confused.

Two new messages were in my voicemail box. Both of them were from Mama. The first message reminded me to pick up some orange juice from the grocery store and the second advised me of a prescription I needed to get from the pharmacy. There's no sense in returning Mama's calls because I know she'll probably be calling back soon with something else for me to do.

I left my office and decided to walk to the company cafeteria to get a hot cup of coffee to get myself going. I'm hoping a good jolt of caffeine can perhaps perk me up until I capture my second wind later in the day.

A strange sensation is filtering through our downtown headquarters. Something shady is brewing within the corporate structure. They're too many company big shots lurking around, and I need to find out what's going on. My body is half asleep, but my instincts are wide awake.

Before reaching the cafeteria, I heard the sound of a high-pitched voice calling my name. It was Christa Roszak, the manager of human resources. Christa's a nice lady, but I find her whiny shrill annoying. I stood near the entrance of the cafeteria and waited as Christa shuffled my way with an arm full of papers and folders.

"Good morning, Christa," I said, greeting her with a corporate smile. Christa is a short, frumpy, white woman with a mop-like haircut that reminded me of the Beatles.

"Hi Lauren," she replied in a shrill which sent a nervous chill down my spine. I bet her kids go nuts every time she calls their names. "I almost didn't recognize you with your new haircut. I had gotten used to seeing you with your braids. You're a very attractive woman Lauren. You're beautiful in any style you wear."

"I wish I could say the same for you," I thought, as I silently critiqued her outdated Ringo Starr haircut. She looked as though she had just had a hard day's night.

Instead I replied graciously. "Thanks, Christa."

"Lauren, will you be available to meet with me and Mark Berlin at ten-thirty?" Christa asked, in a sheepish tone that suggested she was a long way from the hick farm she grew up on. She is one of several employees in the office who commutes an hour and a half each way from Indiana. Christa probably had never even been around black people until she began working in Chicago.

"Sure, Christa," I answered begrudgingly, shaking my head. The last thing I need right now is another meeting to attend. This is going to be a very long day.

Christa read the expression on my face and tried to respond sympathetically.

"I know . . . there's a lot going on around here."

"Where's the meeting?"

"It's in Mark's office."

"Okay, I'll be there."

"Good," Christa said, as she turned and scurried off.

I got my coffee and returned to my office. I'm already behind, but now I feel like I've lost more time with this unexpected meeting with Mark. I must really be tired because I didn't even bother to ask Christa what the meeting is about. Most likely it's concerning some new hires and orientation for new employees coming into my department. I have a half an hour before my meeting, so I might as well use the time to review my adherence reports for the week and enjoy my coffee. At least I can say my department is meeting our quota this month so far.

This isn't the best coffee I've tasted, but as long as it gives me a boost, it will serve its purpose. I opened an Excel Spreadsheet on my computer and printed some documents tracking the number of calls the department has taken this month. The data is impressive because we've exceeded the expectations set by upper management.

The sound of the telephone caught me in the middle of a smile.

"Good morning, Lauren Collins speaking," I answered, picking up the receiver on the second ring with my left hand, with the cup of coffee in my right hand.

"Hi La-La," Mama said, greeting me with a voice of energy. "Did you get the messages I left you earlier this morning?"

"Yes Mama."

"Well when you go to the store to get my orange juice, stop and get me some of those frozen pancakes that come in a box."

That's why I didn't call her back because I knew she was going to call me back with more errands to run, with stuff for me to pick up over here and stuff for me to drop off over there. I looked at the clock as Mama continued to ramble on.

"La-La, are you still there?"

"Yes Mama."

"Baby, were you busy?"

She asked a question, but never gave me an opportunity to answer; she just kept on rolling off instructions.

"I don't know the name of the pancakes, but they come in a big box with waffles and French toast. I like 'em because they're very easy and convenient," she witnessed with the enthusiasm of an old lady doing a food commercial. "I can just stick 'em in the toaster and wait 'til they pop up. I'm able to eat a solid breakfast without having to do a lot of cooking. If you can't find 'em, just ask someone who works in the store."

"Okay, Mama."

"I know you're busy, La-La, but I have to call you and tell you all this stuff when it's on my mind. And since I'm not driving anymore, you know I need you to pick up little odds and ends for me from time to time. . ."

I interrupted her. "I'll talk to you later, Mama," I said abruptly before hanging up the phone. First she calls with a list of things for me to do then she pulls at my heart strings by telling me how much she needs me. Mama's a piece of work. And I already have a lot of work on my desk.

I sucked on a mint to erase the scent of coffee from my breath, and made my way to the ten-thirty meeting with Mark and Christa. My office is nice, but it can't compare to Mark's. Plaques and awards decorate the walls of Mark Berlin's spacious, corner office. I immediately noticed the diplomas from Princeton and the Wharton School of Business. As one of the company's executive vice-presidents, Mark oversees the sales and marketing department, but also has experience as an actuary. Mark is working with serious credentials. He's the epitome of a bean counter, and probably calculates numbers in his sleep.

Mark and Christa are seated at a long cherry wood conference table when I enter the office. I'm early, but it seems like they've been sitting for a while. Mark stands up to shake my hand then offers me a seat at the table. Christa remains seated with the same Dorothy from Kansas look she had earlier in the cafeteria.

"Lauren thanks for attending on such a short notice."

"No problem, Mark."

"First of all, I want you to know we really appreciate the contribution you've made around here within the last several months. You've done an outstanding job."

"Umm hmm," Christa agreed.

"Thanks, Mark," I smiled. "I take pride in always doing my best."

"Indeed you have," he said, as he looked at me through eyes repaired by laser surgery. As usual, Mark is well groomed and nattily attired in a navy pinstriped suit, burgundy power tie with navy and burgundy suspenders. His jelled, jet black hair is neatly in place and looks as though it has recently been touched up with fresh dye. The way gray strands are popping up from my scalp, I need to find out what he's using.

I thanked him again.

"Unfortunately, the company has decided to make some changes," he stated in a matter of fact manner. "And those changes will affect you."

I folded my hands in my lap and tried to refrain from biting my lower lip, but I could feel anxiety taking over my body. Christa still had that puppet like smile on her face. I'm beginning to wonder if Mark is controlling her with strings under the table.

"How will the changes affect me?" I asked with trepidation.

"Well the company has decided to outsource the Member Service Department."

Mark made his announcement without a drop of emotion. Concern nor sympathy were no where to be found. He began the meeting complimenting me as if he was going to recommend me for a promotion to assistant vice-president, but instead he's telling me the company is eliminating my department. I knew something wasn't right the moment I got here this morning. I could just feel it. Christa always acts a little strange in my opinion, but her actions rubbed me the wrong way in the cafeteria this morning.

The news has me feeling dizzy, but I try hard to remain controlled. I'm numb. How can so much stuff keep hitting me from so many different directions? My goodness. Lord, when can I catch a break? My mind raced quickly, but my body sat frozen in time.

Christa continues to nod robotically with a glossy daze covering her innocent eyes. She's uncomfortable dealing these cards to me, but Mark, on the other hand, keeps his poker face intact. I'm sure he's used to playing from a stacked deck. Shuffling and cutting the livelihoods of hardworking people comes easy for him. Also, I bet Jerry Farmer had a role in this.

Mama was right; these companies don't give a damn about folks.

37

JULIAN

I left the courtroom at 26th and California feeling like the weight of the world had been lifted from my overburdened shoulders. Because of the effective motions argued by my attorney, Charles White and Justice Michael Adams on behalf of the Bar Association, Judge Lewis Nathan had finally issued an opinion that quashed the search warrant, forcing the government to return my computer and files to my possession.

I had spent all my years trying to live right and play by the rules, but even with a successful law practice, the system had still treated me like a common criminal. For the court, and its case against me, it had all boiled down to semantics and a bunch of legal mumbo jumbo.

Originally, Judge Nathan made a preliminary finding that suggested the search of my office was reasonable by citing a landmark case in the state of Maryland almost thirty years ago. Fortunately for me, Justice Michael Adams, arguing on behalf of the Bar Association, said the search of an attorney's office should be prohibited if the attorney is not a suspect or target of the investigation.

Once again, Judge Nathan had made the argument stating that when an attorney is a suspect or target of an investigation, the search is more likely reasonable because there is less concern over privilege and confidentiality. He had gone on to say that if an attorney conspires with a client to commit criminal activity, all communications made to pursue criminal intentions are stripped of the privilege by the crime-fraud exception to the attorney-client privilege. Judge Nathan also mentioned his concern was that if an attorney is suspected of crime, he or she is more likely to destroy evidence than an attorney who isn't a suspect. It was a bunch of legal rambling because the bottom line was: the state never had specifically identified me as a suspect.

Attorney Charles White and my legal team made some very strong arguments to support the fact that I was only trying to do my job and was not apart of some criminal scheme. First of all, the search warrant never mentioned me as a suspect. Secondly, I've been present at numerous hearings over the last few months and my name has never been mentioned as a suspect in any of the 157 pages of court transcripts. Also, the State Attorney's Office never identified me as a suspect in any of its written pleadings. Instead, the State had referred to me as a not *totally blameless* third party and a possible suspect. It was all semantics.

Fortunately for me, the language in the State's final brief was believed to be problematic because the State was unwilling to clearly identify me as a suspect. Because of this, Judge Nathan was forced to change his initial position and reached the conclusion the search of my office was less reasonable.

Being apart of this process illustrated how easily an individual without resources can be screwed by the court system. I was blessed to have some brilliant legal minds working on my case. I'm extremely grateful. Thank God I finally have my computer and files back.

Nevertheless, I'm still very angry about how the system has violated me and the privacy of my clients. The officers conducting the search signed sworn affidavits to keep all information gathered from my office confidential, and promised to return all evidence directly to the court for inspection, but the FBI didn't deliver the items they seized from my office to the court right away. While in my office, the agents snapped pictures and delivered three rolls of film to the Cook County States Attorney's Office, but the three dozen photographs were never seen by the court.

Furthermore, the search began before six o'clock in the morning, several hours before I made it to the office. Since I wasn't there to identify the actual files pertaining to the search, the agents were able to go through files not relevant to the warrant. The FBI had even retained a copy of my computer hard drives because they needed an outside technical expert to search my files to retrieve information.

It was a blatant misuse of power. By law, the government had violated my rights because the Fourth Amendment of the United States Constitution deemed the search of my office as unreasonable.

Just think, our government does this kind of underhanded bullshit all the time.

Hell, if J. Edgar Hoover had the unmitigated gall to spy on and investigate a righteous man like Dr. Martin Luther King Jr., then a black man like me doesn't even have three-fifths of a chance.

This is still a white man's world.

I remember my friend Steve Strong warning me to be careful of which clients I chose to represent and not represent. My admiration for Charles Owens ran deep because I respected him for his audacity to stand up to authority and his so-called desire to lift up the little people of the city. Also, I admired the charismatic style that defined his presence, and the confident stride that seemed to open the doors of privilege when he entered a room. Still, the unanswered questions burning within the depths of my soul made me wonder what truly motivated Charles.

Being self-righteous has its place, but so does common sense. I had to face the facts. All of my legal problems were a direct result of my representation of Charles Owens.

Navy Pier's Ferris Wheel provided Vanessa and me with an aerial view of the weekly fireworks show on Lake Michigan. We rotated slowly through the nighttime air in a seat reserved for two overlooking the masses below. Like most places around the country, Chicago was in the middle of a drought and was being scorched with consecutive days of blistering temperatures in the nineties. The sweltering conditions had a crowd of people from all over the city and suburbs hovering close to the lakefront for relief from the heat.

"Thank you," Vanessa said, resting her small head on my shoulder.

"Thanks for what?" I asked.

"For bringing me down here," she replied softly.

"It was something different to do," I grinned as a warm breeze hit me in the face with late night heat. The gentle wind was filled with hot air. It was almost ten o'clock, but the temperature was still warm and humid, and unfortunately, relief was no where in sight. The meteorologists were predicting the temperature to reach as high as 102 degrees by tomorrow afternoon, and cooler temperatures were not in the forecast for several days.

"I like being outdoors," she said.

"I can tell you preferred to be outside," I responded with a sarcastic grin.

"How could you tell?"

"Because when I suggested going to the show you didn't seem that thrilled, but when I mentioned coming down here to see the fireworks I was able to hear the excitement in your voice."

"I was that obvious, huh?"

"I noticed."

"You're very observant."

"I try my best."

Initially, I wasn't excited about venturing downtown on a Saturday night because I knew the area would be crowded with people trying to get near the lakefront. Being in an air-conditioned movie theatre would have suited me just fine, but enjoying the outdoors with Vanessa was proving to be a memorable occasion. And having the fireworks exploding in the backdrop made the evening even more special.

"I love the outdoors," Vanessa exclaimed. "The winters in Chicago are so cold, so I always look forward to summertime."

"Well you seem to be enjoying yourself."

"I am."

"It seems like our first three dates have gone very well."

"They have," she acknowledged with a nod and a smile.

"I'm glad to hear that," I said, putting my right arm around Vanessa and gently massaging her neck and shoulder. I could feel her relax as she moved in closer to me.

Vanessa didn't seem as tense and restricted as she was the first time we went out. I kissed her softly on the cheek and leaned in closer so that our heads could connect like Siamese twins.

"I feel comfortable around you," she whispered. "Normally I don't let guys get too close, but for some reason I feel safe around you."

"That's a good thing right?"

"Yes, that's a good thing," she confirmed.

"I'm glad," I blushed.

"You're an African prince, Julian, with a wonderful spirit."

"You think so?" I asked as the Ferris Wheel continued to loop through the muggy, dark atmosphere in slow motion, while the fireworks continued to light up the sky over Lake Michigan.

"Yes I do," she answered with our heads still joined as one.

"Thanks."

Vanessa's words were soothing and unexpected.

"Julian, I appreciate you for the way you look after your mom. Men who respect their mothers are generally very respectful of the other women in their life. If a man doesn't care about the woman who gave birth to him and brought him into this world, then what makes me think he's going to give a damn about me? I want a man who will respect me. I like good guys, not thugs."

Vanessa's remark about thugs made me chuckle and think about Kendall and all the success he had with women over the years. I didn't want to admit it, but I was jealous of Kendall in some regards. Things seemed to come much easier for Kendall than they did for me.

I excelled in academics because I studied hard and was dedicated, but Kendall was innately smarter and picked things up faster. Fears of getting rejected and not being accepted dominated my adolescent years and followed me into manhood, whereas Kendall was fearless in approaching life and never worried much about what people thought. Even with a law degree and professional letters behind my name, I continue to wrestle with self esteem issues and finding my niche in society. However, Kendall, the junior college dropout, who barely made it out of high school, struts around town with a chip on his shoulder believing the world owes him everything.

Kendall has the brain and bravado to do anything he wants in life, but he chose to be a drug dealer. I'm disappointed because my brother never tried to live up to his potential. He wasted it. Kendall was born with the charisma and confidence that leaders are made of. I just pray his cockiness doesn't lead him to an early grave.

"What are you thinking about?" Vanessa asked, snapping me out of my thoughts as she detached her head from mine to hear my answer.

"To be honest," I shrugged. "I've met some women who seemed like they appreciated thugs more than they did me. I've also met a few ladies who acted as if they were jealous of my relationship with my mother. It was if they felt Mama had too much control over my life. I don't understand it."

"Well I do," she replied sternly.

"Well I wish you would explain it to me then."

"They're selfish," she snapped.

I laughed and pulled Vanessa close again to allow our heads to reconnect. First I kissed her on the cheek and then again on the forehead. Her small head turned in my direction and we kissed each other for the first time. Our tongues explored each other's mouths as the Ferris Wheel reached its peak in the nighttime sky. We ended our kiss, and I held Vanessa in my arms wishing the ride could last forever. Now it was our hearts connecting instead of our heads.

One by one, the compartments of the Ferris Wheel reached ground level and allowed riders to get off. Vanessa and I exited the Ferris Wheel hand in hand. I pulled out my cell phone because I wanted to check the date and time of the moment I thought I had fallen in love. My cell phone confirmed the time as 10:35 p.m., on Saturday, August 13, 2005. It also showed I had one voicemail message. For some reason, I didn't feel my phone vibrate inside my pants pocket when the call came in. Maybe it was because my heart was vibrating more.

I decided to check the voicemail message later and walked hand in hand with Vanessa as we left Navy Pier. The area was congested with people walking, hailing cabs, and boarding buses traveling in all directions, but we strolled slowly in the midst of the crowd as if we were by ourselves. A desire to savor the moment silenced our tongues. We were comfortable around each other so words weren't necessary.

I opened the passenger door to my car and watched Vanessa enter my chariot with a smile. My new title as African prince made me hold my head high. I got in on the driver's side and pulled Vanessa close for a warm embrace. We gazed into each other's eyes and shared a passionate kiss. The vibration of the cell phone interrupted our tender moment. I didn't recognize the number since it wasn't one programmed on my phone's contact list.

"Hello," I answered, expecting to dismiss the call as a wrong number.

"May I speak with Julian Collins please?"

"Speaking," I replied curiously, not recognizing the voice of the caller.

"Mr. Collins, I'm calling from Trinity Hospital on behalf of your mother, Hope Collins. She suffered an asthma attack, and was rushed here by ambulance about an hour ago. Your sister, Lauren is here with your mother and had been trying to get in touch with you, but was unsuccessful. She doesn't want to leave your mother's side so she asked me to call you."

Once again, my tongue was mute, but for a different reason. This time the silence of my mouth was initiated by the fear of days without Mama instead of foreseeing nights with Vanessa. About an hour ago, I was sitting on top of the world, but it only took a few minutes to knock me off my perch. With one phone call, my emotions had fallen from the sky and descended towards a crash landing without a parachute. I broke the silence after I hit rock bottom.

"I'm on my way."

38

KENDALL

A million thoughts soared through my mind as I boarded the plane for my flight leaving Las Vegas. A blonde flight attendant smiled and glanced at me with blue eyes as I walked down the aisle to find my seat. I stopped when I got to row thirteen and searched for a place to put my carry on luggage. I shoved my black duffel bag into an overhead compartment and took a seat next to the window overlooking the left wing. As anxious passengers looked for their seats on the plane, I yawned and stared through the window with tired eyes as the baggage crew loaded our luggage onto the Boeing 757 jet. One of the perky flight attendants announced over the loud speaker that flight 924 leaving for Chicago would be filled to capacity.

The three and a half hour flight from Las Vegas to Chicago seems much longer because of the two hour time difference. It's the middle of the afternoon here in Vegas, but it will be almost nine o'clock by the time I reach Chicago tonight. I tried to get an earlier flight, but I couldn't. I hope I can sleep all the way home since I stayed awake all last night. As soon as I saw La-La's name and number on my cell phone caller ID, I knew something was wrong back home. It seems like Mama always gets sick when I'm out of town. The last time I was in Vegas, Mama had to be rushed to the hospital.

By now, I know Mama has to be tired of being rushed back and forth to the hospital so much; it seems like she's in the hospital every other month. On my last trip out here, La-La was borderline hysterical when she called, but this time, her voice was calm. I guess that's what has me worried. She was too calm. My sister sounded as if she was giving up on Mama. I'm sure La-La and Julian are tired also; not knowing from one moment to the next what Mama's condition is going to be. It drains me mentally and I'm not even around to deal with it. I already know that if Mama dies, people will immediately blame me and say I'm the one who killed her.

That's too much guilt for one man to live with.

Members of the flight crew gave us instructions and demonstrations on what to do in case of an emergency. They checked each row to make sure we had fastened our seatbelts, and that our seats were in an upright position as we prepared for takeoff. I buckled up and stared out the window at the overcast sky. One of the pilots introduced himself and gave us the weather forecast in Chicago. It's almost hotter in Chicago than it is here in Vegas.

It seems like I can't escape the heat these days, it's hot everywhere I go. For all I know, the devil could be piloting this airplane because I feel like I'm on a runway headed for hell. We haven't left the ground yet, but turbulence is dominating my life. I've done too much scandalous shit to call out to God on a wing and a prayer now. Sooner or later bad karma was bound to shoot my ass down for soaring towards a hustler's heaven in a no fly zone. Lately, my conscience has been bothering me. I only wish it had started bothering me sooner.

I could feel the tide turning immediately after Smiley was killed and dumped in the river. Right after that, greedy ass Ronald Green got released from prison and came home wanting a larger piece of the pie. Once Ronald Green hit the pavement, his cousin, Charlie-O got more involved in the day to day activities on the street. Shit got real crazy then because them niggas are ruthless. Then a few days later, I got robbed and jacked up by some crooked ass cops. I should've walked away from this shit then, but I didn't because I was hooked on the action and addicted to the money, power and respect too much to cut it loose.

I realized I was too far gone the night Ray and I kicked in the apartment door of an elderly woman living with her crackhead grandson. It was some foul shit, but it had to be done. For weeks, the grandson, Bruce Franklin had been avoiding us. He owed us over a thousand dollars and was running scared.

Before getting hooked on crack, Bruce had graduated from college and had held down a management position at one of the grocery store chains in the area. He was living well and had a nice apartment in the city's Chatham neighborhood. Bruce drank beer and sipped on Crown Royal occasionally, but had never indulged in drugs. Life was going relatively well for Bruce until he started messing around with this chick by the name of Pam. Bruce, a burly, deep chocolate toned brother with an inferiority complex about his dark skin, was quickly mesmerized by the red bone complexion and light brown eyes of Pam. She had him pussy whipped, paying her bills and buying crack in no time. To make matters worse, Pam is Ronald Green's niece.

Before long, Bruce was spending his entire check on Pam and crack. If he got paid on Friday afternoon his money was gone by Friday night, and his family members wouldn't see or hear from him until Monday or Tuesday of the following week. By that time he was broke, nasty and begging for money. He was addicted. Eventually, he lost his job and had to move in with his elderly grandmother. When he no longer had money for drugs, he gave us the keys to his brand new Chrysler 300C. Once he no longer had a car to give us, he started giving us furniture out of his grandmother's home. We got watches, pendants, toasters, microwaves, radios and televisions. I even saw that nigga on the street one day trying to sell some of his grandmother's church hats for money. And after all the money and household appliances ran out, Ray and I decided to kick the door in.

Our goal wasn't to hurt Mrs. Franklin, but we wanted to beat the shit out of Bruce in front of her. Unfortunately for Mrs. Franklin, he wasn't there so we had to make our point to her. While the old lady screamed and prayed to God for help, Ray and I sprayed the two bedroom apartment with bullets. We fired shots in the kitchen, bathroom and both bedrooms, and even shot a hole in the picture of the late Mayor Harold Washington that was hanging on the living room wall. When we left, Mrs. Franklin was breathing hard and hollering loud enough to go into cardiac arrest. Ray and I laughed the rest of the night.

That was some fucked up shit we did, but it worked because Bruce and his elderly grandmother got the point. The next day, we got all of our money. And Mrs. Franklin moved out of the neighborhood the following month. In the process, we had also gotten our props with Ronald Green.

The commotion of flight attendants rolling stainless steel containers of snacks down the narrow aisles interrupted my thoughts of Mrs. Franklin. In a voice that seemed better suited for radio instead of a cockpit, the pilot announced that we had completed our ascension and were cruising at 37,000 feet. The airplane had me flying high, but by no mean was I floating on a cloud. I got too much shit on my mind.

We've been in the air for over an hour, but I still haven't been able to doze off and take a nap yet. The blonde flight attendant with the sky blue eyes smiles at me and gives me a bag of peanuts and a cup full of ice and Coke. The overweight, white guy, next to me, cramped in the middle seat pulls down the tray in front of him as if the flight attendant is about to serve him steak. The airline should've made his fat ass pay for two seats.

I want to get to the hospital to see Mama tonight, but I know visiting hours are over now. Right now I don't know how serious Mama's condition is. I've tried to reach Julian and La-La, but I'm assuming they've been at the hospital all day because their cell phones are turned off. I don't know who to trust in the game right now, and didn't want to call any members of the crew. I didn't call Tammy because she doesn't have a car and is probably still pissed at me for mistreating her the way I did the night I left her place to go over to Ray's house.

My tasty friend Cookie came to mind, so I decided to call her before boarding the plane and asked her to pick me up from Midway Airport. She said she had been thinking about me and agreed to come get me when my flight landed. Cookie and I haven't hooked up in a while, so it'll be cool spending the night at her place and resting my head on her luscious 39DDs. Maybe after playing with her, I'll be able to get some sleep.

Seeing the tall, tempting and tantalizing Cookie waiting for me when I arrived at gate C14 was a sight for tired eyes. Damn she looked good, and almost made me forget I hadn't slept in almost two days. She greeted me with a wet kiss and squeezed her sexy body close to mine with a tight hug. I was definitely wide awake after that. Cookie was casually dressed in a pair of faded blue jeans and an orange tank top that looked as though it was packing a couple of missiles. Her body was vicious enough to blow an army away. Open toe, high heel sandals displayed a fresh pedicure in a nail color that matched her tank top.

"Welcome home, baby," she said.

"Thank you," I responded with a tired smile. "It's good to be home."

I loaded my luggage into the back of Cookie's green, Ford Expedition and jumped into the passenger seat to relax. It was almost nine-thirty in Chicago, but the weather was still warm and humid. She opened the roof, pressed power for the stereo, and turned up the volume to get the maximum sound of the music by Floetry.

While Cookie darted in and out of the Dan Ryan traffic, I called La-La to get an update on Mama's condition. Once again, the voicemail answered right away. I hated to do it, but I decided to call Julian. At this point, I was worried about Mama and needed to know some answers.

"Hello," Julian answered on the second ring.

"It's me."

The uncomfortable silence dominating the airwaves almost made me think the line had gone dead and the call had dropped off.

"How is Mama doing?" I asked, breaking the silence.

"Not good, Kendall," he answered in a weary voice. "She's in a coma."

Hearing Julian say the word coma almost stopped my heart from beating. I kept the phone to my ear and pressed my hand to my face to keep the tears from flowing out of my eyes. The sound of Julian breathing was the only noise being transmitted over the phone line. I didn't know what else to say. Julian and I need each other right now, but it's been so long since we've been supportive of each other that the whole process seems awkward.

"You still there?" he asked.

"Yeah I'm here," I sighed.

"I thought maybe I had lost you."

"I'm here," I repeated. "I was just . . . Julian."

"What Kendall?"

". . . I'm sorry, Julian."

"It's too late for that, Kendall," he groaned in a tone that increased my guilt. "Man, you should've been thinking about being sorry a long time ago."

"I know," I trembled as a wave of tears poured from my eyes.

"Kendall, right now I'm too tired to have this conversation. I just want to get in my bed and go to sleep, so I can go back to the hospital in the morning."

"Where is La-La?"

"She's sleeping at the hospital."

"Can I meet you at the hospital in the morning?"

"Whatever, man," he sniped. "She's your mother too."

"I'm sorry, Julian."

"Bye Kendall."

I closed my cell phone and reclined in the passenger seat as Cookie drove across the steel bridge on the Bishop Ford Expressway.

"It's gonna be okay," she said, rubbing her right hand on my leg to console me. "You'll be able to get some rest tonight at my place and in the morning, I'll take you to the hospital to meet your brother and see your mom."

"Thanks," I mumbled as I shielded my eyes with my right forearm.

I couldn't wait to get to Cookie's apartment, so I could get in the bed. However I'm still not sure if I'll be able to go to sleep.

Cookie woke me up with some early morning loving. Having her long, lean body next to me during the middle of the night helped to release all of the tension bottled up inside. While I relaxed in her king size bed, I heard her in the kitchen making breakfast and talking to someone on the phone. This is what I need in my life right now;

waking up every morning with a lovely lady next to me who has my back instead of a hootchie trying to get my money.

I glanced at the clock on the nightstand; it was a few minutes after eight. I clasped my hands together and stretched my arms over my head. Cookie returned to the room in a sexy turquoise camisole.

"Didn't you promise your brother you were gonna meet him at the hospital by ten o'clock?" she asked holding a cup of coffee in her left hand.

"Yeah," I nodded.

"Then you need to get up, so I can get you there on time."

"Okay."

I showered and pulled some clothes from my luggage that I hadn't worn while I was in Vegas and joined Cookie in the kitchen for breakfast. She had the kitchen smelling good with grits, link sausages and toast. Cookie's caring and hospitality made me feel good since I knew Julian and La-La were not very pleased with me by the way I had neglected Mama over the years. Cookie sat across the kitchen table from me and looked on as I cleaned the food off my plate.

"You were hungry."

"I guess I needed some home cooking."

"I see," she said, taking another sip of coffee.

"Thanks Cookie."

She took another sip of coffee and smiled back.

"I better get you to the hospital."

"Okay."

The warm, humid weather caused us to ride with the windows up and the air-conditioner on. Once again temperatures were headed for the upper nineties, and were already in the upper eighties and it wasn't even ten o'clock yet.

"You 'bout a no driving bastard!" Cookie shouted angrily when a young guy in a tan Chevrolet Malibu cut in front of her as we exited the Bishop Ford Expressway en route to 95th and Stony Island.

"You okay?" I asked, noticing Cookie's jumpy behavior.

"I had too much coffee this morning."

Cookie turned right at Stony Island and headed east for Trinity Hospital. Usually paramedics take Mama to Roseland Community

Hospital, but this time they took her to Trinity. Mama's house is equal distance from both hospitals, so it's always a flip of the coin on which facility the ambulance will take her to. The closer we got to the hospital, the more my heart raced with anxiety. I didn't know what to expect or what condition I would find Mama in. Cookie made another right turn at 93rd and Jeffery. We were less than a half a mile from the hospital. I was a nervous wreck. I looked for Julian's car as we approached Trinity Hospital, but didn't see it.

"Thanks again, Cookie," I whispered. "I really appreciate this."

"No problem," she mumbled, as she made a U-turn in the middle of 93rd Street, so she could let me out directly in front of the hospital. "Be careful, Kendall."

"I will."

I gave her a hug and a peck on the cheek before getting my luggage and duffel bag from the back of the truck. I pulled my bags to the side of the curb and said goodbye again. She said goodbye, rolled up the window, and quickly sped off.

With a duffel bag on my shoulder and luggage packed with clothes rolling behind me, I made my way towards the entrance to the hospital. I saw Julian standing in the lobby as I made it half way to the automatic doors. Before I could raise my hand in the air to acknowledge my older brother, I heard the screeching tires of a speeding SUV.

Then I heard gunshots!

39

LAUREN

I'm sitting here at my desk, staring at my monitor, trying to analyze our performance numbers for the month, but my eyes are unable to focus and my brain can't compute. My body is here, but my mind is wandering off in space.

Since being advised of the insurance company's decision to outsource the customer service department, I've been feeling like a dead woman walking. My employment death has been a slow one, but knowing my days are numbered makes me feel like I've already been buried alive. Its weird coming to terms with the fact I'm just here to serve out the rest of my sentence before being executed by corporate punishment. The office will remain open for another month while they work to get our replacements in India trained and up to speed. They're killing us while using us to kill time.

At first, I used to try to come into the office everyday and approach the matter in a positive frame of mind, but it's difficult to do knowing I'm about to bite the dust of unemployment. I'd worked so hard and sacrificed so much in my three years here. This job had taken over my life. I'd even put my career before my family, friends and sometimes myself. On many occasions, I'd worked eleven and twelve hour days. I even came in here on weekends. Often I took work home in an attempt to out perform my peers and predecessors in making the department better. At this point, I wish they would just give me my severance package and let me go on with my life, especially since they're forcing me to start over anyway.

As expected, the morale of the department is in the toilet. Instead of upper management flushing us through a drain of defecation, they're forcing us to float in an untidy bowl of corporate waste, while they continue to release their budget balancing bowels on us in a diarrhea of downsizing. Our attitudes can't help but suffer from stinking thinking. We're tired of constantly being shit on.

In today's corporate America, the faces may change, but the game remains the same. For the executives calling shots and padding their bonus checks, it's all about managing the bottom line: money. Despite the restructuring taking place, my department still has to make our members happy by trying to provide them with good customer service. In spite of everything taking place, there are still daily call quotas and adherence objectives to be met, and I'm required to provide weekly reports to the executives unaffected by the company's shift in direction.

At this point, I try not to let it bother me anymore. For instance, when reps like Regina Coleman want to spend time on the phone fussing at her son, I simply act like I don't even hear it. In the past, I had considered firing Regina for having so many personal conversations on company time, but now, I just listen and laugh for sheer entertainment. Why should I reprimand her now? For all I know, we may be standing next to each other at the unemployment office one day. Besides, I have other more important things to worry about.

Knowing Mama is lingering in a coma is sucking the life out of me. I've spent the last two nights at the hospital holding a private prayer vigil at her bedside, while a ventilator did the work her lungs are now too weak to do. I'd talked to her all night long, and thanked her for being my mother, while praying for her to open her eyes one more time. I don't even know if Mama was even aware her baby girl was in the room by her side last night. Her body just laid there motionless the entire time as I reminisced about all the things she had taught me over the years.

Sometimes I wonder where Mama found the time to teach me all the things I wanted to be taught, and made me learn many of the things she knew I needed to know.

While Julian and Kendall were outside doing boy stuff, I was stuck in the house learning how to perform domestic duties. They learned how to do a few things, but it seemed like Mama was teaching me how to do everything. By the time I reached the age of nine, I had already mastered the art of washing and ironing clothes for myself, and sometimes, for my brothers. Back then I used to wonder if Mama was training me to be their loyal servant instead of their loving sister.

When Julian and Kendall came in the house with fresh holes in their pants from playing outside, Mama would make me grab the needle and thread so she could teach me how to sew on a patch. At first, I felt proud being able to do grown-up duties for my older brothers, but later I began to feel like their maid. They were always polite and thanked me while Mama was around, but the teasing started as soon as she left the room. Kendall called me little Hazel and Julian said he was going to use the money in his piggy bank to buy me a maid's uniform.

During the summer, while little girls were outside jumping rope and being chased by boys, I was in the kitchen cleaning greens or in the dining room shelling peas. As soon as I finished shelling one pan and thought I was done, Mama would send me back to the kitchen for another bushel. She would catch me with a frown on my face and warn me not to look at her in that tone of voice. Then, she would follow it up by saying one day I would appreciate what she was teaching me. Mama was showing me how to prepare a dinner for Sunday afternoon on Saturday evening. But more than that, Mama was showing me how to be a hard worker, self sufficient and not lazy. She gave me the tools to survive.

Some of Mama's lessons regarding hard work must have been embedded into my spirit, because while she's at the hospital lingering in a coma, I'm here at the office being diligent to the very end.

Before I left the hospital this morning to go home and get ready for work, I talked to Julian for a little while on the telephone. He was getting dressed and was on his way to meet Kendall at the hospital, so they could talk and go up to see Mama in ICU together. I hope he and Kendall can work out their differences because we all need each other now. So far, I haven't heard from anyone at the hospital, so I'm assuming everything is status quo. Sometimes no news is good news.

Instead of staying inside and going to the cafeteria for lunch, I decided to take a stroll outside and get some fresh air. A relaxing walk by myself always gives me the opportunity to meditate and talk with God while gathering my thoughts and calming my nerves. My mind is going in a million different directions so I'm counting on God to direct my path.

Another day of suffocating temperatures in the mid-nineties has many Chicagoans complaining and hoping for cooler weather, but not me, I enjoy the heat. For me, this would be the perfect day to take a casual stroll on the beach with the one I love. If only I had someone in my life to do the simple things with. So far, the month of August has been very hot, but unfortunately, summer can be the coldest of all seasons when I'm feeling lonely and all alone. Today is one of those cold and lonely days.

It isn't like men aren't approaching me; guys try to talk to me all the time. Sometimes I hear their rhetoric, but most times I don't. Most times they're talking loud and saying nothing, or looking smooth with some kind of hidden agenda.

There are so many things to worry about now as an African-American woman trying to meet and date men in today's society. These days it's hard to tell if a man is switch hitting and swinging his penis on both sides of the net. It makes me leery about some of the men approaching me. If I see something that makes me question whether a man is using his sexual racket as a backhand instead of a forehand to score points, then I'm defaulting all of his efforts. I quickly return the serve and step away from the court. No love match points here. There's no sense in committing any unforced errors.

Brothers on the down low have to be a major concern for women like me, especially since African-American women are the fastest growing group of people being infected with the AIDS virus. That's scary.

Since I hadn't eaten much this morning, I decided to walk down to the corner of State and Jackson and get something to munch on for the afternoon from Garrett Popcorn Shop. As usual, the line inside the popular snack store was long, but it seemed to be moving quickly. I reached the front of the line in a matter of minutes and ordered a half-pound mix of caramel and cheese popcorn. The colored kernels will probably stain my tongue and get caught between my teeth, but I'll just have to brush and floss when I get back to the office.

I left the popcorn shop and strolled north on State Street in the midst of lunchtime pedestrians with hands discolored with brown and yellow stains. Since I was on State Street, I decided to stop in CVS and buy a bottle of juice and some hair care products. I'd never shopped in this store before, so I asked one of the clerks for assistance. He pointed me to the correct aisle to look for hair supplies and continued stocking items on shelves.

"Yo' baby you didn't need to ask the store clerk for no help," said a guy with a husky voice, approaching me from the rear in an orange leisure suit with an orange hat cocked to the side. "I could've told you where to find whatever you needed."

"Yeah right," I snapped sarcastically.

"That's right, but I felt the need to size up the situation to find out what a sista like you is really lookin' fo'," he said, using his manicured fingers to massage his lips.

"Say what?" I asked, observing the stringy hair flowing from under his hat.

"See sometimes a young, tender thang like you need some guidance and a man to point you in the right direction. A cat like me to put you on the right track instead of the wrong track, so you can take a few steps forward and not two steps back. You see what I'm sayin'?"

"No I don't."

He was so ridiculous that I had to laugh. I can't believe I'm being hit on by a pimp looking for some hair products for his perm. You got to be kidding me.

"Yo babydoll I ain't comin' at you like some cat on the hunt, I'm just tryna come to you scraight and be up front," he continued, speaking with more rhymes than the Rev. Al Sharpton at a poetry slam. "I don't mean you no harm Ms. Nubian Princess; I just like how you walkin' and want you to like how I'm talkin' as I try to rise up to be the kang. Baby girl I couldn't lie to you even if I tried, I'm just a man tryna sit on the throne with a queen like you by my side. A girl like you is fine enough to make a cat wanna share his throne. . . Cuz you royalty."

"Are you some kind of pimp?"

"Ha, ha, ha," he laughed. "Nah baby girl, I ain't no pimp. I prefer to see myself as some type of guidance counselor. See I'm 'bout helpin' a honey like you find yo' purpose and get that money."

"Ha, ha, ha," I giggled. "No thanks."

"See that's the problem with some of you young felines," he countered with a slow drawl. "Some of ya'll in such a hurry to make yo' next move that you don't take the time to make yo' next move the best move."

"Whatever," I laughed. "I got to go."

I should've been back in my office over a half hour ago. With all of the stuff already flowing inside my head, I can't believe I'm in a store being encouraged to ho up or blow up by a raggedy pimp in a bright orange suit in need of a touch up.

My next move and best move was to get to the check out line and dash out of here before pimp daddy invites me to the player's ball. I whizzed by him and saw him stagger, as he made one last attempt to counsel me on the ways of the world. It definitely wasn't his best move because he stumbled backwards and knocked bottles of shampoo, conditioners and other hair products off the shelf. The floor looks a mess and the pimp in need of a fresh perm looks even worse.

Attention! Attention! We need someone to clean up the broke face in aisle three!

I paid for my merchandise and got out of the store as quickly as possible. Gobbling popcorn and thinking about the pimp I just saw had me feeling like a kid watching a blaxploitation film. That was some pretty good entertainment.

"Excuse me, ma'am."

I heard the voice trying to get my attention, but I pretended to be deaf and kept on walking, wondering who is it bothering me this time? I just want to finish my popcorn, get back to the office and wrap up the rest of my day, so I can get to the hospital to see Mama. I guess I'm going to have to break his face also and send him on his way.

"Excuse me, ma'am," he repeated the phrase to get my attention.

I turned around to greet the voice with a frown, but my scowl quickly turned into a smile.

"Andre!"

"Hello Lauren."

Andre's strong arms draped around my waist and hugged me tightly. I wrapped my arms around his neck, somehow managing to keep my popcorn stained hands off his light blue shirt. Seeing his chocolate frame standing in front of me was a surprise sweet enough to give me a sugar high.

"I didn't recognize your voice since you were tying to disguise it," I said with a playful grin. "How have you been?"

"Very well," he replied. "I thought it was you, but I wasn't sure because I hadn't seen you since you cut your hair."

"It's the new me, I guess."

"It's looks good on you."

"Thank you," I blushed. "You're looking mighty handsome yourself."

"I'm maintaining."

"What brings you downtown?" I asked.

"I had to come down here to have a meeting with a lender regarding financing."

"Oh you're trying to get a loan for something?" I asked curiously, while not trying to be too nosy.

"Yeah," he answered coyly.

"Are you on your way back to the office?"

"Yes," I replied, admiring his dark brown skin as it glistened under the hot afternoon sun. "I should've been back to work, but they'll see me when they see me."

"You sound like a disgruntled employee instead of the loyal company executive."

"Well soon I'll be a disgruntled former employee."

"Say what?"

"The company is outsourcing my department to India."

"Damn."

"If you're not in too big of a hurry, you can walk me back to the office," I suggested sheepishly, hoping to find the words somewhere along State Street to express how much I miss him.

"You know I always have time to walk and talk with you, La-La."

"Thank you."

"You're welcome."

"How is your family doing?" I asked as we turned east on Madison and walked towards Wabash.

"Everybody is hanging tough," he replied, nodding with a slight smile.

"That's good."

"How's your mom doing?"

"She's in the hospital again," I sighed.

"I'm sorry to hear that La-La," he sympathized with caring eyes. "I know its tough seeing your mother going back and forth to the hospital all the time."

"Its even tougher this time because she's in a coma."

"Oh La-La," he moaned. "I'm so sorry."

"It hasn't been easy, but that's life."

"Yeah, but it still has to be tough on you."

"So what's been going on with you?" I questioned with eagerness to change the subject to something else.

"Just working and trying to put some plans in motion."

"Like what . . .," I hesitated. "That's if you don't mind me asking?"

"Well I just got out of a meeting with a mortgage lender at the Community Investment Corporation because I'm in the process of purchasing a six unit apartment building on the southeast side. My father and a couple of my cousins are going to help me rehab it and use it for rental property. It's been something I've wanted to do for years, however I had pushed it to the backburner, but recently I decided to go for it."

"That's excellent, Dre!" I exclaimed with wide eyes displaying my surprise. "I never knew you had dreams of investing in real estate and rehabbing property. That's incredible."

"Thank you," he grinned modestly.

"You never shared your dreams with me," I stated painfully. "Why didn't you?"

Andre paused before answering my question. We were already standing at the entrance of the high-rise building where the insurance company leased several floors for office space. Before he could resume speaking to give me his explanation, a co-worker from the insurance company got my attention and said hello. I let the co-worker move on and turned my attention back to Dre, and waited for his response.

I repeated my question. "Why didn't you ever share your dreams with me, Andre?"

"I didn't think you really believed in me."

"Why would you say that?"

"Because that's how I felt," he stated with conviction.

"Why?"

"La-La I loved you with everything I had," he declared with honest eyes. "But you didn't feel I measured up to you and met all the items on your check list for the perfect mate. I gave you everything I had and was always willing to stand by you during tough times, but you pushed me away. It seemed as though you didn't think I was on your level because I drove a bus and didn't have your level of education."

"I never said that!" I stated defensively.

"You didn't have to."

"I guess I thought you were just settling for what life was giving you and not reaching to attain more."

"I'm comfortable with who I am, La," he affirmed adamantly. "I may not have multiple degrees and go to work in a suit and tie, but I like the person I am. I may not have a CPA or a MBA, but even though I drive a bus for the CTA, I'm still a good brother. Besides, everyone can't move at your pace and approach life with the same tenacity as you do. People are different La-La."

"I know."

"And although you made me feel like my efforts weren't good enough, I still loved you for being you, La-La."

"I loved you, too."

"Then why did you push me away, La-La?"

"I was going through a lot of stuff and my life was in a state of confusion, Dre."

"That's a cop out La, and you know it!"

Andre's sharp words ripped a hole through my stomach and aggravated old wounds. By asking him these questions, I had opened up a fresh can of pain and now had to swallow and digest the criticism he was shoving down my throat.

"La-La I'm not trying to attack you and lash out at you," he admitted, as he looked down shaking his head. "You hurt me."

"I didn't mean to."

"Yeah and drunk drivers never mean to run over people, but they do."

"I'm sorry," I apologized again, not knowing what else to say.

"Me too, La," he sighed. "Me too."

"Life gets very confusing sometimes," I pleaded. "Sometimes things just don't make sense."

"I guess I just wonder why I hear so many women, particularly African-American women whining and complaining about not being able to meet a good guy whose willing to treat them like ladies and show them a good time; then when they meet that God-fearing, respectful brother trying to do all the right things, it's never enough?"

Before I could ponder the question and respond, Andre spoke again and got more emotions off his chest.

"Women are always ranting about men trading in an older woman for a younger woman, but what about the woman who has a good man in her life and feels the need to trade up for the guy with the bigger house, the more expensive car, the fatter bank account and the better designer clothes? Chicks are always playing *Let's Make A Deal* and want to see what's behind door number two even though they got more from door number one than they ever bargained for. Men are accused of being dogs, but a lot of women want to treat guys like a product in the mall; they're anxious to see what's in the next store where the more expensive merchandise is when they already have everything they've been praying for in the store they're in?"

I should've been back at my desk concentrating on the work in my in-basket, instead of contemplating what was behind door number three, but nothing inside the building seemed very important to me now. Right now, I wanted to wrap my arms around Andre and never let go, but the sting of his words paralyzed me and made me think.

I could've easily countered by asking Andre about all the guys who engaged in multiple relationships and cheated on wives and girlfriends. Some guys even brag about cheating and say they won't turn down anything but their collar. I overheard one of the guys in the office say he always keeps a woman on the side because he didn't want to be stuck on the side of the road without a spare. For him, playing with another woman's feelings was equivalent to pulling a spare tire out of the trunk. To me, it seems like a lot of guys are afraid they're going to miss something if they allow the next freak train to roll by and not jump on. It's as if a lot of men always need to know if the next woman will be better in bed and scream louder than the loving woman he already has whispering in his ear. Those thoughts crossed my mind, but Andre's emotions were running too high for me to take an unnecessary cheap shot, so I kept my comments to myself.

"It seems like you've had a lot to get off your chest since the last time we spoke."

"I'm sorry," he mumbled. "I guess I had a lot of questions."

"Sometimes life is full of unanswered questions," I smirked, while trying to sound philosophical.

"This is true."

"I still care about you a lot, Andre," I confessed. "I've missed you a lot over the last few months and wanted to reach out to you, but I didn't know how to. I was afraid."

"I've missed you, too," he admitted. "What were you afraid of?"

"I wasn't sure you would welcome me back with open arms."

Andre stared at me with the same mischievous eyes that used to signal when he was ready to pin my arms to the mattress and make passionate love to me. I wish he could pin me against the wall of the building and have his way with me now. The look on his face gave me the courage to want to take a chance and open up to him, but before the words could flow from my lips, he spoke again.

"La-La, I would've given you my last breath, but instead of accepting my breath of fresh air, you covered your nose."

I ignored my pride and let my feelings flow.

"Andre, do you think there is any chance we can revive what we had?"

"I don't know, La," he responded with a straight face. "Remember what you said earlier? Sometimes life is full of unanswered questions. Then again, I think I'm where God wants me to be. Since *you* ended our relationship, I've had the opportunity to learn more about myself and how to exist in my world alone. Because of this, I no longer have the need or desire to share your world."

40

MAMA

I woke up wondering how long I been out of it; not sure of where I am or the day and time. It seems like I just been awakened from an intense dream that had my eyes seeing the faces of Kenny, my parents, grandparents, and other folks I ain't seen in a long time. I'm wondering if I had crossed over to the other side. The people I saw looked happy, but they waved at me and sent me back this way. For some reason, they wouldn't let me stay there with them, but I got a feelin' I'll be goin' back real soon.

My eyelids batted a few times as I tried to focus on the unfamiliar surroundings. Beeping machines monitoring my vital signs let me know I'm in the hospital; and the curtains instead of a door tell me I'm in the intensive care unit instead of a regular room. I turned my head to the right and saw Lauren sleeping on a cot beside me. I'm still not aware of the time, but I'm guessing it's the middle of the night.

Several minutes pass as I keep my eyes focused on my youngest child tossing and turning in her sleep. As usual, La-La is restless. I'm guessin' she's been here at the hospital tryin' to watch over me, but instead I'm watchin' over her. Maybe this is why Mudear and Papa sent me back; they want me to watch over my children a little while longer.

La-La looks like she's having a bad dream, but I'm not gonna wake her up; I got faith she'll conquer whatever battle is raging within her right now. I won't be able to save her from life's ups and downs, but I'll be able to watch over her and her brothers in the same way our ancestors been lookin' after me over the years.

I hope my children understand I did the best I could in tryin' to raise them, even though I know I made my share of mistakes in the process. Hospitals don't pass out instruction manuals to us mothers after we give birth to children. They just let us rest in the maternity ward for a little while, and then send us out the door to stumble and fall, making good and bad decisions along the way. An instruction guide would've come in handy because I had to learn all of it by trial and error.

Looking back now, I'm able to see how I'm partly responsible for creating the rift between Julian and Kendall. Lord knows I didn't mean to do it. As parents, we're told how we're not supposed to play favorites or love our children differently, but it happens. It happens all the time. Sometimes it's the make up of the child's personality and the bond that is formed or not formed early on. Perhaps I sabotaged Julian and Kendall's brotherhood.

In many ways, I guess I set Julian up to be at conflict with Kendall by placing too many responsibilities on his shoulders immediately following their father's death. Julian forged an unbreakable bond with me then. Like all boys, he enjoyed playing outside and being with friends, but his main priority was to look after me. Julian was still many years away from reaching his teens, but was already tryin' to fill the role of protector and comforter to a broken-hearted widow. He had become the man of the house. Because of this, he got closer to me than my other two children. Even though I was always a strong disciplinarian to all three, Julian witnessed my depressed behavior and saw my moods change drastically during the days of pain and loneliness. Somehow at a young age, he was already showing maturity and telling me everything would be alright. Julian is a very special man.

While I allowed Julian to view my moments of weakness, I refused to let Kendall see any of my vulnerability. He just saw my strength. Now that I think about it, a lot of Kendall's behavior was probably an attempt to get more attention from me. I should've included Kendall and allowed him to share in the role placed on Julian. It was usually me saying Julian do this or Julian do that, while Kendall sort of faded into the background. I guess calling on Kendall would've reminded me of how much I needed Kenny since they shared the same name.

I made a big mistake in never calling on Kendall when I needed something done, so over the years I guess he figured I didn't need him for anything, and that I would just call on Julian if I did. I sabotaged Kendall by giving him a way out. While Julian was busy making sure everything was okay with me, Kendall was off forming bonds with people he felt needed him more. It's hard to expect a person to be there to save the day when they've never had to do so in the past. Why would Kendall worry about takin' care of me or any other family situation when he knows Julian is gonna be around to do it?

Hindsight always has perfect vision and sees everything.

My eyes ain't been open very long, but La-La has already turned over about five times. It looks like she's uncomfortable tryin' to sleep on that cot, but even more, it seems like she's wrestling with some stuff mentally also. As the only daughter, with two older brothers who don't get along well, La-La is probably already worrying about how she gonna keep the family together after I'm gone. She's always looking ahead.

I'm proud of La-La. She's a very determined woman. La-La has her moments of extreme selfishness, but when the chips are down, she's gonna step in and get the job done. In some ways, La-La's selfishness has been good for her because she's gonna always take care of La-La first. My daughter is a survivor and self sufficient, with enormous pride and a stubborn spirit, committed to doing things her way. I'm wondering how she persuaded the hospital to let her move a cot in ICU. Like I said, she's determined. La-La may toss and turn on that uncomfortable cot for a few hours, but whenever she gets up, she's gonna be ready to take on the world like it ain't nobody's business. However, in this world, my baby needs to realize its okay to lean on someone else every now and then and not try to tackle life alone all the time.

My last prayer would be that my kids don't just go their separate ways, and will work to become closer to each other. I may have raised them differently, but I raised them all under the same roof.

Finally, La-La stops tossing and turning and decides to wake up. I watch silently as she wipes the sleep out of her eyes and sits up on the cot. She stretches her arms and rubs her hands across her face. We resemble each other more since she stopped wearing them braids and cut her hair. She's a pretty girl even with the lines of a restless night on her cheeks. My eyes smile when I see her acknowledge my presence.

"Mama!" she yelled, as tears replaced the sleep in her eyes. "You're awake!"

I smile with my eyes.

"Mama, I'm so glad to see you open your eyes again!" she cried out, as she tried to stop the tears from rolling down her face.

La-La leaned over the bed and kissed me on the forehead. I'm able to look into her eyes and see myself. She's looking more and more like me everyday. Julian has my eyes, my round face, and my smile. Kendall's rich, dark complexion, piercing stare, and broad shoulders are the spitting image of Kenny. La-La's features are definitely a combination of both parents. She possesses the same curvaceous figure and big legs I had as a young woman, and the high cheekbones I have today, however, she's been blessed with the hypnotic eyes her father had.

I wish I could holler out to her with the same excitement she has, but my journey to and from the afterlife has me feeling a bit weary. Besides, I got too many tubes and machines hooked up to my body to say anything. So instead of tryin' to speak, I allow my baby girl to put her head on my breast, so I can caress the side of her face and let my maternal hands do the talkin'. I can feel her shuddering as I wrap my arms around her body and massage her slender back. She's crying uncontrollably. It's been a long time since I seen my daughter cry like this.

Rubbing my hand across her back in rhythm reminds me of how I used to have to burp her as a child after she ate a lot and gulped too much milk. She was a greedy little girl, always wanting more food and more milk, and then, spitting most of it back up before crying herself to sleep.

Thank you, Jesus. The Lord has given me the chance to hold my baby girl one more time. I love you, Lauren Janine Collins. Mama loves you.

Now I need to hug my two sons one more time; especially Kendall.

41

JULIAN

Having Kendall walking around my spacious living room takes away the comfort I normally find at home. Although, he's my brother, this is unfamiliar territory for the both of us. Not once had he stepped foot in my house during the five years I've been here, not even for a can of pop or a hot dog, but now he's pacing the hardwood floors like a hunter afraid of being captured by the game. Kendall isn't comfortable being here, and I'm not thrilled about him being here either. His nervous energy is driving me nuts.

Kendall's nonstop movement is nerve-wracking and giving me the flux, but I'd rather have him marching back and forth through my home than lying stiff on a slab in the morgue. I thought that was going to be the case yesterday. How Kendall managed to avoid the gunshots fired at him yesterday is beyond me because he looked like an autopsy waiting to happen. I guess God even has mercy on people who don't deserve it. La-La called this morning to tell me Mama awoke from her coma. She probably opened her eyes to pray for Kendall.

"Kendall, will you sit down!" I shouted. "You've been pacing the floor ever since you got here."

"You don't understand!" he yelled.

"I understand enough," I countered. "I know our mother is clinging for her life in a hospital intensive care unit and you can't go see her because you got folks shooting at you and shit. Mama woke up out of her coma and your ass is busy dodging bullets. Hell, I understand more than I want to!"

"Yeah right."

"Yeah right my ass!" I snapped. "I knew this Nino Brown bullshit would catch up with your ass sooner or later. How you think you can do this scandalous shit and not have it catch up with you?"

"You think you know everything don't you?" he hollered, staring at me with vicious eyes. "You don't know shit, you wannabe bourgeois muthafucka! We ain't lil' boys no more nigga, I'll fuck you up!"

"You talk like a damn fool!" I shouted, as I got up from the couch, ready to take my brother head on in a fight I know I can't win anymore.

He's bigger, stronger, and madder, but I still take a verbal shot.

"You got thugs shooting at your ass, but you're ready to take your frustrations out on me, when I'm the one trying to help your stupid ass."

"You tryna help me, Julian?" he barked, as he showered my face with spit from a mouth on the verge of foaming like a dog with rabies.

"I don't know if you want to be helped, Kendall," I countered, overwhelmed by the scowl accompanying the intense rage in his piercing eyes. We're staring each other in the eye, ready to go toe to toe in the living room of my house. It's just the two of us. If we start fighting, La-La's not here to go tell, and Mama's not here to break it up.

"You gonna help me, Julian?" he barked again. "You gonna ride in and save the muthafuckin' day super nigga?"

"Fuck you, Kendall!"

"Yeah just what I thought, nigga!" he chided. "You ain't gon' do shit!"

"This is crazy, Kendall," I said, shaking my head and walking away in an attempt to suggest I was too mature for this macho nonsense. "I don't have time for this."

"Punk ass nigga," he mumbled.

"Why don't you just get the fuck out of my house," I replied, waving him off. Kendall is totally out of control. I don't have any good thoughts running through my head about him right now.

"Yeah kick me out your crib," he sniped with his arms folded across his chest and a sinister grin on his face. "Big brother, you don't know the folks you fuckin' with, and it's obvious you don't know your clients very well either."

"Say what?"

"You heard me," he declared, once again pacing across the hardwood floors.

"Why don't you just get out of here, Kendall," I conceded. "I'm not in the mood for this right now."

"A minute ago, you was all up in my face like a frog ready to leap, now you tryna put me out the house. Come on and leap nigga! Raise up and you'll get fucked up!"

"You're crazy!"

"Yeah crazy enough to know you in over your head also, nigga!" he pointed.

"What?" I asked, totally oblivious to what he's talking about.

"Yeah just what I thought," he quipped. "Smart ass lawyer and shit and, you ain't got a fuckin' clue."

"Damn, why don't you just get to the point?" I questioned. "I'm tired of you talking in circles. Just say what you got to say."

"Awight," he laughed. "I'll get to the point."

"Please do."

"The muthafucka shootin' at me is the same muthafucka you been representin' on them real estate deals."

I looked at my brother with a confused expression on my face, but remained silent and waited for him to continue.

"Yeah that's right, nigga," he continued. "The same person collecting drug money from me is the same person you been helping buy property."

"Huh . . ."

"I figured that bit of info would leave you with your mouth wide open," he teased. "See you know that nigga as Charles Owens, a respected man in the community and shit. He used all of his sophisticated words to charm folks like you into believing he was some kind of muthafuckin' Robin Hood. Yeah right, that nigga a hood for sho, but his name ain't Robin. In my world that nigga is known as Charlie-O."

My body sank into the subtle fabric of the living room sofa as my heart plunged into the pit of my upset stomach. Trembling hands covered my face, as I tried to absorb the information coming from Kendall's lips. I didn't want to believe it, but I had no choice.

Finally, Kendall stopped pacing the floor and was now sitting on a lounger adjacent to the sofa I was sinking in. He seemed relieved that he had gotten it out. And I was relieved to see he had calmed down. It took life and death for me to have a serious conversation with my only brother.

"I know that's some heavy shit to lay on you, Julian, but it's the truth."

"Why didn't you tell me?"

"I thought you knew," he answered softly, his words no longer containing the bite they had earlier. "Julian, you hardly even talk to me. Besides, I didn't wanna get in your business, and I didn't want you gettin' in mine."

Questions flooded my brain, but I remained silent, and allowed my brother to continue explaining how our lives are intertwined in more ways than I ever imagined.

"This shit is on an entirely different level, Julian. Real estate and mortgage fraud is like the new crack. Buying a bunch of property is how they keep the game strong; it's the biggest street hustle to ever be invented. Between you and the other lawyers and accountants they got representin' them, the higher-ups done pulled in millions of dollars in mortgage loans. That muthafucka, Charlie-O is tryin' to buy more property than Donald Trump. Soon he's gonna have niggas on the street calling him Charlie Trump. That Charlie-O is one ambitious muthafucka. And that's on the real!"

"Damn."

"Like I said," Kendall smirked. "This here shit here is on a whole 'nother level."

"So why are they trying to kill you?"

"Didn't you just hear me say that they're ambitious? They're tryin' to kill me because they some greedy muthafuckas, that's why," he laughed sarcastically. "They want their corners back. They leased the corners to me, and now my lease is up."

"Unbelievable," I mumbled in disbelief.

"Believe it."

"Wow," I mumbled again, remembering a previous conversation with Charles.

"What?"

"Was Charles involved in Ray getting killed?"

"Listen Julian," Kendall warned. "Charlie-O is involved in damn near everything takin' place on the south side. He's ruthless. I wasn't sure about him killing Ray at first, but once I got away and had some time to think, it begin to make sense. And when I saw that SUV comin' my way at the hospital, I knew it was a hit. The pieces fit."

"How did they know you were going to be at the hospital?"

"Cookie set me up," he admitted, shaking his head in shock. "Everything was cool when she came to pick me up from the airport, but I noticed she was real fidgety yesterday morning. I had a feelin' something was goin' on, but I didn't think that bitch would fuck the shit outta me all night and then set me up the next morning for a hit. Julian, when money is on the line, people might do damn near anything. And Cookie is all about gettin' paid. At least them niggas let me get some of Cookie's pussy before they tried to bump me off."

"You got folks trying to kill you and your mind is on a piece of tail."

"You know me," he snickered. "I'm just glad I had my luggage with me at the hospital to block some of the bullets. Besides, good pussy helps to relieve stress, but you probably wouldn't know nothing 'bout that."

"Your arrogant ass almost found out that being dead relieves stress for good."

"No shit."

"It's starting to make sense to me now."

"What?"

"I remember hanging out with Charles one day after he had done a press conference in the neighborhood to help this senior citizen. I rode around town listening to him talk about cleaning up the streets and addressing the concerns in the community. He said he was going to get to the bottom of some of the problems in the community."

"I guess those problems included me and Ray."

"It sure seems like it," I added. "He was very pissed off about those two children being killed. I think he even paid for their funerals."

"Julian, that nigga, Charlie-O didn't give a rat's ass about them kids. He just don't like shit interfering with his money. Them kids being killed brought too much heat from the cops and took too much cash out his pocket."

"It's all about money, huh?"

"What the fuck you think?"

"Yeah it always is," I admitted.

"Does he know you and I are brothers?" Kendall asked curiously.

"I don't know," I shrugged.

"Did you tell La-La about what happened?"

"No," I answered. "We'll just keep that between ourselves."

"Thanks, my brother."

"No problem, my brother."

"Like I said," he quipped with a serious look on his face. "I'm just glad I had my luggage with me."

"So am I."

In the past, a meeting with Charles Owens would've been a pleasurable appointment on my calendar. On those occasions, I had only seen the brighter side of Mr. Owens' personality, but now I had to view him under a different light. Coming to grips with the fact the man I respected greatly had just tried to kill my only brother was a frightening revelation.

For years, I'd distanced myself from Kendall because of his dangerous drug dealing duties, but over the last several months, I had been involved with one of the men my brother reported to and made money for. For the most part, I had only witnessed the warm, sunny side of Charles' personality, but because of Kendall's life being in danger, I now I had to deal with the cold-blooded, darker element of the man who was once my favorite client.

My instincts had warned me of Charles' goals of being a kingmaker, but I'd never realized he was using Kendall and me in the same game. I didn't know we were just mere pawns occupying separate squares on his board. With the cameras rolling, I had looked on with pride as Charles masterfully coerced citizens to join forces with him, but according to Kendall, Charlie-O was just as competent behind closed doors in ordering the merciless killings of those foolish enough to go against him.

Recent developments were teaching me a valuable lesson. I really didn't know Charles Owens as well as I thought, and wasn't at all familiar with his alter-ego, Charlie-O. Having great admiration and love for people we don't know can be very dangerous. Then again, sometimes I'm guilty of seeing the good things I want to see and turning a blind eye to the bad stuff I want to avoid.

Thinking back, I remember how sometimes representing Charles left me with the feeling of being suspended in mid-air, dangling uncontrollably on an imaginary tightrope that divided good and evil. I'd been under the mental strain of a legal trapeze artist, praying to land on the right side of the law with my conscious still intact. As scandalous as Kendall was in dealing drugs, Charles was even more ruthless in becoming a real estate magnate.

Over a period of several months, I'd represented Charles in numerous real estate transactions and watched him buy distressed properties through a company called G&O Real Estate. Charles would advertise that he could sell properties to buyers wanting to make a purchase with little or no money down. Later, I learned Charles had misled some people by saying he owned properties that weren't in his possession yet. If necessary, he would purchase the property from the actual owner after already having located a buyer. Then, after the property was assessed and overvalued by an unscrupulous appraiser, Charles would subsequently sell the real estate to the buyer at an inflated cost. To make matters worse, the crooked appraisers neglected to inform the new buyers of any of the rehabilitation and repairs needed for the property.

With the help of professional relatives and friends, working in banks, lending institutions and employment offices, Charles was able to assist buyers in submitting inaccurate applications to obtain mortgage loans. The phony documents consisted of false verifications of deposits, fake employment and income histories and puffed up appraisals. The bogus information was then sent to lenders on behalf of unqualified borrowers. All of this had helped to create a record number of foreclosure filings in Cook County. It didn't matter to Charles and those associated with G&O Realty because they had already been paid.

Kendall told me about how the higher-ups used some of the buildings for headquarters and meetings, and used others to store weapons and drugs. He said the higher-ups were even getting Section 8 money from the government.

I had helped Charles buy several large, multi-unit buildings in tax auctions, and watched him take advantage of an Illinois law which allowed him to title the properties to secret land trust without having to disclose his identity for public records. Charles would later sell some of the properties to friends and relatives who had gotten their loans through his connections. Sometimes Charles would buy the property back, but without registering the transactions with the Cook County recorder of deeds.

Charles had mastered the real estate game and used a tactic known as *double sales* to fatten his wallet. Since several weeks can pass before the filing of a property can show up on the computer registry, Charles was able to record a deed, set up a loan, and then filed another deed and set up another loan before the computer system was updated with a record of first filing. In the process, Charles had padded his pocket twice and had shown the real meaning of creative financing. Kendall was right when he said Charles and the higher-ups were working on another level.

I'd worked with Charles on close to two dozen real estate closings, but each of our meetings had taken place at my office, or at the location of the building or home he was purchasing. Never had I been to his home, and to be honest, I was surprised he was allowing me to meet with him here now. I still don't know if he's aware Kendall is my brother. I told him I needed to meet with him as soon as possible and he obliged.

Charles' house is incredible. There's no way the upscale neighbors of Kenwood can know they have a drug kingpin living on their block. Not here. Bounded by East 47th Street, East 51st Street, South Blackstone Avenue and South Drexel Boulevard, the historic landmark district consists of homes designed by world famous architects such as George Maher and Frank Lloyd Wright. Large residences and spacious lots with manicured yards are the norm. This is the community where Muhammad Ali once lived, and where the Minister Louis Farrakhan calls home today. Unbeknownst to them, it's also the home of Charlie-O.

"Where you goin?" asked the stocky street soldier with major attitude as I approached the steps leading to Charles' bi-level home.

"I have an appointment with Mr. Owens," I replied, noticing a vehicle parked across the street monitoring my every move.

"Who are you?" he asked with a round face that had no facial hair, not even eyebrows.

"I'm his attorney," I replied cautiously, trying not to stare at the dressed up hoodlum's peculiar face, while wondering if he had some kind of dreaded skin disease that removed all of his hair and eyebrows.

"Raise your arms and turn around," he ordered without the hint of a smile.

As the funny looking thug frisked me for weapons, I wondered if I should've stopped by Minister Farrakhan's house on the way here and asked some brothers from the Fruit of Islam to come with me for backup. Being patted down by one of Charles' underlings proved he trusted no one; not even his loyal lawyer.

"Go on in," the thug ordered.

I walked through the spacious foyer of Charles' home and immediately noticed his exquisite collection of African artwork. Hand carved masks and shields decorated the mantelpiece with the character and creative flair of the Motherland. Several banana leaf paintings of warriors defended the walls of Charles' kingdom with power and purpose. A beautiful ethnic chess board with African figurines sat atop a wooden table, waiting for an opponent to make the wrong move. For added protection, sharp spears were on hand near the fireplace just in case things got too hot and someone needed to get the point.

The thug with the missing eyebrows led me through the spacious living room and up a spiral staircase made of wood. Once we made it to the second floor, I heard the voice of a lady talking on a cell phone in one of the bedrooms. The voice sounded familiar. I took a quick glance in her direction when I passed by the bedroom and made out the face. She's a weekend news anchor for one of the local television channels. I remember the pretty, light-skinned media darling being very aggressive in trying to get an interview with Charles after a press conference a few months ago. She looked luscious in a pair of blue jeans and a cutoff T-shirt. And by the way she was lounging across the bed I assumed she'd gotten more than just an exclusive interview.

Charles was engaged in a telephone conversation when we reached his office. He continued talking and beckoned for me to enter with his right hand. He leaned back in the oversized, leather chair with his feet propped up on his desk. His tie was loosened and the top button of his monogrammed, French cuff shirt was unfastened. Charles pointed for me to sit down, but the thug who ushered me through the house stayed in the room. Charles concluded the phone call and addressed me in a tone that made me feel as if we were meeting for the first time.

And in some ways we were.

"So how may I help you, Julian?" he inquired in somewhat of a formal manner.

Before replying, I turned around to see if the man without the eyebrows was still in the room with us. He was still standing behind me looking strange.

"Charles may I talk with you in private?"

"Give us a minute," Charles said, ordering the henchman from the large office with a slight hand gesture.

I took a deep breath and tried to compose myself as the door to the office closed shut. Charles remained silent and sat with his index finger touching his mustached lips in a pensive pose. He was studying me as if we were sitting in front of the chess board downstairs. I was afraid to say the wrong thing or make the wrong move.

"So what's so important that made you need to see me right away?" he asked.

"I wanted to talk to you about my brother?"
"Kendall?"
"You know we're brothers?"
"Of course I do," he replied nonchalantly with his finger still over his lips.
"Charles, that's my only brother."
"And your point is?"
"Kendall thinks you're trying to kill him."
"Ha, ha, ha," he laughed arrogantly. "He thought right."
"Please, Charles, Kendall is my only brother."
"This isn't about you, Julian!" he stated harshly. "This is about my money!"
"Please, Charles," I begged with tears streaming down my cheeks. "My mother is in the hospital dying."
"I like you, Julian," Charles said. "It's one thing for you to handle my real estate matters, but now you're getting too deep into my business."
"Charles, I've jeopardized my legal career for you!" I argued. "My office got raided because of my representation of you. I've been dealing with the FBI and the Cook County Sheriffs because of you, Charles!"
"Julian, don't fuckin' insult me with the innocent bitch in the woods routine!" he snapped. "You made a lot of money handling those real estate closings. You got greedy trying to be a big shot lawyer."
"Listen, Charles," I pleaded. "Your business is your business, your other activities aren't important to me. I'm just trying to save my younger brother."
"What you want me to do?"
"Please, Charles, just let my brother out the game."
"Did Kendall send you here to argue his case?"
"No," I answered, shaking my head. "He doesn't even know I'm here. Charles I'm just trying to do right by my family and for my mother."
"You're jeopardizing your own life."

"Charles, my mom just woke up out of a coma," I cried. "I just want Kendall and my mom to make peace with each other before she dies."

"Or before he dies?"

"Please Charles," I pleaded. "I just thought I could come to you in good faith."

Charles folded his arms and grinned. "So you want us to just give Kendall a pass and let bygones be bygones and let him ride off in the sunset with his big ass house in the suburbs and all of his money still in the bank, so he can live happily ever after?"

"Please spare my brother his life."

"Julian you're looking for a fairy tale, but this is an urban drama."

"Charles, I looked up to you like a big brother; I admired and respected you," I urged, wiping the tears from my face as my former role model gazed at me with a blank expression without a trace of sympathy. "I'm not trying to tell you how to run your business or interfere with what you do; I'm just trying to look out for my family."

During our conversation, I always referred to the man across the desk from me as Charles, but the person staring back at me was Charlie-O.

"Tell Kendall to bring me two hundred and fifty thousand dollars, and I'll give him a pass."

42

KENDALL

"Two hundred and fifty grand!" I shouted. "That nigga must be crazy as all get out!"

"Do you have it?"

"Hell yeah I got it!" I bragged. "But that don't mean I wanna give it to that greedy muthafucka. Fuck Charlie-O!"

"Kendall, you're selfish!" yelled Julian. "You're selfish, and you've always been selfish! Why can't you think of someone else other than yourself for a change?"

"Fuck you, too!" I pointed. "You give 'em two hundred and fifty grand then!"

"Kendall, Mama needs to see you," Julian countered with anger and tears in his eyes. "When are you going to realize Mama won't be around forever? Days aren't promised to us, Kendall! Damn, man, you value the money you've made selling drugs more than your own mother's life. They're not going to let you get near that hospital until you pay them off. Kendall, Charles and the rest of the higher-ups are willing to let you out of the game with your life."

"It ain't 'bout the money," I reasoned. "It's the principle."

"Negro please!" Julian countered, as rage replaced the tears in his eyes. "I risked my life going down to Charles' house to speak on your behalf, and now you coming to me with some bullshit about principle. Since when did drug dealers and thugs like you and them have principles?"

"Didn't nobody tell you to speak up for me, nigga," I sneered. "You the one actin' like you on some kinda peace treaty mission like Jesse Jackson or some muthafuckin' body representin' the United Nations and shit! You better be careful before you fuck around and get popped your damn self."

That was the response that came from my lips, but inside, I was shocked by Julian's actions to help me. It's been a long time since my older brother has come to my defense; not since we were young boys. Growing up, I always fought my own battles and didn't lie down for anybody. I never needed Julian's help. Now, my older brother is trying to do the right thing by standing up for his family, but instead of me appreciating his concern, I'm laughing and knocking him down. I can see the hurt on his face and the pain in his eyes. The wrinkles of tension on his forehead confirm the love in his heart. He's afraid. I'm looking at Julian, but I'm seeing Mama.

"Heaven help you, Kendall because you're a lost cause," Julian preached. "I'm going to the hospital to see Mama. I want you out of my house by the time I get back."

"No problem."

"You know what, Kendall?"

"Now what, nigga?" I barked, growing tired of hearing all of his preaching.

"Mama wasted her prayers when she prayed for you."

The bullets fired at me yesterday missed my body, but the verbal shots from Julian's tongue struck its mark. His words hit home and pierced my heart.

I pulled stacks of bills from the safe in my bedroom, which was hidden behind a painting of the Million Man March. The portrait was supposed to illustrate our uniting as a race of men. As a black man, that autumn day in the nation's capitol was intended to represent a day of atonement for the wicked ways of my earlier years. I remember standing shoulder to shoulder with black men from around the country with tears in my eyes and pride in my heart, as we came together with the goal of uniting and atoning in brotherhood.

While standing on the Mall, we were challenged to clean up our lives and rebuild our neighborhoods. We were supposed to take responsibility and commit ourselves to stopping drugs and violence from destroying our homes. As Julian and I flew back to Chicago on a plane full of inspired brothers, I thought about the ways in which I wanted to change my life. I landed on the runway of Midway Airport with a renewed sense of self and purpose. My plan was to go back to school and get my degree. It was time to put Ray and the streets behind me. I was supposed to come home and rededicate myself to doing good deeds, not dealing good drugs.

I didn't keep the pledge I made on October 16, 1995. To be honest, most of my activities since the March on Washington have been a severe slap in the face to all the things millions of brothers stood for on that incredible Monday in D.C.

I closed the safe and hung the portrait back in its place. For me, the painting on the wall symbolized the debt of my past, whereas, the money in my hands, represented a deposit on my future. Banded bundles consisting of ten grand each fit nicely into a large, leather briefcase. Hundred dollar bills in neat stacks meant the difference between me living and dying. Everything in life has a price. Considering all the money I've made over the years, the higher-ups were letting me off cheap.

Julian was right, I need to cash in so I can live to play another day.

A weird sensation accompanied me as I approached the doors of the tavern that doubled as a headquarters for the higher-ups. Its funny how things change; just months ago, Rodney was under my wing and was being picked on by Ray and me. Now, he's standing outside the lounge enjoying his new role as a lookout for the higher-ups; for him it's a promotion.

"What's goin' on, Rodney?" I said, greeting him with an uneasy smile.

Rodney nods, but doesn't say anything. Instead of greeting me with respect I once commanded from him, he stops me at the door and begins frisking me. He makes me open up the briefcase and looks at the money inside. Looking at Rodney now almost makes me forget that I was the one who trained him when he was still just a skinny young kid. I introduced him to the life and made him apart of my crew when he was only thirteen-years-old. At sixteen, he was handling money and monitoring street sales. He was young and loyal. Now at seventeen, he's come of age and ready to make his bones with the higher-ups. Like most kids in the game, he has dreams of moving up the criminal ladder.

Music for steppers played softly as I entered the Debonair Lounge with my briefcase in hand. The strong scent of cigar and cigarette smoke crammed the tiny establishment with a permanent fog. A burly bodyguard by the name of Maurice, who also worked as Charlie-O's chauffeur, frisked me and checked my attaché case again. They must have thought Rodney had missed something or were extremely careful about my visit. I don't know why. It's not like I'm gonna walk in pretending to be John Gotti with goals of killing a boss. That would be a bold ass move, but I would never get outta here alive.

Mirrors lined the walls of the small tavern tucked away on a quiet street on the south side. The Debonair Lounge was where old players, who should've been retired, came to relive their youth and talk shit about what they used to do back in the day. Meanwhile young women whispered sweet nothings in the ears of the old geezers, hoping to lighten the load in their wallets. Regulars of the bar sat at small tables in wooden chairs or at the oval shaped bar in front of televisions hanging from the ceiling. A tiny stage near the entrance of the club provided a dance floor for people in the mood to step and slide. The name of the club is misleading. There's nothing debonair at all about this place. If a person didn't know this hole in the wall existed they would never know it was here because it's nothing more than a dive.

It's four o'clock in the afternoon, so the place is quiet; the party people haven't arrived yet, therefore, only business is being discussed now. A smooth, remixed version of "Stay" by the Temptations filled the air with good vibrations, but the guys here now look like they would rather shoot people instead of dance. Charlie-O and Ronald Green are seated at a long table up against a wall near the dart board. I sit down in front of them and put the briefcase containing my future on the table. I feel more uncomfortable and vulnerable because my back is to the door.

"Did you bring some cash with you, Kendall?" Charlie-O asked, as Ronald Green looked on with menacing eyes.

"Yeah," I responded, as I opened the case and turned it around so that they could see the neat stack of bills inside.

Seeing them sitting in front of me now is just how I envisioned them in my head before I got here; they're as different as day and night. Charlie-O has matinee looks and Hollywood style. Ronald Green has the rugged face of a boxer who had gotten his block knocked off, and he has a prison mentality to match. As usual, Charlie is smooth and shiny, whereas, Ronnie is grisly and grimy. Their opposite choices in fashion reflect differing personalities. Charlie is stylishly attired in a pair of tan, silk slacks and an olive, polo shirt, with fingernails that look as if they just left the manicurist. On the other hand, Ronnie appears as though he just woke up on a farm from a drunken stupor. He's sloppily dressed in a white T-shirt and blue jean overalls, with rugged hands that look like he had just finished fixing a tractor. The two of them remind me of the old television show: *The Odd Couple*. They're the Felix and Oscar of the crime.

Charlie, the personable one with the extensive vocabulary, was always able to put people at ease if he wanted to. Meanwhile, Ronnie, a mumbling man of few words, always seemed to be a ticking bomb on the verge of exploding. No one ever really knows where they stand with Charlie because he's a chameleon who adjusts to his environment. With Ronnie, what you see is what you get. Charlie is smiling as he surveys the briefcase, but Ronnie's expression hasn't changed. I'm more worried about Charlie because he's proven to be a man of many faces. And smiling faces tell lies.

"So what's your next move, Kendall?" Charlie asked with a sneaky grin.

"I want out," I replied. "Just let me walk away."

"I don't think he can, Charlie," Ronnie whispered in a villainous voice. "Hustlin' is in his blood. We let him off the hook and he'll probably go off and try to freelance."

"Kendall, you got dreams of being a free-agent?" Charlie inquired.

"Nah, man," I answered, shaking my head. "At this point, I just want to get out and stay out. I want to be right with my mother and siblings and have peace of mind."

"Ha, ha, ha," Ronnie snickered. "Charlie, did he say he wants peace of mind? What the fuck is peace of mind? Can you buy that shit in stores?"

"It's not sold in stores," Charlie joked, with the tone of an announcer doing voice-overs for a late night television commercial.

"Well that must be some new shit you can buy off the internet then," Ronnie laughed. "Cuz I know they wasn't carryin' that shit in stores before I went to the joint for all them years. Sheeit, if I had been able to buy some fuckin' peace of mind back in the day, then I probably wouldna spent so much time locked up."

"I doubt it," Charlie teased. "They wouldn't have been able to keep enough bottles on the shelves to keep you out of trouble, Ronnie."

"You 'bout right."

"I know I am," Charlie agreed. "You enjoyed robbing and stealing too much."

"And the way you always thinkin' 'bout money," Ronnie added. "You probably woulda bought some stock in peace of mind."

"Hey, you know me." Charlie boasted. "There's nothing like a good investment."

"So tell me, Charlie," Ronnie continued. "How much do peace of mind cost?"

"I'm not sure," Charlie smirked. "But it seems it must be worth at least a quarter of a million dollars, or at least that's what Kendall is willing to pay for it."

I remained silent as the criminal comics cracked jokes and performed an impromptu comedy routine at my expense. They laughed and poked fun at my desire to be a stand-up guy, finally ready to turn my life around. I wanna be able to look at myself in the mirror in the morning, and go to bed at night without sleeping with one eye open and a gun tucked under the pillow.

"Maybe you shoulda ordered him to pay us more money then?" Ronnie added. "Kendall, it's a shame, we damn near had to blow your fuckin' brains out to get you to understand we the ones runnin' this here shit."

"And unfortunately, Kendall, your buddy Ray lost sight of that," Charlie quipped, admitting their involvement in Ray's murder. "Your brother, Julian, came to me crying, begging me to let you off the hook, so I agreed to this parting of the ways because of him. I always liked you Kendall, because you knew how to take care of business, but you and Ray got careless."

"Well I don't give a fuck 'bout your brother comin' to us on your behalf," Ronnie interrupted in an abrasive tone. "Charlie is the one who got a workin' relationship wit' your brother, so I'm respectin' him on this shit. But don't think for a minute we didn't hear that shit on the street 'bout you and Ray wantin' to be the new kings of the hill. That kinda talk didn't sit well wit' me."

Charlie cut in. "You got too big for your own good."

"That's what I'm talkin' bout," Ronnie agreed. "You niggas ain't bigger than the game. Hell, we the reason y'all got a chance to suit up and get in the game in the first muthafuckin' place. It was us, the higher-ups, who gave you niggas playin' time and a court to ball on."

"And since Ray's game got sloppy," Charlie interjected. "We decided to make some roster cuts."

"Kendall, tell me this," Ronnie demanded with a scowl that got meaner by the word. "How the fuck y'all gon' go kill a kid and not expect it to cut into our profits? Do you know how much heat that shit caused us? If you go do some shit like that, you shoulda at least done a clean job."

"The situation got out of hand," I tried to explain, wishing they would return to jokes instead of threats.

"You muthafuckin' right!" Ronnie yelled. "It got outta hand! Y'all shoulda ran that shit by us first."

"We were trying to get to him before the cops did."

"Yeah, but y'all fucked it up," Ronnie scolded.

"That move was bad for business," Charlie lectured.

"You understand that shit?"

"Yeah," I mumbled.

"Speak up nigga and let yourself be heard!" Ronnie shouted, pounding his fist on the fragile table.

"Yeah, man, I understand," I answered humbly, with fear causing my knees to tremble under the table.

"You better fuckin' understand!" Ronnie warned. "Cuz we can take the money and still put a slug in the back of your head. And if necessary, we'll save a slug for your brother, Julian, too!"

"Get out of here, Kendall," Charlie ordered in a calm tone. "We're letting you go, so don't ever think about looking back or coming back. Your business is done, and the turf you once controlled no longer exists. And if you decide to try to reenter our world in any capacity, I won't let a sick mother or a crying brother, affect my decision to put you in your proper place."

The money changed hands, and I ended my sit-down and business relationship with Charlie-O and Ronald Green. They took my cash and sent me on my way. There weren't any goodbye hugs or farewell speeches. Nobody said great job Kendall and good luck in your future endeavors. I didn't get any *"that a boys"* or high fives. In this profession, no one gets a retirement party with a big dinner at the end of an illustrious career. Friends and family can't come and see you receive gifts, and hear people say how dedicated you were to your craft. Meeting annual quotas won't win you any free vacations to Disney World. At the end of this game, the going away present is usually a one way ticket to prison or the cemetery. And I'm not eager to book reservations for either place.

I excused myself from the table and walked towards the door. My former comrades looked at me with contempt. Eyes that used to have respect for me were now filled with resentment; their hands itched with fingers eager to pull a trigger. I headed out the door, praying a bullet in the back of the head wouldn't punch my ticket to the morgue. By no means, am I thrilled about forking over a quarter of a million dollars, but in the grand scheme of things, being allowed a chance to see Mama happy during her last days is more important. I want to be able to tell Mama I'm out for good, and look her in the eyes with a clean slate. Hopefully, I'll be able to clear my conscious in the process. Even if I still have problems sleeping at night, at least turning from my wicked ways will allow Mama to rest in peace. And for me, that would be priceless.

43

LAUREN

For the last couple of weeks, the hospital has been my second home. I leave work and come directly here, usually sleeping on a cot all night, then going to my condo before dawn to shower and change clothes, so I can head back to the insurance company. It's been exhausting. The sacks under my eyes and loss of weight are signals I haven't slept much or eaten well lately. If I went home and got in bed now, I would probably sleep longer than Rip Van Winkle. But there's no way I'm going to leave Mama's side.

Yesterday, Julian and I had a meeting with Mama's primary care physician to discuss placing her under hospice care. It was a tough decision for both of us to have to make. At first, Julian became very upset and resisted the doctor's suggestion. I could relate to what he was feeling. The term hospice had such a negative connotation attached to it. It was a sign of giving up. For us, agreeing to place Mama in a hospice facility was like putting her on a runway to heaven. Nevertheless, we had to be honest with ourselves and realize doctors and medicine couldn't cure Mama's condition; they could only help her to rest better. Watching Mama make her transition is a helpless feeling and a tough pill to swallow, but at least she deserves to be comfortable.

Instead of thinking selfishly, it was time for us to think about Mama and what was best for her. Forcing Mama to surrender to her illness hurt us deeply, but I'm sure, having to suffer through the illness hurt her much more. We were watching our mother put up a courageous fight, but she's the one taking the punishment.

Both of my brothers are avid boxing fans, so I've always been able to appreciate the sport and all of its brutality. As a result, when Julian and Kendall were younger and viewed boxing matches on television, I watched the sport with them, and became familiar with many of the fighters. The two of them loved boxing, but I can never remember them rooting for the same fighter, and always aligned themselves with fighters in opposing corners. Usually they cheered for the boxer who shared similar personality traits with their own. Like in everything else, my brothers were always on opposite sides of the ring.

That's exactly how they were years ago when Sugar Ray Leonard fought Marvelous Marvin Hagler. I remember Julian cheering for Ray Leonard because he liked Sugar's wholesome image and media friendly personality. For differing reasons, Kendall became a fan of Marvin Hagler and embraced Marvelous' brawling fighting style and no mercy disposition. After the bout, Julian was jubilant when Leonard was awarded the controversial decision. Kendall was disillusioned and claimed the fight was fixed.

In later years, Julian admired Evander Holyfield for his tenacity and his ability to take a punch; whereas, Kendall idolized Mike Tyson for his bulldog ferociousness and knack for knocking fighters out. When the two boxers finally faced each other in the ring, Julian and Kendall made predictions and put huge bets on the fight. After Holyfield won the match, Julian requested his money and talked a bunch of crap, referring to Evander as "The Real Deal" Holyfield. As expected, Kendall was pissed off about the outcome and made a lot of excuses. He reluctantly honored the bet, but took pride in seeing Munching Mike Tyson make a real meal out of Evander Holyfield's ear.

These days, it's not uncommon for Julian to host a fight party at his house, or for Kendall to sit ringside at a championship bout in Las Vegas. The two of them probably will still argue over whom they thought the greatest fighter was, but not me.

Mama's the best fighter I've ever seen.

For years, I've watched Mama go toe to toe with the angel of death, taking blow after blow, yet somehow managing to get up after being knocked down so many times by a vicious illness. With a little spiritual maturity, I've to come to realize that it was all God's will; His perfect plan in action.

After being battered by a barrage of asthma attacks, heartaches and weariness, Mama found herself up against the ropes trying to hold on. With death staring her in the face over and over again, she somehow mustered the faith and courage to keep standing. Each time, the Lord was there, embracing Mama in the corner and preparing her for the next round. While the Lord provided her with guidance and strength between rounds, Julian and I stood along the ropes and tried to support Mama with love and encouraging words; doing and saying whatever we could to make her battle a little easier. Because of God's grace and our prayers, Mama answered the bell and met death at the center of the ring for the start of another round. Instead of Mama being a quitter and giving up, she's taking more punches by trying to go the distance. Mama doesn't have to keep fighting to prove anything to me; I already know she's a warrior and a winner.

In my opinion, God should award Mama the victory with a unanimous decision for the battle she's had to endure. However, regardless of the fight's outcome, she'll always be the undisputed champion of my world.

Julian's entrance into the room awakened me from my trance.

"Hey La," he said, kissing me on the forehead. "How are you doing?"

I shrugged. "Oh . . . I'm here."

"Any change in Mama?" he asked.

"She hasn't opened her eyes since I been here," I replied.

"La, why don't you go home and get some rest?"

"I'd rather stay here with Mama," I responded curtly.

"Well if you decide you want to go home and get some rest, I'll stay here."

"I'd rather stay," I repeated, looking over at Mama's fragile body.

"Well it's left up to you, sis."

I nodded and glanced at my watch to check the time. We're still in the season of summer, but autumn is approaching rapidly. It's not even seven-thirty yet, but it's almost dark outside. The days are getting shorter.

My patience for my other brother is also getting shorter.

"Where's Kendall?" I asked tersely.

"I'm not sure," Julian sighed. "I thought he would've been here by now."

"What's going on, Julian?" I inquired.

"It's a long story, La-La."

"I got time!" I snapped.

The sharpness of my words caused Julian to take a step backwards. My tone knocked him off balance and made him stagger to regroup. He looked over at Mama in a way that suggested he thought my tongue was powerful enough to wake her up. Mama's eyes didn't open, and I never took my focus away from Julian. I stared at him with puffy eyes and watched him shift his weight from one foot to the other. He was in a nervous stance.

"This isn't the place, La-La."

"Why not, Julian?" I asked, raising my arms in a combative pose that suggested him to bring it on. "We're all family! Say what you got to say; Mama's not going to wake up and stop you. Are you, Mama? Mama, are you going to stop Julian from telling me about what's going on with Kendall?"

"Not now, La-La," he mumbled, showing signs of mental and physical fatigue.

"Mama, Mama!" I shouted. "Julian has something to say, but he's afraid he may wake you up. Mama is it okay for us to talk? I bet she wants to know what's going on with Kendall also!"

"You need to calm down, La-La!"

"You act like Mama is going to wake up and stop you from talking."

"You need to go home and get some sleep, La . . . You're bugging out."

"And you need to tell me what's going on!"

"This isn't the time!"

"Whatever!"

All of a sudden, Mama woke up and her eyelids began to bat rapidly. The room was quiet as Julian and I stood in shocked silence. Once her eyelids stopped fluttering, she glanced around the room, before finally focusing on me, and then Julian. The anxiety of the moment had me panting heavily. Julian and I stared at each other. My heart was pounding against the walls of my chest, causing my breast to rise and fall. Julian's pupils were dilated to the max, and his body was stiffer than a figure in a wax museum. Both of us were spooked and acted like we had just seen a ghost.

Mama took long gazes at the two of us; then she closed her eyes briefly and reopened them a few seconds later. She didn't say anything, but I knew what she was doing and what she was thinking. Mama was counting heads. She and I were communicating with each other through telepathy. Like me, she was wondering where in the hell Kendall was.

I invaded Julian's personal space, and pressed my finger into his chest. Like an angry military officer, I commanded my oldest brother's attention and barked out orders through clenched teeth.

"Listen here, Julian," I growled. "I don't care what you need to do to find, Kendall, but I need you to find him, and I need you to find him right now!"

Julian's tongue was mute and his eyes were still dilated. It was if he was unable to comprehend anything taking place in the room. The atmosphere was surreal.

"Are we clear, Julian?"

Julian looked over at Mama again. Her eyes were still open, but her tongue was mute also. I was the only person talking. I was in control.

"We're clear," he replied in a monotone voice, which sounded like a robot finally understanding his objective.

"Then you know what you need to do then."

Julian nodded and quickly left the room with the purpose of an android assigned to carry out my orders.

I didn't understand what was happening to me, but a sense of empowerment was beginning to rise up and take control of my inner being. My body seemed as though it was being reincarnated with the spirit of a motivational speaker, and Mama was the person I was trying to motivate. I wasn't trying to do God's job or be His personal assistant, but instead of thinking of the Lord's will, I wanted my willpower to keep Mama alive a little while longer. At least until Kendall arrives.

As Mama stared into space, I paced the floor of the room with renewed energy.

"Hold on, Mama," I preached. "Just hold on a little while longer. I know you're weary and ready for some rest, but hang in here with me for just a few more minutes. Julian went to get Kendall. Just stay with me a little while longer, Mama."

Mama never responded with words, but her eyes told me she understood. She was fighting to hold on. I stopped pacing and sat down next to Mama's bed and began rubbing her forehead. She looked at me and briefly closed her eyes. When she reopened them, a moist glaze of tears covered her pupils.

I continued to rub her damp forehead with my right hand and clenched the sweaty palm of her left hand with mine. Now tears were beginning to fill me eyes. I was holding a bedside prayer vigil. Mama took a deep breath and squeezed my left hand tightly.

"I understand, Mama," I cried. "I'll tell Kendall, you love him."

Once again, Mama grasped my hand.

The woman, who gave birth to me and saw me take my first breath, was now seconds away from leaving me. It was over thirty years ago when Mama heard me cry out as she introduced me to life. Now she was listening to me cry out as she prepared to exit the world she'd brought me into. As a newborn baby, Mama was the first person to hold me and nurture me. Now as an adult, I was holding on to her during her final moments. I laid my head on Mama's chest and listened to her last breaths. Mama gasped as I felt her chest rise beneath my head. Her body relaxed as she released the grip she had on my hand.

I couldn't hear Mama breathing; her body was still. She had exhaled for the last time.

"Mama," I whispered, wiping fresh tears from my eyes. "Mama, are you gone?"

I already knew the answer. I put my head down on her chest and savored one last private moment. My intimate moment was interrupted by the sound of Kendall and Julian running into the room. I got up from the chair and tried to compose myself with rubbery legs. I staggered into Julian's arms and buried my face full of tears into the same chest I had pointed a directive finger at minutes earlier. He held me close and rubbed the back of my head. Grief and relief was overtaking us. It was no time for us to be selfish. Mama's headed for a better place.

Julian and I departed the room of our dearly beloved, seeking solace in each other's arms. Kendall was left alone with Mama to have his private moment. I wish he had gotten here sooner, but I guess it wasn't meant to be. Kendall ran out of time. He raced against the clock and the clock won.

Kendall is no different from a lot of people, foolishly believing their loved ones will live forever. Never taking the time to mend broken relationships or fully appreciating the solid relationships already in place. In the process, we cheat those we love and we cheat ourselves. But most of all, we cheat life. As a result, we're left with the emotional scars of being forced to live with words never said, feelings never expressed, and hearts never touched. We need to appreciate our special moments while we have them instead of waiting until they become a part of our memory.

Unfortunately, for Kendall, he appreciated his outside world more than he did his family. Julian and I allowed a few minutes to pass before returning to the room to console our grieving brother. I could hear him wailing loudly and apologizing over Mama's lifeless body as we reentered the room. His tears and apologies are too late. They have about as much power as a room full of flowers that can't be smelt. He's saying all the things he should've said months ago.

Julian and I put our arms around Kendall. He's hurting deeply and guilt will cause him to hurt for a long time. Nevertheless, we still love Kendall even though he's disappointed us. He's still our brother. The three of us have shared too many things over the years not to love each other.

As children, Mama made us share everything we had with each other. We didn't always want to do it, but we were forced to share

French fries from McDonald's, bicycles, roller-skates, jackets and hats, and some of our other favorite things. And if we made Mama mad enough, we even had to share whippings and punishments. Now in death, Mama was forcing us to share in our grief.

I guess that's the way it should be. We were raised under the same roof.

CPSIA information can be obtained at www.ICGtesting.com
Printed in the USA
LVOW080241171112

307702LV00002B/3/A